# THE
# AUGUSTINE WAY

# THE

# AUGUSTINE WAY

*RETRIEVING A VISION FOR*
*THE CHURCH'S APOLOGETIC WITNESS*

## JOSHUA D. CHATRAW & MARK D. ALLEN

**Baker Academic**
*a division of Baker Publishing Group*
Grand Rapids, Michigan

© 2023 by Joshua D. Chatraw and Mark D. Allen

Published by Baker Academic
a division of Baker Publishing Group
www.bakeracademic.com

Printed in the United States of America

Library of Congress Cataloging-in-Publication Control Number: 2022050413
ISBN 978-1-5409-6248-5 (cloth)

Unless otherwise indicated, quotations from Augustine's works are from the Works of Saint Augustine series by New City Press; references can be found in the bibliography.

Baker Publishing Group publications use paper produced from sustainable forestry practices and post-consumer waste whenever possible.

23   24   25   26   27   28   29       7   6   5   4   3   2   1

For the weary and heavy-laden

# Contents

# Acknowledgments

Saint Augustine could not be happy without his friends. They became a conduit of God's grace for him as they listened to and challenged him. The bishop of the inward turn perpetually turned outward to his friends. In his *Rule of Saint Augustine*, a guide for communal life, he gave sage advice for life's journey: "Whenever you go out, walk together, and when you reach your destination, stay together."[1]

Through writing this book we have deepened old friendships and made new ones. We could not have completed this literary journey without the critical eyes and supportive hands of our friends. They have walked alongside us and made our work better. We happily acknowledge our friends who have traveled in "the Augustine way" with us.

Student workers and graduate assistants at the Center for Apologetics and Cultural Engagement at Liberty University researched details, put together bibliographic data, toted books back and forth from the library, and provided much-needed moral support. Among them were my (Mark's) student assistants: Adebukola "Bukky" Adebayo, Jesse Alker, Dennis Nicholson, Seth Pryor, and Zane Richer. I would also like to recognize the insights I gained from table discussions with those bright, budding theologians in my Augustine independent study course: Gabe Magan, Joseph Carson, and Cameron Hayner.

I (Josh) am grateful to the Center for Public Christianity and Holy Trinity Anglican Church for their support and partnership in this project. To the fellows of the New City Fellows program, thank you for giving me such joy over the past four years.

1. The *Rule of Augustine* can be found at https://www.midwestaugustinians.org/roots-of
-augustinian-spirituality.

Many readers of earlier versions of the manuscript gave pertinent feedback: Connor Schonta, Alysia Yates, Justin Bailey, Keith Plummer, Joey Sherrard, Collin Hansen, John Sehorn, and those of the Center for Pastor Theologians, St. Anselm Fellowship. We appreciate the reality checks and affirming words. We both also recognize the wisdom and insights we have gained from hundreds, if not thousands, of conversations with our good friend Jack Carson.

Thank you also to our acquisition editors, Dave Nelson and Anna Gissing, to our copyeditor, Eric Salo, and to the entire team at Baker Academic. You made the journey a pleasure.

Thank you to these and many other friends for the grace of God we have experienced through you. May we "stay together" in this Augustinian vision for the church's apologetic witness.

# Introduction

## Time to Make Room at the Table

Saint Augustine of Hippo is arguably the greatest postbiblical theologian in the history of Christianity. And given the sheer quantity and historical impact of his apologetic works, he is at least to be considered the "greatest apologist of the Latin west."[1] This is high praise, though not misplaced. So it is surprising that Augustine's works have remained in the background of the debates on apologetic methodology that have taken place in the past century, rarely ever being positioned to address the shape of our contemporary Christian apologetic witness directly.[2] The aim of this book is to recover the great pastor-theologian's mature apologetic voice in order to address the challenges facing the church today.

In carrying out this apologetic retrieval, our organizing questions do not locate us primarily in the past but rather place Augustine in our present age, that he might speak to us in ways that are resonant. This means we are not simply asking, What *were* Augustine's arguments? or, How *did* Augustine interact with doubters and unbelievers? Though these are critical questions, our work of retrieval involves animating questions that are in the present tense: What can we learn from Augustine—his own journey, context, theology, and approach—to resource apologetics for our present context? This is an imaginative enterprise through which we ask, If Augustine were here with us, what might he say? With

---

1. McGrath, introduction to part 1 of Forrest, Chatraw, and McGrath, *History of Apologetics*, 29.
2. Curtis Chang's treatment of *The City of God* in *Engaging Unbelief*, 13–93, is a wonderful exception. After submitting our initial manuscript, I (Josh) was sent early proofs of Christopher Watkin's excellent book *Biblical Critical Theory* and was delighted to see him use Augustine's *The City of God* to frame a "biblical social theory for today" (xx).

this aim of offering an Augustinian *ressourcement*, we frame each chapter with scenes from our contemporary context.

We have chosen to center our attention (though not exclusively) on *Confessions* and *The City of God* for several reasons: the need for focused attention given Augustine's voluminous output, the structural and thematic connections between these two works, their relevance to our contemporary setting, their importance within his canon, their wide readership and multiple audiences in view (compared to the specific audiences of his works against particular groups), and Augustine's seasoned theological and pastoral maturity represented by both.

Our choice to retrieve *The City of God* is unlikely to take anyone by surprise, for it is Augustine's apologetic magnum opus. However, claiming that *Confessions* is relevant to apologetics might raise some eyebrows, but it shouldn't. We agree with Chad Meister, who notes that while *Confessions* is clearly a "profession," the book is also attempting to "persuade readers of the beauty of God, of the goodness of following God and the Christian path, and of the madness of following someone or something else."[3] *Confessions* narrates how Augustine himself rejected Christianity and traveled through competing philosophies of life, only to finally discover the wisdom of Christ. Through his story-shaped prayer, he sets out to persuade readers to follow him on the cross-shaped path to the good life.

By paying close attention in *Confessions* to what it felt like for Augustine to journey away from and back to faith and by paying close attention in *The City of God* to how he approached ministering as a pastor-theologian-apologist in the wake of a resurgent paganism, we hope to recover ancient wisdom to meet the challenges of our day with theological faithfulness and renewed apologetic imaginations.

In his eminent biography, Peter Brown traces the shifts Augustine experienced throughout his life, underscoring that he lived "in an age of rapid and dramatic change."[4] Mindful of the pronounced changes taking place in society and the challenges Christians felt, Augustine believed it was his pastoral calling to meet the demands facing the church brought about by the tectonic shifts of his own time.[5] The ideas Augustine offers in *Confessions* and *The City of God* are the outworkings of this pastoral calling and still ring true today in our late-modern

---

3. Meister, "Augustine of Hippo," 151. According to Henry Chadwick, "In the *Confessions* there is an undercurrent of apologetic addressed to a critical pagan intelligentsia, in whose eyes the Church was a collection of largely uneducated people." Chadwick, "On Rereading the *Confessions*," 15.

4. Brown, *Augustine of Hippo*, ix.

5. "Augustine was above all a pastor, that is to say, a man whose words and writing responded to the pressures of the moment, to requests which were made to him, to the needs of the faithful, to events taking place, or to the demands of the liturgy." Gilson, *Introduction à l'étude de Saint Augustin*, 244–45, quoted in Harrison, *Rethinking Augustine's Early Theology*, 283.

world. Hence, after getting his feet on the ground in late modernity—and acclimating to a world of electricity, mechanical horses, and microcomputers—he would certainly have a few things to say, and we'd be wise to listen. The wager of this thought experiment is that by welcoming Augustine into our context, we will hear sage words for a new apologetic day. This may strike some as an audacious endeavor, for it is challenging enough to understand Augustine as he speaks to his contemporaries. Nevertheless, we're convinced it's worth the risk to strain our ears to imagine what the bishop might say if he joined us at our apologetic table.

## A Word with the Pastors and Theologians

To begin with, Augustine might want to have a word with many present-day pastors and theologians, who, though inheritors of his tradition, have sold off their apologetic birthright, mistakenly assuming apologetics is synonymous with a flattened Enlightenment-style rationality and seeing it as irrelevant to their ministry. Though these criticisms can find targets, they aren't actually aimed at apologetics per se. If they were, someone must have forgotten to tell the church fathers, Augustine chief among them, who saw "apologist" as part and parcel of their identity as leaders and theologians of the church.[6] In *The City of God*, Augustine, as he himself puts it, seeks to "persuad[e] a person either to enter the city of God without hesitation or to remain there with perseverance."[7]

With so much attention being paid to the political and theological implications of *The City of God* in recent scholarship, it is important not to miss that Augustine's stated purpose is to persuade skeptics and reassure doubters. He ends up doing more than this—but certainly not less. He made clear in a letter, penned after the completion of *The City*, that he wanted his apologetic work distributed to those who despise Christians and to the pagan seekers of his day. These are the wishes of an aging bishop who, almost a decade and a half after he started writing the book and with only a few more years left in his life, had finally finished what he promised to do in the opening pages: "I have taken up the task of defending the most glorious city of God . . . against those who prefer their own gods to its founder."[8] From beginning to end, apologetics was

---

6. As Avery Dulles points out, "After the first quarter of the second century . . . apologetics became the most characteristic form of Christian writing." *History of Apologetics*, 27.

7. Augustine, *Letter* 2*.3. The asterisk indicates a special numbering for the more recently discovered letters. See also Brown, *Augustine of Hippo*, 511. Unless otherwise indicated, quotations from Augustine's works are from the Works of Saint Augustine series by New City Press; references can be found in the bibliography.

8. Augustine, *The City of God*, preface to book 1.

always at the center of *The City of God*. Apologetics was the great theologian's capstone project.

To those who have recently called for cultural withdrawal, "strategic" or otherwise, our book doesn't exactly offer a response. Instead, we take it as a given that, as members of a religion born within a hostile Greco-Roman world and called by its founder to go make disciples of all the nations, we are still called to venture into the messiness of a fallen world even as we confess we are citizens of a different kingdom. Given this calling, the "Augustine way" gets on with the task of asking how we might go about the hard work of persuasion.

Apprenticing ourselves to Augustine might also help us learn to work together in carrying out this mission. Augustine captured the attention of people on both sides of the Reformation, with both Catholics and Reformers claiming him as their own. Though he was a source of division, with the two sides appealing to different aspects of his thought, perhaps now Augustine could bring all parties back to the table, giving rise to ecumenical apologetic efforts similar in spirit to C. S. Lewis's *Mere Christianity*.[9] This would be a salutary result for us in post-Christendom, for the chief cultural rivalry in the West is no longer Protestantism versus Catholicism but Christianity versus a variety of other options. It's a bit like the experience of a Christian missionary who, in facing a local population hostile to Christianity on top of the myriad language and cultural barriers, finds immediate kinship upon meeting a believer—even one from a different Christian tradition. The fact that these two Christians would have found each other (and their respective sects) disagreeable back home is less of an issue on the mission field, where their meeting is viewed as a divinely appointed partnership. So, too, today we need this missional mindset.

This is not to paper over theological differences. They do exist and are important to acknowledge, but our desire is to also recognize the catholicity we share and to discern ways to work together to persuade people, as Lewis put it, into taking steps toward the hallway of the Christian house.[10] Augustine, as one of the fountainheads of both Western traditions, might just spur a deeper conversation with pastors and theologians from opposite sides of the same table, to put this Lewisian apologetic vision into practice today.

---

9. On the topic of Augustine's legacy in Lewis's thought, see Watson, "Enlarging Augustinian Systems," 163–74. To see traces of Augustine's semiotics and understanding of human desire in Lewis's work, see McGrath, *Intellectual World of C. S. Lewis*, chap. 5.

10. Lewis, *Mere Christianity*, xv–xvi. By "catholicity" we mean not the Roman Catholic Church but the universal faith held by Christians throughout the history of Christianity. This is what we have in mind when we use the term with a small *c*.

## A Word with the Apologists

Augustine would also want to have a long conversation with modern-day apologists. For, while he would likely be pleased to observe how some of his apologetic seeds have blossomed through the ages, he would surely raise some concerns that would keep everyone at the table for extra rounds. Augustine would join a conversation that, over the past century, has largely consisted of the back-and-forth between evidential/classical and presuppositional apologists.[11] Apologists from these contemporary approaches offer many valuable insights. However, the way contemporary methodological debates are often framed has left our apologetic imaginations entrenched *inside* certain systems; meanwhile, the cultural winds *outside* have been rapidly changing. Our late-modern communities have been inhaling ways of thinking, believing, and living—not by way of logical syllogisms or analytic argument but through the oxygen given off by stories, symbols, and artifacts—that have made Christianity seem not only irrational but oppressive and dangerous. Today, then, the aesthetic and moral vision of Christianity, which can't be neatly bracketed off from the critiques against its rationality, is now being called into question. Our cultural air is far different from what it was even fifty years ago. A changing culture would not surprise or exasperate Augustine; he saw it in his own time. But the idea that we would be unwilling to adapt how we attempt to persuade likely would have.

A growing number of voices have begun to reflect seriously on the contingency of persuasion, as our thinking, believing, and committing is always embedded in a historical context and inextricably linked to human affections. An appreciation of these complexities has caused some to at least recognize the need to shift conversations about apologetic methods to better meet the challenges of late modernism by engaging not the abstract, universal person but rather the particular person—heart, mind, and soul—standing before us. Yet, an alternative apologetic school has yet to coalesce. This book is an attempt to rally such voices together, neither by breaking from the past in the name of novelty nor by negating more recent insights but by retrieving an ancient vision capable of helping us meet Christianity's present challenges.

---

11. At least this rings true for North America. In Great Britain these competing schools have not cast the same shadow over methodological imaginations, which may be one of the reasons why many of the central figures in British apologetics do not fit neatly within these contemporary classifications and have felt the freedom to explore more contextual and creative approaches. We are thinking in particular of figures such as G. K. Chesterton, Dorothy Sayers, and C. S. Lewis, as well as current intellectuals such as N. T. Wright and Alister McGrath. We are using "evidential" and "classical" apologetics here to denote what is sometimes called a "one-step approach" and a "two-step approach," respectively.

What if the resources and inspiration to move forward wisely have always been hidden in plain sight in the form of the most influential theologian in the church? What if the future of apologetics is to be found back in premodern North Africa?

PART 1

# Going Back
# for the Future

# 1

# A Prodigal Son Returns Home . . .
# as an Apologist

Imagine a prodigious boy who grew up in the 1990s. Let's call him John. John was born and bred in the sticks of south Georgia among a certain kind of people. The cosmopolitan intelligentsia might call these people simpletons and claim they do little more than cling to "guns and religion." This kind of sneering, reinforced by widening educational and economic gaps, caused the people of John's community to live with a chip on their shoulder. But, while despising the smug self-importance emanating from the so-called elites, more than a few secretly coveted their social standing and prosperity.

The Christians in John's small town were Fundamentalists with a capital *F*: a potluck of authoritarian leaders, hard-and-fast rules, "literalist" interpretations of, well, everything, and a helping of snake handling. You'd have to squint to maybe catch a glimpse of the distant family resemblance between these communities and C. S. Lewis's Anglicanism or Alvin Plantinga's philosophically robust Reformed tradition. Yet these are the people, these hardy Fundamentalists, who preached from the pulpits and sat in the pews of the churches that John bounced to and from throughout his childhood. His mother taught children's Sunday school and vacation Bible school while making sure young John attended Royal Ambassadors—a Christian version of Boy Scouts meets Bible sword drills—every Wednesday night. Her faith was simple yet deep.

John's dad was another story. He was an Enlightenment man: Voltaire, David Hume, and Ludwig Feuerbach were his luminaries. For him, the whole Christianity thing was a leftover half-baked myth. He felt it necessary to keep his opinion on these matters within the family, however, for such ideas would not have been good for business. And while John went along with his mom to church, his dad's skepticism was never lost on him. Even as a child he could see the possibility of growing up and staying home with Dad. He could imagine one day not believing.

With a degree from a second-rate law school, John's dad was one of the town's few attorneys. He couldn't make it in the big city, so he had moved the family to this little town, where the competition was thinner. Though he had once been personally ambitious, he now resigned himself to living out his ambitions through his son. Everyone agreed that John was the smartest kid in town. And, although his parents didn't agree on religion, they agreed on one thing: the American Dream. At first John resisted his parents' designs, for the supposed dazzling lights of achieving upward mobility through hard work paled in comparison to much shinier interests such as sports and girls. But John, as a result of hundreds of parental nudges through the years, eventually came to inherit his parents' ambitions as his own.

With John on board, his father scraped up enough money to send him to a premier prep school in New England. There John entered a community of the elite. It might as well have been located on a different planet from where he grew up. Dinner parties, poetry readings, professors who lived and breathed refined and cultured sentiments, plus some upscale parties over weekends where everyone could play fraternity. John, of course, was an outsider with humble roots, a funny southern accent, and a hesitancy to cause too much trouble. All of this made him stick out, though he desperately wanted to fit in.

By this point the ambition that John's parents had drilled into him from an early age was being reinforced by everyone around him. The American achievement story had become the driving narrative of his life. He didn't just dream of a home with a white picket fence, three kids, and a car. He craved admiration. He longed to be revered.

Around such secular and educated teachers—with "secular" and "educated" nearly serving as synonyms at boarding school—John was increasingly embarrassed by his mom's quaint Christian piety. Sensing that he was coming of age, John eventually concluded that he simply must leave his mom behind, along with her Fundamentalist Christian community. Predictably, John harbored a mostly unconscious bias against other Christian traditions, since the strict preachers of his childhood had so often warned him about those other, twisted versions of Christianity that attempted to make the faith palatable to cultural elites. The effect was that he never gave much thought to other Christian options. He occasionally attended church services, but only to pick up girls. Ambition, coming-of-age rationality, lust—these are the strands of John's story.[1]

Though the specifics will vary, John's story is one whose basic plotline is all too familiar in our late-modern world. And yet it is also a narrative that finds resonance within Augustine's world. In fact, John is our modern-day portrait of the young Augustine. In entering Augustine's story we find ourselves in a world that feels different from the one soon to be *fully* absorbed by Christendom, which arrived after Augustine's death and reigned in the West for over a thousand years.[2] For while Christianity was a growing force in late antiquity, certain winds make Augustine's waters strangely familiar to Christians in the West today: an elite, anti-Christian community leveraging moral and civic denunciations against believers; a society experiencing the uncertainty and angst of tectonic cultural shifts; and the prophetic, existential particularities told in Augustine's personal story.

By merging several modern people we've known into a composite character, John, we've depicted in contemporary terms some of the present-day cultural riptides that we will turn to again later in this chapter: a pluralized environment where no single worldview has absolute dominance, the rationalistic coming-of-age story that shapes the imagination of those in our cultural centers, and the stories packaged in everything from car commercials to graduation speeches that beckon us to find cosmic significance in this-world achievements. In this chapter we will see that Augustine is swimming in and against a current that looks surprisingly familiar. And because Augustine has to navigate these waters himself and instruct doubters and believers on how to make it through them, he is uniquely equipped to speak into contemporary apologetics. By paying close attention to the opening books of *Confessions* as well as zeroing in on the cultural upheaval in the Roman Empire that led to *The City of God*, we will see why Augustine's voice has renewed relevance for us today.

---

1. While we both (Josh in Georgia in the '90s and Mark in West Virginia in the '60s and '70s) felt similar pressures, John is not a pseudonym for either one of us but is rather a composite character that allows us to synthesize different experiences and the observations of other people we grew up with.

2. The start of Christendom is often signaled by the reign of Constantine and, more specifically, the Edict of Milan in AD 313. While we do not disagree that these are significant historical markers for the beginning of a trajectory toward what would eventually become Christendom, it is important to note that neither development automatically made catholic Christianity the default option for people in the Roman Empire. The early stages of late antiquity were yet to be fully absorbed by Christendom. True, Christians had growing and significant institutional and cultural power in Augustine's time, but Christianity still did not dominate the social imagination, especially among many elites, in the way it would in the medieval period.

## A Coming-of-Age Story . . . and Back: The Context for Augustine's Deconversion

### An Identity Crisis

As the philosopher Charles Taylor explains, "No one acquires the languages needed for self-definition on their own."[3] We are always defining our personal identity in dialogue with our community. Consider, for example, the hero stories our communities and traditions tell us and how we embrace these narratives and seek to live them out. But what happens when our competing national and local stories blow us in different directions?

Augustine was born into a certain kind of incoherence, and thus his early life lacked a larger, unifying narrative from which he could build a secure identity. We might call this Augustine's disorientation, and it began with his birthplace: Thagaste, North Africa. It was a small, unremarkable town where three worlds, each with its own cultural identity, intersected and vied for space to flourish.[4] First, the Berbers, originally a seminomadic people, made up most of the native population. They spoke Lybian and valued emotion, spontaneity, locality, and family. The Berbers viewed the Romans as imperialists who justified their law and order with a slanted rationality. Second, there were the Punics, who had colonized the area centuries before Augustine's birth. They had subjected the Berbers to high taxation and relegated them to less-respected occupations, often involving manual labor. But the sun was beginning to set on them, and by the time Augustine was learning Latin in school, the Punic language was disappearing from streets and homes. Third, there were the Romans. They had invaded and dominated the region after the Punics, administering the area, and especially the large landholdings, with a strong arm. Their language, Latin, was the language of the empire. They valued reason, order, natural law, and, of course, their empire. Naturally, then, they considered the impulsive Berbers to be uncivilized, and their estimation of the Punics was barely higher.[5]

Augustine's personal identity was not grounded solidly in any one of these cultural stories but rather was pushed and pulled within this cross-pressured local context, where heritages overlapped, competed, and grated against one another in confusing ways. By analogy, imagine growing up in the rural American South, with its festive patriotic holidays and civics classes teaching a glorified national history rooted in the notion of America's divinely inspired exceptionalism, only to go to university and hear this story deconstructed as a fiction and

---

3. Taylor, *Ethics of Authenticity*, 33.
4. Ellingsen, *Richness of Augustine*, 7, 11.
5. For Augustine's early multicultural background, see González, *Mestizo Augustine*, 21–32.

replaced with one that makes the nation's history about oppression. It is easy to imagine the effects, which could culminate in a sort of identity vertigo after years of being tossed to and fro.

In addition to lacking a single, obvious local narrative to inhabit, Augustine experienced competing cultural and spiritual differences within his own family. His father, Patrick (Patricius), was Roman. He was employed as a Roman official with the responsibility of collecting taxes, which would have made him unpopular with the native Africans. Religiously, he was pagan, only converting to Christianity shortly before his death. Patrick was not a person of means, but—in Augustine's words—his "shameless ambition" pressured him toward fame and wealth in the Roman world.[6] Augustine's mother, Monica, was a Berber and an extremely dominant presence in his life, pushing constantly for his salvation, professional success, and ascent up the Roman social ladder. She was a devout Christian with, above all else, an unrelenting passion for her son's conversion to the faith. The unhappy result for Augustine was that he felt disoriented and wrangled by these competing expectations of him: Roman and Berber, pagan and Christian, success and salvation.

During adolescence, Augustine began seeking the carnal pleasures on offer in a highly sexualized culture. He also made friends with people whose favorite pursuit in daily life was to gain all sorts of social advantages over others. This turned out to be a noxious mix of sexual and social pressure, unmooring Augustine from any sense of wholeness. At the beginning of book 2 of *Confessions*, Augustine admits to his fragmented life: "I will try now to give a coherent account of my *disintegrated self*, for when I turned away from you, the one God, and pursued a multitude of things, *I went to pieces*."[7] Augustine's affections were being pulled in impossible directions. Contorting himself to follow each one left him miserable.

Later, he turned to philosophical wisdom but found that this alone did not have the power to heal and integrate his fragmented self.[8] Augustine despaired of ever making meaningful sense of the vast chasm of his complicated desires and mysterious inner workings: "A human being is an immense abyss. . . . Even his hairs are easier to number than the affections and movements of his heart."[9] During this time a close friend of his died, leaving Augustine's soul bleeding and tattered: "I had poured out my soul into the sand by loving a man doomed to

---

6. Augustine, *Confessions* 2.3.5.

7. Augustine, *Confessions* 2.1.1 (emphasis added).

8. Augustine would later come to see God as offering grace to heal humanity, such that while a full restoration was not experienced in this life, the medicine of Christ and its effects did begin to work in the present. More on this in part 2.

9. Augustine, *Confessions* 4.14.22.

death as though he were never to die."[10] Augustine was at the end of himself: "I had roamed away from myself and could not even find myself."[11]

It is worth stopping to introduce a point that we will feature more prominently later in this book: persuasion happens not in the abstract but in the particular—a specific person or persons with their own personal time-bound experiences speaking to others, who have their own culturally embodied stories. In this sense all apologetics is cultural apologetics, because persuasion always happens within a particular culture, responds to particular challenges, and addresses particular maladies. Augustine's own struggle to find a unifying story and a place to call home while experiencing soul-crushing disillusionment and a disintegrated self makes his voice particularly relevant to us, for we are living through what has been labeled the "age of anxiety"—a society absent a coherent, sustainable, unifying narrative. The similarities between Augustine's anguish and our modern malaise will prove useful in later chapters; from Augustine we will learn an apologetic that offers a way to heal and a reason to hope.

### Coming of Age

Today we tend to think of a coming-of-age story as an account of someone maturing beyond the Christian faith. Generally speaking, on an experiential level, coming of age feels like an honest and brave quest for truth that involves advancing beyond belief in primitive Christian myths that, contrary to what so many preachers insist, seem naive and unhelpful in the real world. Science, logic, and objectivity combine to help a person shed the remnants of Christian innocence. Rationality demands we grow up and face the cold, hard facts of life, sometimes with deep angst and other times with optimism fueled by the prospect of human achievement. Professional ambitions play a larger role than many will admit, as so often the "maturing" we're talking about revolves around earning acceptance from the "who's who" in respected fields of work. Like so many of our late-modern versions, Augustine's quest consisted of desires for what was certain amid a plurality of choices and what was intellectually respectable and financially profitable among the elites of his day.

The adults in Augustine's early years baptized him into the waters of a kind of ancient meritocracy. Stern discipline and the right education in the best schools were to be paired with Augustine's natural talent in order that he might earn a life of wealth and fame. According to Augustine's later reflections, his parents and teachers "thought only of sating man's insatiable appetite for a poverty

10. Augustine, *Confessions* 4.8.13.
11. Augustine, *Confessions* 5.2.2.

tricked out as wealth and a fame that is but infamy."[12] Their main concern was decidedly not Augustine's personal character but "that I should learn to excel in rhetoric and persuasive speech,"[13] for these were the chief means to achieve success in the Greco-Roman world of this time. And what was success? Money and notoriety. In time, personal hubris and peer pressure piled on top of the controlling messages coming from his authority figures, and the three together shackled Augustine to the pursuit of these ambitions. He admits that, along with a company of students similarly affected, he began to study "treatises on eloquence," longing "to excel, though my motive was the damnably proud desire to gratify my human vanity."[14] A while later, in his twenties, he joined a cult of ambition, a society of deceived and deceiving idolaters who devoted themselves to their twisted ambitions: "We pursued trumpery, popular acclaim, theatrical plaudits, song-competitions and the contest for ephemeral wreaths. . . . I pursued, these things I did, in the company of friends who through me and with me were alike deceived."[15]

A fascinating example of what we might call the sociology of being led astray is found in Augustine's famous pear story. In his adolescence, Augustine, along with some friends, stole some pears out of a tree and then destroyed them; the thrill was in the theft. Upon reflection, Augustine realized there was a certain allure in outsmarting others and belonging to an exclusive, empowered group. He explains, "I most certainly would not have done it alone. It follows then that I also loved the comradery with my fellow-thieves." Then he confesses, "But since my pleasure did not lie in the pears, it must have been in the crime as committed in the company of others who shared in the sin."[16] The satisfaction was found not in the thing but in the special friendship of those who pursued it together, plus the thrilling feelings of superiority attained by "outwitting people who had no idea what we were doing."[17]

Long before Friedrich Nietzsche interpreted the world through a "will to power," Augustine confessed that "commanding and dominating other people" was an intoxicating motivator and the desire to do so greatly affected his reasoning.[18] To use Jonathan Haidt's metaphor, the elephant (emotions) and the rider (reason) were in this quest together.[19] While reflecting on his early life, Augustine admitted that lurking behind his youthful self-confident claims to

12. Augustine, *Confessions* 1.12.19.
13. Augustine, *Confessions* 2.2.4.
14. Augustine, *Confessions* 3.4.7.
15. Augustine, *Confessions* 4.1.1.
16. Augustine, *Confessions* 2.8.16.
17. Augustine, *Confessions* 2.9.17.
18. Augustine, *Confessions* 2.5.10.
19. Haidt, *Happiness Hypothesis*, 1–44.

have mastered the world through reason, the elephant had been running wild. Given these factors—his ambition to be admired by the cultural elites, his need for certainty, and his *libido dominandi* (the dominating lust to dominate)—it's no surprise that he, like our composite character John, turned away from the Christian faith of his childhood to what he felt was a more intellectually mature option. In short, Augustine had to be humbled to see that there was much more happening epistemologically than a simple rational quest to follow the evidence.

Augustine famously turned toward wisdom upon his reading of Cicero's *The Hortensius*. He described the volume's profound impact on him: "The book changed my way of feeling and the character of my prayers to you, O Lord. . . . With unbelievable intensity my heart burned with longing for the immortality that wisdom seemed to promise. I began to rise up, in order to return to you."[20] In his search for wisdom, Augustine explored the faith of his childhood but was profoundly disappointed. He rediscovered a Bible that was offensively crude and common. The Old Testament Scriptures recounted worldly and immoral stories. The New Testament contained contradictions in places critical to the person of Jesus Christ. Further, a narrow "fundamentalism" characterized his home church. Obstinate bishops used the Bible as the basis for their oppressive rule and wielded its words as a means to stamp out challenges to their authority and to skirt difficult questions.

For certain spiritual seekers at that time, this ecclesial traditionalism and literalism made them thirst for an unmediated spiritual encounter with Christ, one in which divine Wisdom would speak directly to the longing soul and the curious, contemplative mind captured by the arts and education. Along with others in his social and intellectual circles, Augustine enthusiastically extricated himself from the confining beliefs of the church and opened himself up to the possibilities of a new kind of freedom, one found in a reimagined Christ (a name in his "deepest heart" to which he still clung),[21] based on reason instead of faith, and leading to what he thought would be a true knowledge of himself.

Manicheism provided Augustine with this alternative fundamentalism to the Christian fundamentalism of his childhood. It promised him the universality, spirituality, and certainty he desired. The Manichees saw themselves as rationalists and took great pride in following "science."[22] Yet, for Augustine, it was the Manichees' enlightened posture that drew him in more than the details of their strained system of beliefs. Augustine hoped that by associating with the Manichees he would have a sophisticated justification for putting his childhood

20. Augustine, *Confessions* 3.4.7.
21. Augustine, *Confessions* 3.4.8.
22. We don't mean to suggest that "science" meant to the Manichees what the word means today. Our focus here is on an analogous posture between modern rationalists and the Manichees.

religion completely to bed. Better yet, since he feared being duped, the Manichees' habits of mocking the old wives' tales of his mother's Christianity and promising a rational, manly philosophy of life made Manicheism an altogether enticing, albeit illusory, option. The community was also appealing, for in it Augustine could flourish side by side with people who valued objective truth over fanciful myths and would allow him "to slough off any beliefs that threatened the independence of his very active mind."[23] Plus, he would now be identified with the intelligentsia of his day; these "Brights" carried themselves with the epistemological confidence of today's New Atheists, possessing cultural power beyond their limited numbers (and scholarly depth).[24]

Manicheism was a variegated sect. It could mean many things to many people in many places. Augustine's Manicheism "was of a specific group, of the cultivated intelligentsia of the university of Carthage and of the small-town notables of Thagaste."[25] Manicheism associated him with an exclusive group of young men who possessed superior intelligence and an argumentative spirit. Young Augustine reveled in being part of a group that could outwit and embarrass ill-equipped, naive Christians. He later recalled the thrill of victory:

> I almost always gained a certain harmful victory when I argued in discussions with Christians, who were unlearned but still striving to defend their faith in combat, as well as each of them could. My youthful ardor increased along with this frequent success and unwisely brought me by its impetus into the great evil of stubbornness. . . . My love for [the Manichees] was daily renewed as a result of my success in debating. From this it came about that in certain strange ways I approved as true whatever they said, not because I knew that it was true but because I wanted it to be.[26]

It's easy to imagine a modern version of young Augustine in his Manichean stage riffing off popular atheists like Richard Dawkins and Christopher Hitchens, mockingly dismissing Christians on his personal YouTube channel.

Augustine was still a young man at this point, but along with his Manichean friends, he took great pride in his advancement beyond the faith of his childhood. Together, they deconstructed traditional faith in the Scriptures and discovered more rational, ethical, and spiritual ways of living in the world. They reveled in their superiority. For Augustine, these efforts provided the elite comradery and worldly esteem he longed for. Even after he became disillusioned

---

23. Brown, *Augustine of Hippo*, 38. This coming-of-age section relies on two chapters in Brown: "'Wisdom'" (chap. 4) and "Manichaeism" (chap. 5).

24. J. Smith, *On the Road with Saint Augustine*, 146.

25. Brown, *Augustine of Hippo*, 43.

26. Augustine, *The Two Souls* 9.11.

with Manichean thought, he was "more comfortable in friendly association with Manichees than with others not of that heresy."[27]

Two episodes from Augustine's life illustrate what he was leaving behind and what he was striving toward. First was the death of the aforementioned lifelong friend, whom Augustine had grown up with in Thagaste. At some point Augustine convinced his friend to leave the catholic faith and join him in following the Manichees. Later, there came a time when this friend was battling a fever that left him unconscious and "sweating at death's door." As hope for recovery faded, the friend's family had the baptismal rites administered to their unconscious son. A short while later, and to everyone's surprise, he began to recover, rallying to a sentient state. Augustine wrote that soon afterward "I attempted to chaff him, expecting him to join me in making fun of the baptism he had undergone while entirely absent in mind and unaware of what was happening." It's a telling scene, Augustine eagerly awaiting this fresh and dramatic opportunity to mock his former faith with a good friend. But to Augustine's surprise his friend took the baptism seriously and was thus offended by Augustine's scorn and condescension: "He recoiled from me with a shudder as though I had been his enemy, and with amazing, new-found independence warned me that if I wished to be his friend I had better stop saying such things to him."[28] Though taken aback, Augustine was confident that he could persuade his friend of his naivete once he was fully restored to health. Augustine never got the chance. Just a few days later his friend died.

Augustine lamented the death of his friend with bitter tears. But, like turning over rocks to find a mass of ugly, crawling things, this traumatic incident exposed ugly qualities in Augustine that were otherwise hidden. Much later, in frank self-reflection, he concluded he had been trying to fulfill his innate thirst for God by way of a thick, even twisted, love for his friend. "I was miserable, and miserable too is everyone whose mind is chained by friendship with mortal things, and is torn apart by their loss, and then becomes aware of the misery that it was in even before it lost them." At the time, however, Augustine probed no deeper than his broken heart. The result was a hardened resolve to shed the religion of his childhood. In support of this were his comrades, and together they pressed deeper into the pursuit of a more elegant and sophisticated existence.[29] With the death of his dear friend, Augustine turned not to the Christian God but to the comforting spoils of an elite group of friends: hearty conversation seasoned with witty banter, penetrating debates about important ideas, and,

27. Augustine, *Confessions* 5.10.18–19.
28. Augustine, *Confessions* 4.4.8.
29. Augustine, *Confessions* 4.6.11.

most importantly, a shared love of fine books. But these friendships were disordered, fragile, exclusive, and weighed down by the heavy ego each participant carried. They reinforced Augustine's departure from the church and ushered him on his quest for intellectual and vocational success. And to Augustine, these companions were just what he needed to overcome the limitations of his past and become somebody great.

The second episode came at a time when Augustine was writing some works on beauty. He decided to dedicate them to Hierius, a Roman orator. What's interesting is that Augustine never knew Hierius personally; he loved Hierius for his reputation as a learned man. This is telling, for as much as Augustine believed he desired wisdom and rational truth, his thinking was unduly shaped by fixations on reputation. Beyond admiring others for the respect they commanded, Augustine desperately wanted others to respect him, as they did Hierius. Here, then, Augustine betrayed his own stated aims, for what he was really interested in was not discovering truth through a learned man's ideas but rather using the man's sterling reputation for his own benefit. If he could praise the right people, then he, too, might climb the intellectual ladder all the way up to a nice perch on which he could rest as intelligent people dedicated books to him. Hence, while he was indeed moving away from his childhood faith, it was not for purely rational reasons. His longing to achieve something great and to be respected for it in elite circles shaped his likes and dislikes, his research and conclusions, and what he published and to whom he dedicated it; these malformed motivations shaped the judgments of a discontented soul.

Morality and guilt also played an important part in Augustine's coming-of-age story, as he desperately sought a way to maintain a sense of moral superiority while minimizing any dissonance he felt over seeking pleasure to the point of repeated carnal failures. Augustine saw in the Manichees a way to alleviate the guilt brought on by his morally rigid religious upbringing, the stern warnings against bodily pleasures in Cicero's *Hortensius,* and his own moral shortcomings. He needed something to assure him of his essential goodness while helping him to deal with the guilt of his sexual failings. As an adherent of Manichean anthropology, Augustine could view himself as an essentially good person encroached upon by evil. His mind and soul were eternally good but temporally harassed by violent attacks of the bad. Peter Brown explains, "For Augustine, the need to save an untarnished oasis of perfection within himself formed, perhaps, the deepest strain of his adherence to the Manichees."[30] Later, as a bishop, he admitted, "I liked to excuse

---

30. Brown, *Augustine of Hippo,* 40.

myself and lay the blame on some other force that was with me but was not myself."[31]

As Sigmund Freud and Nietzsche understood many years later, guilt is a powerful force that drives humans intellectually and emotionally. Aldous Huxley understood this too, as we see in his famous confession concerning the motivation behind his doctrine of meaninglessness: "The liberation we desired was simultaneously liberation from a certain political and economic system and liberation from a certain system of morality. We objected to the morality because it interfered with our sexual freedom."[32] Somewhat analogously, Manicheism seems to have allowed Augustine to pursue the austere morality of the philosophers without, at least in theory, the nagging inner shame that haunted him when he failed to live up to his own standards.

Augustine's analysis in *Confessions* of his journey from his mother's quaint faith to a kind of fourth-century hard rationalism reveals just how varied the psychological, social, and moral factors were in his deconversion. His analysis, so appreciative of the human complexities at play when one comes of age, helps us make sense of what happens today. It's common to hear, especially among secular urbanites, that humans have a moral imperative to push culture beyond antiquated religious ideas; this notion is buttressed by polls suggesting a rapid increase in the number of "nones," those with no religious affiliation. But Augustine reminds us that coming-of-age stories are not simply matters of following the evidence as we cast off religion. As Charles Taylor's account of the West's five-century journey from Christianity to secularism makes clear, such stories, both the societal and individual versions, told in the name of science are actually reductionistic "subtraction stories."[33] Though people may claim that coming of age today is as simple and neutral as basic math—just subtract religion from society and "follow the science!"—in actuality they are pushed along by moral, psychological, and social beliefs that aren't scientifically provable and are chock-full of assumptions leftover from metaphysical stories they deny.[34]

---

31. Augustine, *Confessions* 5.10.18.

32. Huxley, *Aldous Huxley: Complete Essays*, 4:369.

33. Taylor, *A Secular Age*, 26–29. We are using "secularism" along the lines of Taylor's secular 3, which he describes as a society that has moved from belief in God being "unchallenged and indeed, unproblematic" to religious belief being "understood to be one option among others, and frequently not the easiest to embrace" (3).

34. In the West, the most impactful of these stories has been the Christian story. See Holland, *Dominion*.

### Plot Holes Emerge in the Coming-of-Age Story

Returning to Augustine's inner life, despite Manicheism's promises and its teaching on the essential goodness of humans, it did not, in the end, assuage his guilt. Rather, by depicting both God and human beings as victims of evil's power, it left him unsatisfied. And while it's true that many people identify primarily as victims in order to "experience a profound sense of moral release, of recovered innocence,"[35] embraced as a fundamental identity, victimhood actually diminishes agency, personhood, and the ability to look to a God who is able to save one from evil forces. The Manichees emptied God of his omnipotence and turned humans, whose souls were merged with the divine, into passive, violated weaklings. Blaming an external force for personal moral failings never cleanses consciences in a positive or sustainable way. Later, upon reflection, Bishop Augustine realized how Manichean anthropology had undercut the therapeutic power of confessing sin before God: "When I had done something wrong it was pleasant to avoid having to confess that I had done it, a confession that would have given you [God] a chance to heal this soul of mine that had sinned against you."[36] Augustine eventually discovered that Manicheism could offer only a hollow rationality and failed to satisfy. His soul remained guilt ridden and restless.

Instead of directing him back to his orthodox Christian faith, Augustine's disappointments with Manicheism turned him toward the skepticism of the Academics, who, at least in Augustine's understanding at the time, doubted everything and denied that the human mind could comprehend any part of the truth.[37] And while an elegant and civilized skepticism would have helped him move within the circles of well-educated Romans,[38] Augustine learned soon enough that it "could never provide an honest seeker after truth like [himself] with the peace of mind he craved."[39] He had reached an intellectual, spiritual, and moral dead end.

Augustine's ambition and rhetorical prowess, along with some connections to Manicheism he kept up for social and professional reasons, landed him the job of professor of rhetoric in the city of Milan, the seat of the imperial court. Hearing of Bishop Ambrose's reputation as an eloquent preacher, Augustine,

35. McClay, "Strange Persistence of Guilt," 48.
36. Augustine, *Confessions* 5.10.18.
37. Augustine, *Confessions* 5.10.19, 5.14.25. Augustine is not using the term "*Academics*" the way it is used today to describe people who are intellectual or have advanced degrees. Rather, Augustine is referring to a particular kind of intellectual who, after his conversion, he would write a treatise against.
38. Chadwick, *Augustine of Hippo*, 18.
39. Bray, *Augustine on the Christian Life*, 23.

ever an admirer of quick, sharp thinking and speaking, began listening to Ambrose, interested to see whether the bishop's skills matched his reputation.

Ambrose was a learned man. He had received an elite education—"grammar, Latin and Greek literature, rhetoric, and law"—and as a bishop he was well versed in "the Eastern Fathers, the Neoplatonic philosophers, and the pagan writers of antiquity."[40] More than that, he was a pastor-apologist who helped his flock by tirelessly defending the faith with a rhetorical flare and robust learning that matched the times and addressed the pressing challenges to Christianity. Although Augustine was not immediately convinced, in listening to Ambrose he found himself with fewer reasons not to believe. For instance, Ambrose's figurative interpretations of the Old Testament satisfied Augustine's concerns about the Law and the Prophets. Furthermore, Ambrose's "emphasis on the spirituality of God and the soul"[41] freed Augustine from the confines of fourth-century materialism.

As he sat under Ambrose's teaching, some of the fixtures of Augustine's coming-of-age narrative proved quite flimsy. In the bishop he had discovered an articulation of the faith that was far more sophisticated than the one he had grown up with in Thagaste. Augustine later admitted he had made certain assumptions about the Christian faith that were simply untrue: "I was filled with joy, albeit a shamefaced joy, at the discovery that what I had barked against for so many years was not the Catholic faith but the figments of carnal imagination. I had been all the more foolhardy and impious in my readiness to rant and denounce where I ought to have inquired and sought to learn."[42] After some time in Milan, Augustine assessed Ambrose's case for the catholic faith as being "defensible" (fairly high praise coming from Augustine) and the content of that faith as "intellectually respectable." Still, he did not commit himself to that faith. "I did not yet consider the Catholic way the one to follow simply because it too could have its learned proponents, men who were capable of refuting objections with ample argument and good sense."[43]

Yet, "while doubting everything and wavering," Augustine decided "to live as a catechumen in the Catholic Church . . . until some kind of certainty dawned by which I might direct my steps aright."[44] After a period of deep mental anguish, he was famously converted in a small garden while reading Romans 13:13–14. Thereafter, he renounced his career ambitions, was baptized by Ambrose, and returned to Thagaste, primarily for the purpose of prayer, meditation, simplicity, good works, and teaching in the company of a few companions.

40. Trapè, *Saint Augustine*, 75–76.
41. Trapè, *Saint Augustine*, 82.
42. Augustine, *Confessions* 6.3.4.
43. Augustine, *Confessions* 5.14.24.
44. Augustine, *Confessions* 5.14.25.

Immediately, however, his path took a drastic turn. While he was on a trip to Hippo hoping to find a place to establish a monastery, the local congregation seized him and, in spite of his objections and tears, ordained him as a priest. Eventually, he became bishop of Hippo and necessarily took on the many burdensome duties of a bishop, perhaps the most burdensome of all being the task of leading people to and keeping people in the faith. This responsibility would become even harder when the world was turned upside down. What he would come to see, however, was how much his own journey away from and back to the faith eased this burden. For his soul had gone astray and come home, and he could thus speak to the complexities therein with profound conviction capable of comforting the believers in his flock and pricking the hearts of the skeptics in their midst.

### One Option among Many

Charles Taylor has described our current secular age as one in which Christian theism is only a possibility among many competing options—and one that in some quarters is increasingly marginalized. This is a far cry from the worlds of the medieval and Reformation periods, when Christianity was the dominant option and, in most cases, was simply taken for granted. It should be noted, however, that while Christianity is now only one among many options, it is still *an* option. In fact, there are currently 167 million confessing Christians of some sort in America,[45] and 91 percent of people living in Western Europe have been baptized.[46] Clearly, Christianity, at least some form of it, remains widespread in the West. But it's becoming an increasingly strange option for elites in our various cultural centers. Similarly, the pagan intelligentsia in Augustine's time— a group that harbored serious contempt toward Christianity and, as a result, found itself in Augustine's apologetic crosshairs—were making condescending jabs similar to those one might expect to hear about "Bible thumpers" at enlightened cocktail parties in today's upscale urban high-rises.

Despite Christianity's growth throughout the third and fourth centuries— a transformation that prevented critics from ignoring it outright—heroic and nostalgic tales of Rome's former glories, circumscribed by the eminence of her ancient philosophers, continued to cast long shadows over people's imaginations. (The divide between the church and the pagans was even sharper in the Greco-Roman world of the second century, especially among elites who easily

45. "In U.S., Decline of Christianity Continues at Rapid Pace: An Update on America's Changing Religious Landscape," Pew Research Center, October 17, 2019, https://www.pewforum.org /2019/10/17/in-u-s-decline-of-christianity-continues-at-rapid-pace.
46. "Being Christian in Western Europe," Pew Research Center, May 29, 2018, https://www .pewforum.org/2018/05/29/being-christian-in-western-europe.

dismissed Christians as a bizarre people moving about the unsavory margins of society and possessing nearly zero cultural influence.) Augustine practiced apologetics at a time when catholic Christianity had become a significant cultural force, but it was still one option among many (and when, to large swaths of pagan elites, the idea of choosing was met with condescension). Today, as Christianity faces decline in the West, we find ourselves on the opposite end of Christendom from Augustine and in a faraway world. Yet it is a world with some surprising analogues to that of the bishop. For both worlds—Augustine's and ours—are deeply impacted by Christianity but are outside Christendom's dominance.

In 397, by which time Augustine had been bishop of Hippo for only a few years, he composed *Confessions*. He desired to bolster the faith of those who might be struggling with issues similar to his own. He had experienced a coming-of-age story marked by a desperate pursuit of professional achievement, social standing, personal spirituality, assuaged guilt, and truth grounded in material proof and naked rationality. In his reflections on each of these pursuits, *Confessions* offers us many different treasures, though they have rarely been mined for apologetics. So far in this chapter, we've seen how Augustine's journey and his subsequent analysis provided a pastoral apologetic for his congregation, which has the potential for offering us relevant resources for persuasion today. While keeping a close eye on the parallels between Augustine's context and our contemporary situation, we'll now fast-forward in Augustine's life to the historical and cultural background for *The City of God*.

## The Cultural Crisis: The Context for Augustine's Magnum Opus

### Loss of a Coherent Narrative

Augustine ministered during an epochal change. With the sack of Rome in August 410 by Alaric and his Gothic forces, the angst in the empire grew palpably. Many blamed Christianity for the fall of Rome and questioned whether its ethic was actually livable. Would Christianity be sacked too? Would traditional pluralistic paganism, always poised to regain power, take over at the expense of Christianity's influence?

Augustine responded to the challenge of the massive changes happening during his life by paying close attention to and developing a nuanced understanding of them. Consequently, he is well suited to speak into our context and help us understand the epochal changes we are living through. Curtis Chang, finding analogues in Augustine's context, reminds us that our time "is not the first time Christianity has needed to figure out what to say when the Western civilization it is attached to seems to be in danger of dying."[47] To see how Augustine is relevant today, it is instructive to contrast the era that preceded Augustine with the one that was unfolding while he served as a bishop. The contrast reveals at least two important shifts within the history of the Roman Empire that help us understand the unique epochal changes, and the resulting apologetic challenges, Augustine encountered. In other words, contextualizing Augustine in this way sheds light on his apologetic innovations and why they are helpful in addressing our own shifting culture.

We might term the first era the pre-Christian Roman era. Paganism was well established historically, politically, and philosophically within the Roman Empire. A kind of pluralism was allowed as long as each religion could fit within the bounds of Caesar's lordship, a kind of forced accommodation strategy that diluted religions by mixing them. Christianity, though just a small movement, caused some concern in that it didn't fit well within these parameters, since Christians denied all other gods, refused to participate in pagan worship, and recognized only the lordship of Jesus Christ.

At times Christians in the Roman world literally had to run for their lives. It was normal for Christians to perceive themselves as a small minority within a hostile society. Christianity also lacked any mature institutional presence. Apologetics, then, was necessarily defensive and reactionary. Most unbelievers didn't feel serious pressure to weigh the claims of Christianity because it was generally not considered a serious option. A new era finally dawned during Emperor Constantine's rule, which saw Christianity become a tolerated religion before being instituted as the empire's leading religious force.

The second era we might term the Christian Roman era. In it, many aspired to wed the Roman Empire with the kingdom of God; what developed was the narrative of the Christianized eternal city. For example, the ancient Christian bishop and historian Eusebius of Caesarea (265–339) celebrated Emperor Constantine as the culmination of God's universal saving work begun in Jesus Christ. The Roman Empire would now advance the work of God on earth and unite all people into one great, harmonious order that would forever worship the one true (Christian) God: one empire under one God, advancing God's peace and purposes throughout the earth. Eusebius's convictions about the eternal city were given credence by two subsequent Roman emperors. Emperor Gratian discontinued the empire's funding and sanction of pagan cults. Emperor Theodosius I declared Christianity the state religion of the Roman Empire. Both imperial acts occurred during Augustine's lifetime.

---

47. Chang, *Engaging Unbelief*, 25.

Yet not all in Rome shared Eusebius's enthusiasm over the marriage of Rome and the kingdom of God. Emperor Julian the Apostate led a short-lived campaign to rid the empire of Christian influence, and many intellectual traditionalists did not go along with the new religion but held on to the old Roman politic, philosophy, and religion. Such pagan elites controlled the educational system and shaped the way society perceived much of its history and contemporary events. Thus, we should not confuse the Christian Roman era with what would later be called Christendom.

Even after Theodosius had declared Christianity the official religion of the empire, many pagans in North Africa stubbornly resisted the teachings of the church. In the new edition of Peter Brown's biography of Augustine, Brown admits he changed his mind about Augustine and the challenges of his ministry context. With the discovery of Augustine's Dolbeau sermons and Divjak letters, Brown decided to take a closer look at "the more humdrum, the less successful and the more gentle, painstaking aspects of Augustine's life as a bishop in North Africa,"[48] the place where pastor-apologists had to actually practice the craft of persuasion. This fresh look at Augustine called for a closer examination of his sermons and letters. Brown states that Augustine's sermons were not authoritarian *ex cathedra* declarations but were more like "dialogues with the crowd." We see in them Augustine pastorally and patiently persuading the unconvinced. "One senses in them the constant presence of the unpersuaded, the indifferent and the downright disobedient."[49] Further, Brown describes Augustine's fluid and contingent ministry context in this way:

> Paganism, although officially suppressed by Imperial laws and frequently declared by triumphant Christian writers to be virtually non-existent, had by no means given way to Christianity in the cities of Roman North Africa. . . . The medieval Christianity to which Augustine's thought contributed so heavily was still a long way away from the North Africa of Augustine. . . . This new picture of Augustine the Bishop [reveals him] at work in a more fluid environment than we had thought.[50]

Triumphant Christian claims may have denied paganism's vitality in the cities of North Africa, but the actual facts on the ground reveal that paganism was yet alive and well, even within Augustine's flock. On at least one occasion he felt compelled to abandon his proposed sermon topic because of

---

48. Brown, *Augustine of Hippo*, 446. Brown admits, "I have found the Augustine of the Dolbeau sermons and the Divjak letters to be considerably less the authoritarian, stern figure that my reading of the evidence available to me in the 1960s had led me to suspect" (445).

49. Brown, *Augustine of Hippo*, 446.

50. Brown, *Augustine of Hippo*, 447.

the unyielding obstinacy of the crowd.[51] Still, the bishop maintained a hopeful approach, grounding his sermons in the narrative of Scripture.[52] He believed that by enduring in the face of the hardships caused by the hard hearts of his hearers, he would find that the mercy and grace of God was slowly but powerfully transforming their hearts, producing within them a love for God and for their neighbors.[53]

Even in the face of strong opposition, Augustine envisioned the transformative power of the Christian faith. He imagined a Christianity expansive enough to capture the heart of an entire society,[54] bringing healing, unity, and peace to the world.[55] For a short while he insisted that the pagans needed to wake up to the fact that Christianity was a universal religion with the capacity to carry the weight of an entire society. Even though it had begun with fishermen, the catholic faith had now gained the attention and allegiance of emperors and kings, fulfilling Scripture's prophecy. In the year 404, preaching to the people of the little town of Boseth, he declared optimistically and forcefully,

> Kings lately, are coming to Rome. It's terrific, brothers and sisters, how it was all fulfilled. When it was being uttered, when it was being written, none of these things were happening. It's marvelous. Take note of it and see, rejoice. . . . They're astonished, you see, at the way the human race is converging on the name of the crucified and streaming together, from kings to ragamuffins. . . . Every age has been called to salvation, every age has already come, every degree, every level of wealth and property. It's high time for all and sundry to be inside. Now just a few have remained outside, and they still go on arguing; if only they would wake up some time or other, at least at the din the world is making! The whole world is shouting at them![56]

Here we have what turns out to be an overly optimistic notion expressed enthusiastically in a rhetorical flourish. Augustine's vision of Christianity's redemptive capacity was right, but he seemingly overreached in declaring just how expansive it had become. Within a few years, his hopes for a full-throated merger of Christianity and the empire had dissipated. Perhaps his enthusiasm cooled because Christian bishops turned out to exercise precious little clout in

51. Brown, *Augustine of Hippo*, 447.
52. Brown, *Augustine of Hippo*, 448, 455.
53. Brown, *Augustine of Hippo*, 448.
54. Brown, *Augustine of Hippo*, 459.
55. Brown, *Augustine of Hippo*, 460.
56. Augustine, *Sermon* 360B.25. See O'Daly, *Augustine's City of God*, 47. O'Daly notes that Augustine had enthusiasm for a Christianized empire as early as the 390s: "Augustine was attracted to the idea of a radically Christianized empire under Theodosius in the 390s, but had retreated from it by the time he came to write the *City of God*."

everyday Roman affairs, having to "reckon with a deeply entrenched tradition of resistance, often by officials who were still pagan in their allegiance."[57] But even before the sack of Rome, Augustine began to rethink the relationship between the earthly city and the heavenly city while remaining convinced of the catholic faith's ability to impact society in meaningful ways.

With the sack of Rome, the Christian eternal-city narrative proved fragile and temporary. Pagans vigorously challenged Christianity as a transitory, foreign intrusion into the glorious history of Rome. Even worse, the tide turned against Christianity as pagans blamed Christians for Rome's fall. Reaching back into the sources of their ancient history, Roman conservatives argued that Rome fell because its people had turned from their political, philosophical, and religious traditions.[58] With Rome reduced to rubble, many of these pagan Roman traditionalists fled to North Africa carrying with them criticisms that would be felt by Augustine's own parishioners.

It was an unsettling time in which ancient and contemporary conceptions of the nation and the world were in flux. Many Christians were deeply distraught over the threat of a divorce between Christianity and the empire. Jerome, the Christian translator of the Latin Vulgate, mourned the lost optimism of so many who had hoped that the merger between Christianity and the empire would bring peace and the reign of the Christian God throughout the world. He wrote, "When the brightest light of the world was extinguished, when the very head of the Roman Empire was severed, the entire world perished in a single city."[59] He, and many other Christians, sobbed with crushing disillusionment.

During these times, when the legitimacy and livability of the faith was in question, Augustine reflected deeply on Christianity, ancient history and philosophy, and contemporary rivals to the faith to provide a way for his congregation to inhabit the world, stay true to their faith, and stand up against pagan attacks. This called for more than a reactionary apologetic like that of the Christian apologists before the Christian Roman era,[60] although many of the arguments of these pre-Constantinian figures were brought forward. It called for a contextualized apologetic that reflected deeply on the sweep of history, critiqued culture, and presented a reimagined way for Christians to inhabit the emerging world.

---

57. Markus, *Christianity and the Secular*, 34.

58. Chang, *Engaging Unbelief*, 46–49.

59. Jerome, *Letter* 126.2. The translation is from Kelly, *Jerome*, 304.

60. See O'Daly, *Augustine's City of God*, 39–52: "The post-Constantinian Christianization of the Roman empire had altered the context of apologetic. Rome had a new public religion, and the question of its efficacy in protecting Rome called for new arguments. Yet many elements of earlier apologetic could be, and were, exploited by Augustine" (39).

This new apologetic needed to tackle big questions. Would catholic Christianity collapse with the fall of Rome? Should Christians revisit old patterns of Roman thinking? Was that even possible given Rome's fall?

Concerned Christians and skeptics alike brought such questions, along with theories about the relationship between Christianity and the empire, to Augustine.[61] The inquiry that most stubbornly occupied Augustine's mind was sent to him in a letter, around 411 or 412, by a friend and imperial official named Marcellinus. Marcellinus noted a very specific objection from an "illustrious lord" named Volusian. In Marcellinus's own words, the following is Volusian's objection to Christianity's relevance and practicality in the public square:

> Moreover, the preaching and teaching of Christ is in no way compatible with the practices of the state, since, as many say, it is clear that it is his commandment that we should repay no one with evil for evil, that we should offer the other cheek to one who strikes us, give our coat to one who insists on taking our cloak, and go twice the distance with someone who wants to force us to go with him. He states that all these are contrary to the practices of the state.[62]

For Volusian, Christianity simply could not work in the real world. The kind of Christian virtue expressed in the Sermon on the Mount was wholly impractical in public life.

Augustine, avoiding the delights of a quick and clever but simplistic answer, developed a response so patient and thoughtful that it's hard to think of a modern comparison: a sweeping tome more than a decade in the making—*The City of God*. He referred to it as "a massive work, and arduous" and regarded it as a promise kept and a payment of a debt to his friend Marcellinus, who was falsely accused of a crime and tragically executed in 413. In writing *The City of God* for his beloved Marcellinus, Augustine asserted that he took up the primary "task of defending the most glorious city of God." In the preface to *The City of God*, he stated his purpose clearly and succinctly: "I have undertaken to defend [the city of God] against those who prefer their own gods to its founder."[63]

With his purpose set, Augustine developed *The City of God* with three kinds of readers in mind. The first were "pagan critics of Christianity and 'these Christian times.'"[64] Such people, eager to blame Christianity for the sack of Rome, never liked the wedding of the empire to Christianity in the first place. Rather,

---

61. Portions of what follows in this section have been adapted from Mark Allen, "The City of God and the City of Man," *Faith and the Academy* 6, no. 1 (Fall 2021): 8–9. This article is used with permission.

62. Marcellinus to Augustine, *Letter* 136.2.

63. Augustine, *The City of God* 1, preface.

64. Babcock, introduction to Augustine, *The City of God*, xiii–xiv.

they were pagan traditionalists who had long sought a return to the glories of Rome that had existed before Christianity. They blamed Christianity for many of society's ills, vigorously challenged the religion's fittedness for the actual world, and doubted that it had any hope of bringing about peace and prosperity. More zealous members of this camp opposed any remnant of vibrant Christianity, arguing that its ethical norms were out of step with broader society, particularly the universal Christian call for people to embrace the claims of the gospel. Such exclusiveness was insufferably narrow, denying people the freedom to worship their own gods and enjoy culturally sanctioned pleasures.

Second, Augustine wrote to "Christians who have, in one degree or another, turned against their faith."[65] In today's terms we might say they had "deconverted." Under the pressures caused by Christianity's diminishing influence and increasingly fragile place in culture, some were walking away from the faith altogether, convinced it did not belong in the emerging world.

Third, Augustine considered "Christians who stand in need of a wider vindication of their belief over against the accumulated weight of the Roman religious and political tradition which represented Christianity as a betrayal of all that had made Rome great and, most especially, as a betrayal of its gods."[66] Even among the faithful, doubt crept in, loosening their confidence in the tenets of their Christian faith.

### Christianity as a Major Civic Problem

In significant ways the complicated landscape of the fourth and early fifth centuries that Augustine had to navigate is more similar to our context than the second century, the one that, at least recently, has often been compared to the West of today.[67] For one, Christians were a marginal group in the second century. Today, things are different. Still fresh in our minds as we write this is the image of President Donald Trump posing for a photo op in front of a church with Bible in hand during the racial unrest of summer 2020, President Joe Biden's 2021 inauguration speech sprinkled with Christian references, and Jeep's 2021 Super Bowl commercial featuring Bruce Springsteen honoring a church in Kansas as the symbolic center of America (there were even images of a cross flashing across the screen). One would search in vain for parallels in the second century; at this point emperors didn't use biblical allusions, and there was no Christian symbolism in the empire's propaganda. Meanwhile, recent

---

65. Babcock, introduction to Augustine, *The City of God*, xiv.

66. Babcock, introduction to Augustine, *The City of God*, xiv. See also O'Daly, *Augustine's City of God*, 36–37.

67. See, e.g., Trueman, *Rise and Triumph of the Modern Self*, 406–7.

polling here in the West suggests that Christianity is still a cultural force, even if the numbers are trending downward and Christian assumptions about goodness, truth, and beauty can no longer be taken for granted. As Ross Douthat has noted, "For all its weaknesses, Christianity remains institutionally significant, at least for now, in America and Europe on a scale no rival faith can match."[68]

Rather than the second century, it's to the fourth and fifth centuries we should go to find a closer historical setting to ours today. By the fourth century Christianity had begun to make a dent in the elite structures and institutions of society. Once Augustine entered the scene, Christianity had enough institutional power to be a significant cultural force and thus also to be attacked as *the* big civic problem by its critics. While Christians in the second century were accused of being immoral, no one had reason to argue that Christians had exploited outsized power to do broad social and civic damage. In the aftermath of Rome's fall, however, the pagans could argue just that. Seeing an opportunity in the cultural chaos, they blamed the Christians for the mess, in essence saying, "Look at what just happened in Rome—the *rise of Christians to power* is at the root of this evil that plagues our glorious civilization." This polemic, perhaps familiar to modern ears, could never have been levied against Christians in the earlier centuries of the church.

In order to defend Christianity, Augustine worked to out-narrate those who accused the catholic faith of being detrimental to the empire and impractical and unhelpful to individuals and families in daily life. Understanding this dual accusation, Augustine critiqued the pagan narrative before narrating the scriptural plot—a story of hope, social cohesion, and eternal justice; a story grounded in God's love and loving one's neighbor; a story that, as he sought to tell it, could appeal to the hearts and minds of his contemporaries. Augustine claimed that the Christian faith better explained history, made more sense of the material world, gave substantial meaning to everyday lives, and offered a hopeful realism that addressed both human suffering and death. Christianity, he argued, was good for humanity and lined up with the way people actually experienced the world. Today, for most skeptics, the question of Christianity's truth is closely bound up with the question of Christianity's goodness. Augustine can help us wisely navigate both.

## From Georgia to France

We started this chapter in post-Christendom, specifically late-twentieth-century Georgia, with a composite character named John. We then went back to the

68. Douthat, *Decadent Society*, 233.

Roman Empire at the turn of the fifth century to explore the landscape facing Augustine, a confusing time before Christendom fully absorbed the West. Now we end in seventeenth-century France with Blaise Pascal, a prodigy and intellectual disciple of Augustine who was forced to grapple with the beginnings of the end of Christendom.

Peter Kreeft, in *Christianity for Modern Pagans*—in which he describes himself as offering "festoonings"[69] of Blaise Pascal's *Pensées*—writes, "Most Christian apologetics today is still written from a medieval mind-set in one sense: as if we still lived in a Christian culture, a Christian civilization, a society that reinforced the Gospel. No. The honeymoon is over. The Middle Ages are over." He quips, "The news has not yet sunk in fully in many quarters."[70] Quite a lot hangs on Kreeft's use of the word "fully." For most apologists do recognize that things have changed and certainly that the Middle Ages have ended. And yet we should consider carefully the spirit behind Kreeft's point. As we will see in our next chapter, there is still much work to be done to understand the currents of post-Christendom and integrate this deeper awareness into the way we teach apologetics.

Kreeft makes this point in support of his argument concerning Pascal's uniqueness: "[Pascal] is the first to realize the new dechristianized, desacramentalized world and to address it."[71] To respond effectively to the shifts in his own day—including both the epistemology of his rival, René Descartes, and the project of "immanent contentment" envisioned by the skeptic Michel de Montaigne and subsequently metabolized by many of Pascal's contemporaries—Pascal recognized that the church could not afford to swallow the Cartesian pill or attempt to repristinate medieval approaches.[72] Simply dusting off Aquinas's five ways[73] or accepting the emerging Enlightenment-style rationality or accommodating modern diversions that mask the human predicament were not going to work. So to whom did Pascal go for inspiration? Instead of turning his back on the past in pursuit of complete novelty, a hazardous ploy that usually spells disaster, Pascal went further back: he returned to Augustine.

Pascal forged a path that transcended the limits of rising rationalism while avoiding skepticism, making him a timely figure for our character John to meet. For in owning his own contingency, Pascal offers those made fragile by our

---

69. Kreeft defines this as "free flowing extensions of his [Pascal's] thought." *Christianity for Modern Pagans*, 17.

70. Kreeft, *Christianity for Modern Pagans*, 12–13.

71. Kreeft, *Christianity for Modern Pagans*, 13.

72. For more on Montaigne's project of "immanent contentment" and Pascal's response, see Storey and Storey, *Why We Are Restless*, 10–98.

73. This is not to say that Aquinas's five ways aren't instructive in certain ways for us today. For more on this, see chap. 2.

secular age "a critical shift in perspective," as Benjamin and Jenna Storey describe it.[74] With Pascal, "traversing the uncertain passage of a human life looks less like needless risk-taking than purposeful adventure. . . . Armed not only with doubt but also with reason, honesty, and relentless hope, Pascal burns away every petty attachment in his search for real knowledge, solid happiness, and genuine love. He shows us that the true adventure of the human soul begins not on study abroad but right here—alone in our rooms."[75] But Pascal was not really alone. In addition to the biblical authors, he took Augustine along with him.

Yet Pascal never finished his major apologetics project. He left us only his notes, which have led to some powerful reflections.[76] Overall, though, Pascal's Augustinian approach has remained on the periphery of the most popular contemporary apologetic schools. The rest of this book follows Pascal in going back before the "medieval mind-set" to hear from the great fifth-century pastor-theologian-apologist. Of course, as we adjust our ears to catch Augustine's voice in the subsequent pages, we do so for *today*—far more distant from the enchanted medieval world than Pascal's time. If anything, we now live in a time plagued by a more perplexing malaise than what Pascal saw in his contemporaries, for our wealth and technological innovation have enabled diversions at a scale far beyond what Augustine or Pascal could have imagined. Yet, as they would have predicted, our discontentment doggedly persists. We continue to be both wonderful and wretched creatures, though the expressions of and responses to this mysterious paradox of human nature have continued to take different shapes into the present. Attending to this contemporary world—both its challenges and our responses to it—is what we turn our attention to in the next chapter.

74. Storey and Storey, *Why We Are Restless*, 180.
75. Storey and Storey, *Why We Are Restless*, 180–81.
76. See, e.g., Kreeft, *Christianity for Modern Pagans*; Storey and Storey, *Why We Are Restless*; G. Hunter, *Pascal the Philosopher*. In light of some common misunderstandings, Hunter clarifies that Pascal rejects only certain forms of philosophy rather than philosophy per se (26).

# 2

# An Augustinian Assessment
# of Contemporary Apologetics

It was the late 1980s. I (Mark) was taking a class from the well-known evangelical apologist Norman Geisler. I had first heard him on a Moody radio affiliate while in college and was soon hooked. I picked up his book on ethics and devoured it. I can remember him making me feel like I could be a Christian without unscrewing the top of my head and removing my gray matter. When I first visited Dallas Theological Seminary while still a student at a fundamentalist Bible college, I sat in on one of his classes. An hour or so later, I left mesmerized. After matriculating at the seminary, I made sure to enroll in his class on Christian apologetics. To his credit, I still remember his lectures almost thirty-five years later.

His course was one long, continuous argument. He took the entire semester to unpack his methodology:

Logic → Proof for the existence of God → Evidence for Jesus's resurrection → The authority of Jesus → The inerrancy of the Bible[1]

I looked forward to every class as he built toward the completion of what seemed at the time to be an airtight argument for the Christian faith. As future pastors, Christian educators, and missionaries, my classmates and I furiously wrote notes while he gave us the artillery needed to defend our faith and train others for combat.

I entered my first pastorate armed with Geisler's method. The people in my congregation in Richmond, Virginia, genuinely needed apologetics as they

---

1. I would later realize that this approach functions somewhat similarly to what Stephen Evans calls an "algorithmic method," which operates under the illusion that it "if properly followed would guarantee truth." Evans, *History of Western Philosophy*, 579.

dealt with the complexities of modern society and their personal doubts. I sometimes preached using this method, and I even tried teaching it in a small group. Only, it didn't seem to help them much. We were a suburban church of educated and accomplished professionals, so it wasn't because our congregation couldn't understand it. The method's failure to connect didn't have to do with their mental capacity; it had to do with motivation and desire.

The people were having babies, raising teenagers, chasing vocational dreams, and burying parents while also dealing with the disappointment and loneliness of a culture driven by meritocracy, consumerism, and efficiency. Consequently, the method could feel arid and out of touch. This approach seemed like it belonged in a courtroom or laboratory—or, worse, in another age—more than it belonged in my context, ministering to the restless and jaded. Plus, as a pastor who didn't just preach to them but lived among them, when I used the method, I felt like I was wearing an ill-fitted suit. They knew it didn't fit me, and I knew it too. Eventually, after fifteen years of pastoral ministry, I had to own up to the fact that it wasn't working, at least not in my context. Only later did I realize it wasn't working for many others as well.

Recently, I was discussing apologetics with my colleague Chad Thornhill. In the course of our conversation, Chad, a PhD in theology and apologetics, recounted an experience in teaching apologetics that challenged his assumptions about how to practice and teach apologetics. His classroom experience supported the point I was trying to make. Here's his account, which serves as an illustration of how popular construals of apologetics often fail to consider the importance of context:

> Early in my teaching career, I taught a semester-long graduate introduction to apologetics. We covered everything from arguments for God's existence and historical Jesus studies to the coherence of the Trinity and the problem of evil. The class was globally and ethnically diverse, with students from different backgrounds in the US, South Korea, Africa, and South America. Near the end of the course, I vividly recall a student from Africa giving an impassioned critique of how we had spent our time. He lamented that the issues we had addressed were not the issues his own social location demanded. I realized at that moment a painful lesson, that in coming to the course with my preconceived goals, well-intentioned though they were, I hadn't actually taken into consideration the starting points, plausibility structures, and questions of my own students. In doing so, I hadn't really given them a model of apologetics to take and replicate in any social context. I had given them a Western, academic model that, formed by the academy, may or may not have much concrete value in the ministerial contexts to which these students were headed.[2]

2. Chad Thornhill, email message to author, April 28, 2021.

We've both come to see that the most popular apologetic approaches today lack an integrative model—a *way of doing* apologetics—that is responsive to cultural and historical variances and, in the words of Charles Taylor, our social imaginaries. As we will see in more detail in the following section, the social imaginary is the intuitive and contingent cultural soil in which our plausibility structures are rooted and grown. Although I came to sense that the approach I had been taught was not quite right, I never could diagnose the root of the problem. But later, as I went searching for ways to help others—including my own son—deal with unbelief and overcome their barriers to Christianity, I began to realize that the approach I had inherited lacked an awareness of the contingencies in how different people reason. Moreover, I had been trained to treat others one-dimensionally, basically as logic processors, people who, as I had imagined when I was coming out of seminary, would be waiting for me to fill them with the right data. What I discovered through personal experience I also came to see reflects a more general weakness of contemporary apologetic methodologies to give due consideration to the West's shifting social imagination. This has contributed to approaches that are insufficiently contextual and anthropologically thin.

In this chapter we will imagine that Augustine has joined us at our contemporary apologetic table and is allowed to speak into areas he would find concerning. We'll first take up the context problem and its implications and then relate this issue to the reductionism underlying the anthropologies that are at least tacitly at work in much of today's apologetics; here we will be particularly interested to see what contemporary apologetics often looks like in practice rather than simply in the abstract. This will open the way for us to explore the potential gains and possible limitations of two recent works that rightly emphasize the challenge of the late-modern social imaginary for Christian persuasion. Finally, we will conclude with some reflections on the context out of which the problems surveyed in this chapter developed.[3]

## The Need to Persuade in Light of Social Imaginaries

A social imaginary consists of pre-reflective assumptions that shape our loves, provide the framework for what is believable and what is unbelievable, and

---

3. The examples in this chapter are meant to be illustrative of concerns about how the dominant approaches are applied and what they assume in practice. They are not meant to be an exhaustive account of their abstract methodologies. For a more general survey of the contemporary apologetics schools, including their potential strengths and weaknesses, see Chatraw and Allen, *Apologetics at the Cross*, 105–31.

contribute to the context for which arguments and evidence are meaningful and which are insubstantial and unconvincing. Or, as Taylor puts it, social imaginaries are "broader and deeper than the intellectual schemes people may entertain when they think about social reality in a disengaged mode." They include "the ways in which [people] imagine their social existence, how they fit together with others, how things go on between them and their fellows, the expectations which are normally met, and the deeper normative notions and images that underlie these expectations."[4] Social imaginations are powerful, tacitly inherited frameworks that feel natural, even basic, for most who inhabit them—in Augustine's Rome no less than in contemporary America.

Few cultural artifacts permeated the Roman imagination more than Virgil's poetic narrative the *Aeneid*. Like other society-defining myths, the *Aeneid* captured the collective imagination of generations, providing shared symbols and language for Rome's citizens as well as a normative framework for navigating their life. The historian of late antiquity Henri-Irénée Marrou writes that Virgil's work represented "the categories of Roman thought, the forms of Roman sensibility, the imperatives of the Roman moral conscience, . . . the most profound aspirations of Roman personal religion."[5] In similar fashion, Gillian Clark summarizes why Augustine himself took "Virgil as the representative of Roman culture and belief":

> For Latin speakers of the late fourth century, education was based on Roman classical authors of four or five centuries earlier. Everyone who could afford more than primary education read some Virgil, and in later life could evoke this shared culture by references to him. Augustine himself read Virgil as a schoolboy, taught Virgil . . . , and knew how teachers could use Virgil as the basis for instruction not only in literature and history, but also in religion.[6]

Virgil, we might say, was something like the Walt Disney of the Roman Empire. Well, not exactly Disney, but indulge us. Disney's legacy, to mention just one dominant economic and spiritual institution of late modernity, reflects and molds "the categories of [American] thought, the forms of [American] sensibility, the imperatives of the [American] moral conscience, . . . the most profound aspirations of [American] personal religion."[7] By its fictional narra-

---

4. Taylor, *A Secular Age*, 17. Taylor is getting at the communal nature of our imaginations compared to the individualized way the term is sometimes used. The two, of course, are interconnected: our individual imaginations are largely limited and opened by way of the communities we inhabit.

5. Marrou, *Histoire de l'éducation dans l'antiquité*, 341, quoted in O'Meara, "Virgil and Augustine," 30. O'Meara describes the *Aeneid* as representing "the ripeness of Pagan Rome."

6. Clark, "Paradise for Pagans?," 166.

7. Marrou, *Histoire de l'éducation dans l'antiquité*, 341, quoted in O'Meara, "Virgil and Augustine," 30 (slightly modified).

tives, the Walt Disney Company reinforces modern-day therapeutic consumerist culture while also spreading its assumptions beyond the West and to the next generation. Just as Disney has bolstered and spread the message of optimistic individual self-determination—captured by one of Disney's iconic quotations: "All our dreams can come true, if we have the courage to pursue them"—so, too, the poetic narrative of the *Aeneid* promulgated a message that defined the lives of generations of Romans: "On them I set no limits, space or time: I have granted them power, empire without end."[8]

Augustine understood the power of such culture-shaping myths to distort desires. In *Confessions* he personally testifies to how Virgil's characters captured his younger self such that they brought him to tears, and in book 1 of *The City of God* he tips his hat to the illustrious poet: "Their small children read Virgil precisely so that—once their tender minds have soaked up the great poet, the best and most famous of them all—he cannot easily be forgotten or fade into the oblivion."[9] "For Augustine," Sabine MacCormack explains, "Virgil was not an author of the long distant past from whom he could abstract himself in order to arrive at some objective and detached interpretation. . . . For Augustine, Virgil spoke of values and ideas that were alive and powerful, however much he disagreed with them."[10] Augustine recognized that skipping over Virgil's narrative and ignoring its influence over the culture's imagination, failing to speak to those who were under the great poet's spell, would be apologetic malpractice.[11]

Our social imaginary shapes the way we experience the world, interpret events, reason, and make decisions. Yet many apologists still give only a polite nod, if that, to the social imagination of late moderns. By doing so, they risk bypassing the way people navigate their life and imagine the world to be. People reason within the images, stories, and myths they've inherited through their social setting.[12] Indeed, they will use a kind of logic, but it will be one that fits the larger framework that they live and move within.

In late modernity, the default is no longer that humans are made to discover meaning that is universally existent within creation; rather, in our day each person imagines themselves creating their own unique meanings out of the raw material of a universe devoid of any necessarily true, universal purpose.

---

8. Virgil, *Aeneid* 1.333–34 (trans. Fagles, 56).

9. Augustine, *The City of God* 1.3.

10. MacCormack, *Shadows of Poetry*, 226.

11. In the first five books of *The City of God*, Augustine cites Virgil over seventy times. Chang, *Engaging Unbelief*, 71; cf. O'Meara, introduction to Augustine, *The City of God*, xxii (London: Penguin, 1987).

12. Taylor explains, "I adopt the term imaginary (i) because my focus is on the way ordinary people 'imagine' their social surroundings, and this is often not expressed in theoretical terms, but is carried in images, stories, and legends." *Modern Social Imaginaries*, 23.

Truth is equated with expressing their own authentic self by living according to their own feelings. Left alone—without a common source from which to derive meaning, purpose, and significance—the contemporary world has found a common telos in the project of feeling better.[13]

In the consumeristic pursuit of personal therapeutic ends,[14] many have sought a tribe where they can be most like themselves, feel comfortable, and be affirmed in who they are. Such a tribe must use a language and a kind of rationality. Those living within the middle and upper class of Western meritocracy are often consumed by a need to give an account for their life, their achievements, and their decisions—both to themselves and to those around them. Their specific tribe provides the social context for them to experience such self-actualization as accomplished individuals. Their tribe affirms and celebrates who they have chosen to be and what they have decided to do. Thus, thrusting upon them a "meta" norm external to them or their community is received as an act of violence to their personal identity and an attack on their particular tribe.

Unlike previous "worlds," today's is increasingly viewing itself as closed off from transcendent norms that must be discovered externally. Our world no longer assumes that an ultimate ethical rationality or a divinely given moral imperative beyond the individual is necessary or plausible. In this context a transcendent God gradually becomes unnecessary, as each individual *apparently* self-authenticates their own truth and morality. The guiding ethical question is, Does an action or disposition induce within me a feeling of well-being? Late moderns increasingly make ethical decisions based on their own preferences. "I know in my heart it is true" and "It just feels right" are stock phrases that most of us will recognize. However, as we noted in the previous paragraph, there is more going on beneath the surface. For what "just feels right" has operative social dimensions.[15] Consequently, what feels right to the individual is always negotiated socially and, ironically, ends up often functioning as a norm that others are measured against.

We'll return to this admittedly brief sketch of the late-modern social imagination at the beginning of chapter 5 to explore how Augustine's approach to his own challenges might help us today. For now, this brief sketch will do, because our present point is more limited: the West's social imagination has changed, and yet apologists have been slow in engaging productively with these changes— which leads us back to Augustine.

---

13. Rieff, *Triumph of the Therapeutic*, 25.
14. Burton, *Strange Rites*, 9.
15. Taylor, *Ethics of Authenticity*, 31–41.

In chapter 1 we explored Augustine's own context and its touch points with our own: the pluralized environment, the coming-of-age story, and the longing for cosmic significance derived from this-world achievements. Augustine lived in a time of epochal shift, as do we, and he developed an apologetic approach that was nimble enough to handle these shifts. Recognizing these salutary connections and Augustine's intuitive understanding of the power that epics such as the *Aeneid* can have over the imagination of a society, the wager of this book is that if we welcome him to the apologetic table, the old bishop can breathe new life into the discipline.[16] But first it is necessary to give some examples from prominent sources to show why we need to hear from him afresh.

Perhaps no one alive today has done more to advance classical/evidential apologetics than William Lane Craig. And yet, while Craig is not known for his emphasis on cultural analysis, he does admit the value of what he terms "cultural apologetics" in his highly influential book *Reasonable Faith*. In a chapter titled "The Absurdity of Life without God," he surveys and assesses cultural apologetics. He finds it can be beneficial, but mostly as a negative apologetic used to show skeptics the logical inconsistency of their worldview and the ultimate unhappiness to which that worldview leads. Craig suggests that by working with a person's embeddedness and the predicament in which they find themselves, we can raise their critical awareness of their lack of meaning, value, and purpose. Some non-Christians will come to faith if we help them see the absurdity of their modern life without God. Thus, early in this work, Craig demonstrates a willingness to nod approvingly toward cultural apologetics and the human predicament, which is commendable. We hope this will pique the interest of some of his peers and followers who rarely go down this road at all. But we do have some concerns about how Craig isolates "cultural apologetics" from the rest of his approach and, as Paul Gould has pointed out, how Craig can at times seem "less enthusiastic about the emergence of cultural apologetics."[17]

For what it is worth, we don't find the label "cultural apologetics" particularly helpful. For what kind of apologetics isn't cultural? We are always doing apologetics in a culture of some sort, whether we admit it or not. The philosophy department at any university is just as cultural as your local pub. We agree with Edward Carnell's statement, written over half a century ago: "Whenever a philosopher speaks of mankind in the abstract, rather than concrete individuals

---

16. Our claim is that Augustine intuitively understood the force of something along the lines of what Taylor refers to as the "social imagination" and calibrated his arguments to engage his audience in light of their particular imaginaries.

17. Gould, *Cultural Apologetics*, 21.

at home and in the market, he deceives both himself and all who have faith in his teaching."[18]

Moreover, it is wrong to claim, as Craig does, that an "apologetic for Christianity based on the human predicament is an extremely recent phenomenon."[19] As the rest of this book will make clear, some sixteen hundred years ago the most important theologian in the Western tradition focused on the human predicament in his apologetic approach and offered a critique of the underpinnings of Roman society. To the extent that any apologist is doing this, they are in line with an ancient approach to philosophy and persuasion.[20]

These differences between us and Craig likely contribute to why Craig doesn't go as far as we do in integrating cultural analysis into an apologetic approach. While affirming the potential usefulness of a negative critique of the current cultural situation, once Craig moves on to his two-step approach, which is the bread and butter of his apologetic, such analyses don't play a critical role. At one point, he even goes so far as to deny that postmodernity is real; indeed, he thinks that "getting people to believe that we live in a postmodern culture is one of the craftiest deceptions that Satan has yet devised."[21] He continues, "Meanwhile, modernism, pretending to be dead, comes around again in the fancy new dress of postmodernism, masquerading as a new challenger. 'Your old arguments and apologetics are no longer effective against this new arrival,' we're told. 'Lay them aside; they're of no use. Just share your narrative!'"[22] While we do not dispute the questionable value of the label "postmodern" itself (the label has the potential of at times concealing more than it reveals), in common usage it is at least nominally communicating some general societal shifts.

Granted, most would admit that modernity is alive and well within postmodernity (or whatever one decides to call it) and that a kind of pre-postmodernity already existed within modernity in various forms, such as Romanticism; but

18. Carnell, *Christian Commitment*, 2.

19. Craig, *Reasonable Faith*, 65.

20. To explore in detail how Augustine actually applied the classical philosophical tradition using an assessment of the human predicament to form his arguments for Christianity, see Kolbet, *Augustine and the Cure of Souls*.

21. Craig, *Reasonable Faith*, 18. For many, "postmodernism" seems to be often used as a shorthand for something close to simple relativism or nihilism. Therefore, postmodernism is either all bad or even a facade created by the devil. Augustine would certainly not be opposed to reflecting on possible demonic activity; however, this overly simplistic critique of postmodernism is a caricature of complex historical developments. A more productive approach is to see the gains and losses within different movements and time periods. Christianity sits at ease—in simple denunciation or affirmation—during no time period, as we live in the *saeculum* (the time between Jesus's first and second comings).

22. Craig, *Reasonable Faith*, 18. We have had difficulty finding a serious voice in apologetic methodological discussions suggesting that one should "*just* share your narrative."

few would deny that some kind of shift has happened with the rise of Jacques Derrida's "deconstructionism," Jean-François Lyotard's "incredulity toward metanarratives," and Michel Foucault's "power-knowledge."[23] We prefer the designation "late modern," because it recognizes the complexity of an epochal change while acknowledging that with such a shift there are always continuities and discontinuities. In the words of Carl Trueman, "There is always a temptation in social criticism either to attenuate the differences between past and present in a manner that misses new developments and distinctives in social practices and thought, or to emphasize the alleged uniqueness of today so much that the roots of current ideas and behaviors are sidelined and ignored."[24] If we have understood him correctly, it appears that Craig could be in danger of the former.

Our concern is that when cultural shifts are minimized and not fully taken into account in building an apologetic model, it will have adverse implications. Or, to put this slightly differently, if we do not sufficiently grapple with our culture's growing denial of the goodness and beauty of Christianity and the impact this has on how people reason as an apologetic issue, ministers on the ground will often be left flat-footed. Take, for example, Craig's On Guard. In this accessible volume he adapts the basic content of Reasonable Faith in order to equip Christians to defend their faith reasonably and advance faith conversations intentionally. The book presents a cumulative-case argument that addresses important questions related to creation, life, morality, suffering, and Jesus's resurrection, culminating in an argument for Jesus being the only way to God. Craig offers many valuable insights that can be used effectively—particularly for conversations with someone who is already open to such argumentation. Yet he tends to compartmentalize his analysis of and interaction with culture to an early chapter. The social imaginaries inherited through culture, however, shape the way people reason, what they think is plausible to believe, and what they desire. Because Craig neglects to integrate ways of interacting with these deeper cultural frameworks into his main model, readers may conclude that others simply need to objectively review the applicable logic of the arguments presented. This would, however, be an unfortunate conclusion for readers to draw.

For what is perceived as "rational" by any person is not determined simply by logic. Basic logic is an aspect of rationality that is generally recognized "to be independent of a given individual's cultural location."[25] However, as Alasdair MacIntyre explains, while

---

23. For more on the apologetics gains and challenges with the "postmodern" shift, see Chatraw, Telling a Better Story, 32.

24. Trueman, Rise and Triumph of the Modern Self, 102.

25. McGrath, Territories of Human Reason, 25.

no one who understands the laws of logic can remain rational while rejecting them, observance of the laws of logic is only a necessary and not a sufficient condition for rationality, whether theoretical or practical. It is on what has to be added to observance of the laws of logic to justify ascriptions of rationality . . . that disagreement arises concerning the fundamental nature of rationality and extends into disagreement over how it is rationally appropriate to proceed in the face of these disagreements.[26]

What is added to the laws of logic includes the available evidence for a historical person or community, what evidence they focus on and deem relevant, and the prevailing cultural metanarrative or social imaginary—with the latter being less formally reasoned and more absorbed through the stories, symbols, relationships, and institutions of a particular community. And our social imaginary heavily influences what data we deem relevant and affects how we interpret the data we focus on.[27]

Thus, Charles Taylor explains how an apologetic that integrates a robust understanding of the social imaginary differs from one that does not:

My account doesn't leave much place for the five ways of proving the existence of God, . . . provided . . . that they are meant to convince us quite independently of our moral and spiritual experience, that one can take them as an unbeliever would, as showing the inescapable rational cogency of certain conclusions, regardless of their spiritual meaning to the thinker.[28]

We need to be careful we don't go beyond what Taylor is saying here. Aquinas's five ways are not completely out of the question for Taylor—and given Augustine's dexterity in persuasion[29] and his reflections on the natural world and eternal truths,[30] our guess is that the ancient bishop wouldn't take something similar off the table for us today.[31] A rich array of philosophical arguments (in-

---

26. MacIntyre, *Whose Justice?*, 4.

27. McGrath, *Territories of Human Reason*, 25.

28. Taylor, "Reply and Re-articulation," 228. See also Ashford and Ng, "Charles Taylor," 689–90, esp. for Taylor's epistemological indebtedness to Michael Polanyi's "postcritical arguments against classical foundationalism and its commitment to neutral, abstract laws of logic."

29. On Augustine's improvisational nature in response to critics and the particulars of his audience, see Fitzgerald, "Jesus Christ," 108–24.

30. On Augustine's use of such evidences, see Meister, "Augustine of Hippo," 147–49.

31. Aquinas and Augustine both offer apologetic resources we can and should learn from, and they certainly share some common ground, with Aquinas being Augustinian in his theology. A certain reactionary response among some Protestants to Aquinas, even pitting him squarely against Augustine as well as later Protestant theology, has been misleading and unfortunate. Yet, it is also problematic to skim over the real differences, reading Augustine through the lens of Aquinas or even later Thomisms. For, as Edmund Hill explains, to give just one example, Aquinas opts to say

cluding possibly both Craig's and Aquinas's), properly framed, are not something Augustine would have us shy away from. But Taylor cautions against using the five ways as universal, stand-alone proofs with the expectation they will carry the same weight they once did. Augustine would likely agree. For as an effective rhetor and preacher, Augustine understood that in aiming for conversion—whether intellectual or spiritual or both—arguments and communication should be calibrated for particular audiences.[32]

The extent to which such proofs "work" is largely contingent on the shared social imaginary between the apologist and the other person. Yet, in an increasingly post-Christian context, with vastly different imaginaries from the medieval era or even from a century ago, such proofs in isolation are less likely to prove effective. Typically, many other types of apologetic appeals will need to be offered before the average late modern will feel their weight. For such arguments in today's context often lack what Graeme Hunter refers to as "mass":

> When candidate arguments present themselves before the court of our mind, asking to be believed, they may or may not be equipped with mass. They possess it when they are not only intuitively clear and plausible but also anchored in the assumptions and practices of ordinary life and connected to habitual pathways of thought. We easily bestow belief upon arguments that are in tune with our established convictions and conventions. Arguments that do not fit in so easily, however, lack mass and are unlikely to be believed.[33]

It is no wonder, then, that many students who take apologetic classes eventually find themselves frustrated when they use them in their ministry contexts. The arguments might be cogent and even compelling to the Christian students, but they end up discovering that these arguments don't have enough "mass" to move many non-Christians as we slouch further into post-Christendom. In fact,

---

we have "a certain knowledge of God as a cause in its effect." "Augustine," in comparison, "takes a more subjective line, and says in substance that we have direct knowledge, and not in terms either of genus and species, of certain values, truth, the good, justice, and hence an indirect knowledge of God as the guarantor of these values, or the source from which they derive." "Introductory Essay on Book VIII" in Augustine, *The Trinity*, 295.

32. In his introduction to Augustine's *The Trinity*, Edmund Hill, after explaining the medieval scholastic distinction between faith and reason, corrects the misreading of this later tradition into Augustine's work (Hill, introduction to Augustine, *The Trinity*, 7). For a similar point, contrasting more broadly the ancient apologists with later systematic approaches, see Cavadini, *Visioning Augustine*, 241.

33. G. Hunter, *Pascal the Philosopher*, 28.

sometimes even the leaders of these schools find themselves exasperated by the unenthusiastic reception of, and even the lack of interest in, their arguments.

In a recent interview, William Lane Craig is perplexed with people's attraction to other forms of persuasion:

> The odd thing though I find is that some people do find Jordan Peterson's approach more persuasive than the approach that I take, which is to give arguments and evidence in support of the truth of the Christian worldview. I don't understand this, frankly. I have to admit I'm mystified. Why is it that Jordan Peterson telling young men to sit up straight and make their bed in the morning is something that's so appealing and arresting to them? It gives them, I guess, a sense of confidence and maleness that perhaps eventually leads them in the direction of Christian faith, but it seems to me at the end of the day there's just no substitute for asking the question "but is it true?"[34]

We agree with Craig's point about the importance of questioning the veracity of a view. Christianity works because it is true, not the other way around. Yet, since Christianity claims to be in line with the universe and thus tells us how to live most fully as humans, to be "happy in hope," as Augustine puts it, why not try starting with this fact and use it in a positive apologetic, inviting the unbeliever to try on Christianity—not solely as a set of propositions to affirm but as a way of life that is, yes, intellectually capacious but also existentially robust, offering wiser resources with a more ancient pedigree for human flourishing than does Jordan Peterson or other secular representatives of late modernity? Such questions of wisdom and the good life are part of the human experience, have an ancient philosophical pedigree, and are at the heart of Augustine's apologetic.[35] To put off such questions, or to not fully integrate them into our

34. William Lane Craig and Kevin Harris, "Has Christian Apologetics Failed?," September 29, 2019, in *Reasonable Faith*, podcast, https://www.reasonablefaith.org/media/reasonable-faith -podcast/has-christian-apologetics-failed.

35. This emphasis on human flourishing and philosophy as a "way of life" is a difference, as Jonathan Pennington points out, between ancient philosophy and some forms of modern philosophy. Pennington, *Jesus the Great Philosopher*, 17–36. This wisdom-based approach is also on par with a Socratic dialectic philosophy, which, as James Peters describes, "holds that the primary reason for engaging in philosophy is thus deeply practical: philosophy's primary purpose is to cultivate the virtue of self-understanding through critical conversation—not to gain power over others in a competitive agon of conflicting selves, or to achieve intellectual or material advantage, but to promote human excellence in all persons." Peters, *Logic of the Heart*, 45. And particularly within apologetics, Alister McGrath notes the historical shift with Descartes in the seventeenth century and then "the rise of the Enlightenment in the eighteenth century," which "generated new pressure for a demonstration of the veracity of the Christian faith, [and] created a new intellectual context within which 'proofs' for God's existence assumed an important cultural and apologetic role. In contrast, most pre-modern writers regarded the human experience of desire as something that could be integrated satisfactorily within a Christian framework affirming the rationality of

approach, and instead concentrate on theoretical proofs to those who aren't accustomed to such forms of reasoning misses an opportunity to offer arguments with "mass"—in this case, living arguments that are much more likely to carry weight in today's context.

Consider an episode of a popular podcast, *Armchair Expert*, in which pop-culture celebrities Russell Brand and Dax Shepard discuss the problems in their life—addictions, anxiety, stress, broken relationships, attraction to chaos—and their ongoing recovery.[36] Brand invokes prayer, meditation, spirituality, the divine, and a reinterpretation of Buddhism's four noble truths, critiquing contemporary culture as not working and referring to "super powerful and successful people as utterly broken." Shepard, who chimes in throughout with testimony about his journey to get better, reflects on how community and greater self-awareness have been instrumental in his recovery. Yet, he laments, "What a shame that the only real option other than that [referring to his recovery program] is to go to a church on Sunday to get that experience." He adds, referring to communities of healing, "There are no options out there for people." Why did this thoughtful man in his midforties not entertain the idea of showing up in a church to find such resources? He puts it bluntly: "I did not want a Christian God. I didn't want an all-knowing God. I didn't want a God that said some people go here and some people go there. I didn't like any of those options."

Notice three things. First, Brand and Shepard are representative of many late-modern non-Christians. At least in this conversation, they are not following the path of the New Atheists; both seem open to their need for resources beyond the flattened, naturalistic world on offer from the likes of Christopher Hitchens and Richard Dawkins. Brand in particular is immersed in spiritual ideas and language. This is representative of what Charles Taylor has labeled the Nova Effect—the explosion of different types of quests for "fullness" in response to the lack of resources available from strict secularism.[37] Second, both have accepted that something is wrong with the world and themselves. Their response is to seek recovery—to figure out how to feel right, to live mentally healthy lives, and to find peace. The central question for both men throughout the conversation is, to put it in our own words, Where can late-modern people like us turn for resources that will help us flourish? This is representative of a host of recent important cultural analyses that describe the late-modern person as highly individualized, internally focused, and aiming to achieve personal psychological

---

faith in a *prudential* rather than an epistemic sense." McGrath, *Intellectual World of C. S. Lewis*, 108 (emphasis added).

36. "Russell Brand," June 7, 2021, *Armchair Expert*, podcast, https://armchairexpertpod.com /pods/russell-brand.

37. Taylor, *A Secular Age*, 299–422.

happiness. In the words of Philip Rieff, instead of being a society of people who see themselves as "born to be saved," we now see ourselves as "born to be pleased."[38] Third, the reason Shepard gives for his rejection of Christianity is not that it is irrational or intellectually lacking but that it is something that he doesn't "like" or "want." Christianity isn't even plausible enough to try out. It is undesirable and distasteful.

Like Augustine himself, the young men who have been drawn to Peterson on the one hand and those exemplified by Brand and Shepard on the other have had social experiences that led to identity crises and lives filled with fragmentation and anxiety. In response, they're looking for a sustainable and meaningful *way* to live, which includes practices that will provide stability, wisdom, and peace. This is a potential opportunity to step into rather than a problem to lament while wishing that people would come to Christianity on our preferred terms. Rather than lamenting how this late-modern search for a way to find peace doesn't resonate with our apologetic systems, we could instead turn back to look afresh at the Christian tradition. For the tradition has the resources that lead to true peace; our apologetic task is to learn how to integrate this ancient wisdom into our contemporary approaches. Apologetics can reveal their wrong turns, point to the story of reality, and help them see that Christianity is something they should "want." Apologists can persuade by showing that Christianity is *the way* to truly thrive if only we don't remain trapped in narrow approaches and reductionistic anthropologies. The good news is that Augustine can help set us free.

The reluctance of some contemporary apologists to reconsider their method could be due in part to their quest for universal and rationally coercive arguments for demonstrating the truth of Christianity.[39] For example, Norman Geisler employs the "leaky bucket analogy" against combinationalist approaches to epistemology. In his response to these approaches, Geisler seems to indicate that arguments for truth must be rationally airtight or else they are unable to provide the certainty he is pursuing.[40]

The dissatisfaction with arguments that fail to achieve certainty is also evident in some presuppositionalists as well, such as Scott Oliphint, who stresses that historical arguments can't give "absolute certainty" but rather "provide only

---

38. Rieff, *Triumph of the Therapeutic*, 25. "You be you" is now the path to healing. More academic labels include "expressive individualism" (Robert Bellah), the "ethics of authenticity" (Charles Taylor), and the "psychological man" (Philip Rieff).

39. The trend among Christian philosophers across various traditions is to acknowledge, rightly, in our view, that such rationally coercive proofs are unavailable. For two examples of well-regarded philosophers on this point, see Evans, *History of Western Philosophy*, 577–85; Plantinga, *Knowledge and Christian Belief*, x.

40. Geisler, *Christian Apologetics*, 127.

a probable conclusion."[41] So, while according to Oliphint the historical data "can support our belief in the resurrection," the emphasis in his work is on its limits rather than its effectiveness; for with historical data, all we can affirm, says Oliphint, is that "we believe in the probability of the resurrection" with "some level of doubt" always remaining.[42] Later in the same work he stresses again what he sees as the problem with arguments that reach only probability: "[Jesus] is not probably risen or probably alive. If he is probably risen, then our faith is probably in vain."[43] (Though this drive for absolute certainty can be found within both schools, it is by no means an essential characteristic of everyone who describes themselves as a classical/evidential or presuppositional apologist.[44])

The problem with these quests as well as the residual posture they leave behind—even at times with apologists who rightly tap down such ambitious claims—is that they betray a faulty epistemology that casts a shadow over methodological imaginations. Even if one's chain of arguments doesn't quite lead to *absolute* certainty, contemporary apologists still often simply assume a universal, common-sense rationality. This assumption results in, as Chad Thornhill confesses earlier in this chapter, a fairly straightforward transferability of their approach to any time or place or people.

Yet, as the work of Alasdair MacIntyre has made clear and as Alister McGrath has emphasized in relation to apologetics, it is no longer sustainable to build a methodology on the understanding of the task of apologetics "as an attempt to justify the 'rationality' or 'reasonableness' of Christian beliefs *on the basis of the classic notion of universally valid patterns* of reason and thought."[45] This does not deny that there are "degrees of overlap" between traditions of rationality. Nor does it deny the use of universally accessible logic to arrive at certain basic, unquestioned truths, such as "Three plus seven equals ten"—an example that Augustine himself gives. Basic math and the law of noncontradiction can be spoken of in such terms, but larger conceptions of rationality are dependent not only on basic logic but also on the evidence available at a particular time and the shifting social imaginaries or assumed metanarratives of different social milieus.[46] We affirm that God, the transcendent and objective Logos,

41. Oliphint, *Know Why You Believe*, 90–91.

42. Oliphint, *Know Why You Believe*, 91, 93.

43. Oliphint, *Know Why You Believe*, 101.

44. For example, Craig recognizes that "one's apologetic case for Christianity yields only probability rather than certainty." *Reasonable Faith*, 55.

45. McGrath, *Genesis of Doctrine*, 199 (emphasis added). See also Taylor, "Reason, Faith, and Meaning," 13–27; MacIntyre, *Whose Justice?*, 39; MacIntyre, *After Virtue*, xii–xiv.

46. See McGrath, *Territories of Human Reason*, 24–26. We're expanding on McGrath's model to explicitly include "social imaginary."

holds all things together as the universal and personal rationality; yet as finite and contingent beings, our particular social and historical locations cannot be bypassed in our attempt to access this rationality. Yet when our contingency is tacitly seen as a barrier to truth rather than an inescapable feature by which humans must discern truth, there seems to be less incentive to build into our apologetic models the resources needed to read and engage with shifting cultural landscapes.

Others believe they have discovered *the* biblically supported approach, leaving themselves methodologically stiff in the face of contexts that call for nimbleness. An example of such an assertion is made by those who claim a theological mandate for a presuppositional apologetic in the legacy of Cornelius Van Til (at least as his approach is narrowly conceived), who grounded his approach in the claim that the ontological Trinity provides "the necessary foundation of 'proof' itself."[47] Yet, as we argue elsewhere, the Bible does many different things apologetically—it provides patterns, offers wisdom, and narrates a theological drama that can be synthetically organized—but it never mandates a single universal method.[48] So, while Van Til and his followers are absolutely correct to argue against notions of disinterested neutrality, one will search in vain through Scripture and the earliest apologists for, in the words of Timothy Paul Jones, the "claim that the ontological Trinity is necessary, whether consciously or unconsciously, for rational predication."[49] It does not appear to have even occurred to the apostles or the fathers that their apologetic arguments might require such reasoning.

Looking at an example illustrates how such philosophical commitments can lead to apologetic stiffness in practice. Consider, for instance, the reason Scott Oliphint gives for believing Jesus's resurrection.[50] While noting that historical evidence can be helpful, he omits providing any actual historical evidence in support. In a book titled *Know Why You Believe*, he references evidentialists who make historical arguments, but he does so by stressing that, because of the nature of historical investigation, such works can't provide certainty, and

---

47. Van Til, "My Credo." Timothy Paul Jones summarizes Van Til's central thesis: "Every fact in the universe proves the truth of Christian theism, according to Van Til, because every fact and every description of facts relies on the reality of an ontological Trinity." Jones, "Apologetics: Did Cornelius Van Til Really Teach That Non-Christians Know Nothing?," TimothyPaulJones.com, February 11, 2020, https://www.timothypauljones.com/apologetics-what-critics-of-cornelius-van -til-get-wrong.
48. See Chatraw and Allen, *Apologetics at the Cross*, 27–61.
49. See Timothy Paul Jones, "Apologetics: How Much Intellectual Common Ground Is There between a Christian and a Non-Christian?," TimothyPaulJones.com, September 19, 2020, https:// www.timothypauljones.com/apologetics-is-there-any-common-ground-between-a-christian-and -a-non-christian.
50. Oliphint, *Know Why You Believe*, 90–91.

he neglects to summarize for his readers the specific historical arguments. In his own defense of the resurrection he expounds on 1 Corinthians 15:1–9, but without making a case based on the eyewitnesses—which Paul himself stresses—instead focusing on the theological implications Paul draws from the event to be the reasons for believing the resurrection: "The reason that Christians believe in the resurrection is because, since sin came into the world, the fact of Christ's resurrection, together with its meaning, comprises the center of God's entire plan for the world."[51] A more nimble and holistic approach would be willing to leverage wholeheartedly the historical, theological, and existential evidence for the resurrection, as Augustine himself did, as reasons for believing in the resurrection.[52]

## The Need for a Holistic Anthropology

Steven Smith observes, "The question—'What are we?'—is one that law, politics, history, and the social sciences seldom ask but always answer, at least implicitly."[53] The same is true of apologetics. Much of contemporary apologetics has answered the question with approaches that suffer from reductionistic anthropologies, focusing on one particular aspect of personhood to the neglect of others.[54] Though lip service is occasionally given to the affective facet of our humanity, it has largely been ignored. The result is that, too often, contemporary apologetic models have remained beholden to reductionistic anthropologies, which, as we will see in this chapter, is particularly problematic when combined with an inattentiveness to changes in our social imaginaries.

James K. A. Smith suggests that "there are different, competing models of the human person that we can see throughout the history of philosophy and theology."[55] He offers three models that address the human person as *thinker*,

51. Oliphint, *Know Why You Believe*, 94.
52. We will discuss Augustine's apologetic approach to the resurrection in chapter 5 with the help of O'Collins, *Saint Augustine on the Resurrection of Christ*.
53. S. Smith, *Pagans and Christians*, 17.
54. In particular, we have American evangelical approaches in mind. Yet, the American evangelical methodological sandbox might prove more parochial than most ministerial students who have been taught to play within these dominant models realize. When one compares many of the leading twentieth-century evangelical American apologists with those from the same time in the British contexts (e.g., G. K. Chesterton, Dorothy Sayers, C. S. Lewis, and Lesslie Newbigin), it seems these British apologists were less interested in or constrained by the modern-day fault lines that emerged between contemporary apologetic schools in America.
55. J. Smith, *Desiring the Kingdom*, 41. Readers of Smith will recognize in our work more of an emphasis on the importance of verbal communication in persuasion and transformation. This is likely due in part to the differences in the nature of our projects but is also probably because of a different proposed solution (at least in emphasis) for a problem we would both agree upon. The

*believer*, and *lover*.[56] Though he is not writing about apologetics, Smith's three models provide a taxonomy that can be adapted to help us think through several apologetic approaches.

Before moving forward with our concerns about the major approaches, note that we do not mean to imply that everyone within these apologetic schools falls prey to the functional anthropologies that have often characterized the application of each model in practice. We have recently been encouraged by some of the movements within these camps, counteracting the potential weaknesses we explore below.[57] Another way forward, however, and the one we have taken in this book, is to go back deeper into the history of the church to retrieve an apologetic option that predates these contemporary models and reframes the methodological conversation.

Modern classical and evidential apologists are prone to attend to people primarily as *thinkers*. This is the anthropological assumption behind the approach I (Mark) once took. People are persuaded to the "truth," which is characterized chiefly through analytic reasoning and facts. The danger is that humans are only contingently embodied; they are treated, at least in practice, as essentially "immaterial mind or consciousness," with their central problem being their failure to follow the evidence or process the logic.[58] In this way of conceiving of people, apologists risk engaging people as "brains on a stick"[59] or information processors in search of the right data. This minimizes the affective side of their humanity, appealing almost exclusively to their ability to objectively follow the evidence.

A more holistic view of human personhood would take into account the reality that human reason is tied to humans' (fallen) affections and operates within their context of a tradition of beliefs and practices. We are not denying that apologetics should strive to give a rational warrant for faith; we are

---

Augustinian path forward, as we will see in part 2, is an approach to apologetics that emphasizes both the practices of the church and the hearing of different kinds of verbal arguments as part of the church's "word ministry." Communal practices play an important role both in the formation of apologists and in an embodied apologetic, which produce the right kind of speaker and the right kind of encounter (see particularly chaps. 3–4), but we will also emphasize the importance of verbal persuasion (chap. 5).

56. J. Smith, *Desiring the Kingdom*, 41–47.

57. See, e.g., Gould, *Cultural Apologetics*. Also, we are encouraged by the group of scholars from the Dutch Reformed tradition who draw on Augustine to emphasize the importance of the existential impact of sin and appeal to the affections. See, e.g., the Bavinck scholar James Eglinton, "Voetius: Can We Classify Sin?" (lecture, International Presbyterian Church Catalyst Conference 2021), available at https://youtu.be/o-v6lhPc5Tk. Eglinton appeals to Voetius's use of Augustine, but one might also appeal to Pascal, who is inspired by Augustine to similar effect. Likewise, in the opening chapter of *The Wonderful Works of God*, Herman Bavinck summarizes anthropological insights from Augustine and Pascal as seemingly foundational for his project (6).

58. J. Smith, *Desiring the Kingdom*, 42.

59. J. Smith, *You Are What You Love*, 3.

saying that in answering the big questions of life, one's perception of the good and the beautiful cannot be neatly or simply set aside without impoverishing rationality. The danger would be to functionally separate out and focus on one valid aspect of personhood while undervaluing other aspects and their role in thinking and deciding.

Presuppositional apologetics tends toward engaging people primarily as *believers*. Its proponents challenge what they see as other apologists' functional ideal of an objective "view from nowhere." Emphasizing that all reasoning operates on the basis of faith, they see humans foundationally as "believing animals." By faith a person must first assume a whole constellation of interconnected beliefs making up the Christian worldview before being able to consistently reason their way within and to the truth. This approach criticizes the ideal of neutral rationality and, due to the noetic effects of the fall, chastens expectations about what typical evidences by themselves can achieve. However, it still often ends up focusing on the question of how one *can* (by way of the Christian worldview) or *cannot* (by way of any other worldview) ground rational predication, normally paying little attention to the affections. By challenging the unbeliever's warrant for trusting their own cognitive faculties without a triune God, the presuppositionalist seeks to undercut their trust in their worldview at the very root.[60]

Yet, here again the danger is a reductionistic anthropology—in this case, attending to people as essentially containers for beliefs, with one set of beliefs grounding rational predication and with all other sets of beliefs failing to do so. If narrowly applied, it also fails to address the practical problem of relevance: most people, especially today, don't sense an existential need to find such a grounding. Most people simply take practical reasoning for granted, using their reason to help them get what they *want*. At the societal level today, most use reason to achieve what feels to them like common-sense goals all humans should share (e.g., peace on earth, modern comforts, and entertaining gadgets). In this context, abstract philosophical arguments that propose to ground rationality in a belief in the Trinity lack the "mass" needed to persuade.

The thinker and believer anthropologies each capture an important aspect of truth, but taken by themselves they are reductionistic, failing to emphasize humans as worshiping beings, and miss an opportunity to speak to the heart of what drives people to make their deepest commitments. For, indeed, we reason and we believe—but we also love. Each aspect impacts the other. Thus, they

---

60. Asking an unbeliever why they trust their own reasoning abilities given their worldview, especially if they believe materialistic naturalism and evolution to be true, can be useful for conversations with certain people. However, one does not need to subscribe to presuppositionalism to make this move. See, e.g., Plantinga, *Where the Conflict Really Lies*, 314; Lewis, *Miracles*.

cannot simplistically be separated. How we reason impacts what we worship. What we worship impacts what we believe. What we believe shapes how we reason and worship, and so on. The feedback loop is an inescapable dynamic of human cognition and decision-making.

By neglecting—at least functionally—the importance of humans as doxological creatures, the first two approaches underestimate the power of connecting with the unbeliever's deepest aspirations, the effects of sin on these desires, and the extent to which an individual's ultimate aims impact their reasoning. For, as we will explore in more depth in the next chapter, "Augustinian reasoning is not a neutral technological process but is an ethical and teleological activity. . . . Reason by its very nature seeks to know and thus possess and enjoy the good."[61] The unified nature of the three aspects of humanity means that we have an opening for apologetics: engaging over the central pursuits of our shared existence as worshiping beings, which includes such experiences as our quest for meaning, our need for an identity, our longing for communal devotion, our yearning for happiness, and our desire to love and be loved. Though these quests take different, historically diverse forms because of the diversity of sin and varied cultural expressions, the quests themselves are universal features of our humanity.

However, it is not only the *content* that is adversely affected by these models' reductionisms; they also result in problems of *form*. Too often, in classical/evidential and presuppositional apologetics, the "what" to say has been elevated too far above the "how" to communicate. Aesthetics takes a back seat while depersonalized modes of discourse supposedly free of the biases of historical particularities are allowed to sit in the driver's seat. Narratives and poetics are looked on with suspicion, and syllogisms take precedence. And yet, in order to capture the imagination of the late modern, we need *content* and *forms* that are aimed at the "gut" and the "head" together. We need "stronger spells," as C. S. Lewis once put it, that pay close attention to the "charms" of our day. This means developing an approach that seeks to understand our current malaise and to know which spells show signs of bringing the hypnotized to their senses.[62] In fact, however, it has not been uncommon for us to hear that leading apologists testify with some pride to not reading poetry and fiction. These are the very forms, as Lewis and J. R. R. Tolkien both realized, that have the potential for

---

61. Peters, *Logic of the Heart*, 71.
62. We are thinking here of a line from C. S. Lewis: "Do you think I am trying to weave a spell? Perhaps I am; but remember your fairy tales. Spells are used for breaking enchantments as well as for inducing them. And you and I have need of the strongest spell that can be found to wake us from the evil enchantment of worldliness which has been laid upon us for nearly a hundred years." *Weight of Glory*, 31.

opening up more possibilities to those whose plausibility structures have been shaped by an ostensibly disenchanted or anti-Christian social context. Narratives in particular are able to implicitly ask the question "What if?" in a form that speaks to the human experience as a narrative creature.

The problem for these normalized forms of apologetics is this: impoverished imaginations result in impoverished rationality. As Colin McGinn argues,

> *Rational, reflective* belief is selection from imaginative alternatives. . . . Imagination is crucially implicated in this kind of selective belief formation; it is not some separate faculty that has nothing directly to do with the serious business of believing things. [Imagination] is bound up with the very essence of rational, reflective belief formation—and hence with arriving at knowledge of the world.[63]

Moreover, as James K. A. Smith has emphasized, before one desires, one must imagine. And stories and the narrative scripts we inhabit through our habitual practices[64] play no small role in forming desire, imagination, and perception: "Stories capture our imagination precisely because narrative trains our emotions, and those emotions actually condition our perception of the world."[65] Stories, therefore, play a crucial role in the integration of reason, belief, and desire. By failing to give enough attention to the imagination—in either its social or its individual form—and the kinds of persuasion that better appeal to human imaginations and desires, apologetics has too often attempted to persuade within a reductionistic view of rationality and failed to register on the street level of the post-Christian West.

Thus we have much to learn from Augustine's interaction with the *Aeneid*, but we may also find his own creative use of story to be instructive. While his corpus includes various different forms, *Confessions* and *The City of God* both include love stories as central threads. *Confessions* is the story of how Augustine the prodigal son searched for love in the wrong places only to come back home and find the true love of the Father. *The City of God* tells the story of God's city, a people defined by their love for him, who are on a journey home to him.[66]

---

63. McGinn, *Mindset*, 142.

64. We will say more in the following two chapters about the relationship between ecclesial practices and apologetics.

65. J. Smith, *Imagining the Kingdom*, 32.

66. G. Ward, *Unimaginable*, 98–106, traces the development of Augustine's thought regarding the "imagination" from his largely negative account of the word *imaginatio* in an early letter to his friend Nebridius to his more mature reflections in *The Trinity*, where "it is the Trinitarian mind of God that guarantees a relationship between truth, memory and image making in us. It also guarantees psychological integrity; for is not Christ the self-image of the Father and we the image of His image? Such theological thinking, beyond and beneath psychological reasoning, will help

In spite of all this, practical apologetic manuals too often remain on the surface level of what is needed for effective persuasion. For example, in the popular book *Tactics*, Gregory Koukl implicitly provides an example of approaching people primarily as thinkers. He identifies a primary need for the apologetic task: "We need a plan to artfully manage the details of our dialogues with others."[67] While we appreciate many of the clearly thought-out arguments in *Tactics* and Koukl's attempt to keep conversations civil, the way that he explains terms like "tactics" or "maneuvers" exposes the dangers of what seems to be, at least functionally, a reductionist anthropology.

In chapter 1 Koukl promises "to teach you how to navigate in conversations so that you stay in control—in a good way—even though your knowledge is limited." He continues, "I am going to introduce you to a handful of effective maneuvers—I call them tactics—that will help you stay in control."

Koukl offers a personal anecdote to illustrate what he means:

> Several years ago, while on vacation at our family retreat in northern Wisconsin, my wife and I stopped at a store in town to get some photos digitized. I noticed that the woman helping us had a large pentagram—a five-pointed star often associated with the occult—dangling from her neck.
>
> "Does that star have religious significance," I asked, pointing to the pendant, "or is it just jewelry?"
>
> "Yes, it has religious significance," she answered. "The five points stand for earth, wind, fire, water, and spirit." Then she added, "I'm a pagan."
>
> "So you're Wiccan?" I continued.
>
> She nodded. Yes, she was a witch. "It's an earth religion," the woman explained, "like the Native Americans. We respect all life."
>
> "If you respect all life," I ventured, "then I suppose you're pro-life on the abortion issue."[68]

At this point she was trapped by her inconsistency, since she affirmed life but was pro-choice. The conversation continued with a discussion about "killing babies."

Unfortunately, Koukl's approach quickly took the interchange in a direction away from persuasion of the life-giving message of the gospel. Abortion is a very important issue, but this method moved the focus away from more relevant apologetic questions, like, Who is Jesus Christ? What did he do? And what difference does it make? It moved straight for an intellectual and logical trap.

---

Augustine to come to terms with the way imagination is fundamental to active understanding and communication as they operate at levels both human and divine" (105).

67. Koukl, *Tactics*, 33.

68. Koukl, *Tactics*, 26–27.

Koukl admits, "True, I hadn't gotten to the gospel, but that was not the direction this conversation was going."[69] However, it seems by his own account that the conversation didn't go toward the gospel because the questions he asked did not take their discussion toward the heart issues. He later states that he steered "the exchange in the direction that I wanted it to go, which was not hard at all using my tactics."[70] Actually, his verbal exchange with this woman lacked the sensitivity and nimbleness that would have allowed him to adjust to get to the heart of the matter.

The problem with this approach is *not* that it requires another person to think or asks them to consider the contradictions in their beliefs. Koukl's advice on this front is sound. No Christian should be against thinking or unwilling to point out contradictions. The shortcoming with this methodology has to do with the assumptions it makes about what a human is and how people process information and are ultimately persuaded. Most people do not change the way they think by being backed into an intellectual corner in discussions like this; it's especially ineffective when trying to discuss the big questions of life. This approach keeps the intellectual exchange at a surface level. The woman probably "thought" her way to her religious beliefs from her heart—what she desired, the hurts she had experienced, the love and community she felt. She was thinking and deciding, but not in the framework and categories the person "in control" of the conversation was assuming. Wicca was apparently offering her something she believed she needed and was good for her. If so, why ask her about abortion instead of asking her what attracted her to paganism?

Koukl's question assumed she was a Wiccan due to its basic logical coherence and that catching her in this contradiction over abortion could open the door to deeper apologetic conversations. This seems unlikely. The question about what attracted her to Wicca would have left her some space to reply in a number of directions. She could have replied, "I am attracted to it because after searching for years I have found it more rationally consistent than any other system," but we doubt it. It is much more likely that she would have replied that becoming Wiccan enabled her to resist the evil forces of a male-dominated society or that it allowed her to tap into a life force and community that empowered her. Either of these responses is much more likely to be the primary reason, and it would have called for a different type of approach than the one Koukl seems to have assumed. But you don't know unless you ask.

Basic questions that would move the thinking to a more holistic place would be, "How did you become a pagan?" "What about paganism appeals to you

69. Koukl, *Tactics*, 30.
70. Koukl, *Tactics*, 31.

most?" "How do you perceive paganism as helping you?" "What is your community like in paganism?" You could say something like, "I would love to hear a bit about your religious background." (Sure, you do not have much time at the one-hour photo shop, but even a little human love and connection, which is so rare today in our combative society, can come back later like healing waves to the person.)

These questions get at the core of the person's motivations, express respect for her, and create space for her to respond candidly. We are asking, as Sarah Coakley has asked, the ancient question, "What do you seek?"[71] Granted, we may have to risk losing a certain amount of "control" in the conversation, but the potential payoff is the ability to move beyond maneuvers that settle for the surface and to connect our persuasion more personally to her life. Thus, when we share the logic of the gospel it will require more than just assent to an intellectual takedown; it will be the living truth that leads to true flourishing. We are suggesting that we challenge conversation partners to think holistically and invite them to try on the logic, theology, and ways of Christianity. This is not simply a difference in style but a fundamental disagreement rooted in different anthropologies, one that affects how people are instructed to engage others and the apologetic moves that will be made in real life.

Augustine would see both the humans-as-thinkers and humans-as-believers approaches as saying something that is true but alone not encompassing the whole story. Augustine, however, offers us the resources for an integrated approach that includes the thinking and believing aspects of our humanity but does not skim over our doxological natures. Understanding people as beings who desire to love and be loved and who reason toward a certain telos they believe will make them happy will change our apologetic encounters.

But what, you might be asking, does recovering a holistic anthropology have to do with social imaginaries?

By studying social imaginaries we learn about the assumed visions of the good and beautiful and how the universal features of personhood are being pursued in a particular context and by specific people. This enables us to engage the deepest aspirations, miseries, beliefs, and logic of a person and culture in order both to challenge that person and to show that what they

---

71. For an eloquent example of appealing to the seeking heart for the sake of apologetics, see Sarah Coakley, interview by Robert Lawrence Kuhn, *Closer to Truth*, episode 1103, "Why Believe in God?," aired July 14, 2015, https://www.closertotruth.com/episodes/why-believe-god. Coakley affirms a variety of traditional arguments for God, but—displaying Augustinian apologetic sensibilities—she recognizes she is better off first spending her time exploring existential pressures. We will explore her approach from this video more in chap. 5. Thanks to Justin Ariel Bailey (*Reimagining Apologetics*, 242–46) for bringing the Coakley video to our attention.

are ultimately looking for is to be found only in Christ. However, if we don't understand the particular local expressions of such desires and malaises along with the reasoning and beliefs intertwined with these existential realities, in practice we'll struggle to effectively connect our arguments to these universal features.

Again, the dominant contemporary approaches, which at least tacitly view people as thinkers or believers, are not all wrong; rather, they don't say enough. Especially within our contemporary Western context, with its emphasis on expressing the authentic self and its quest for healing and happiness, an apologetic approach can't afford to bypass these realities.

Thus, in turning to Augustine's focus on our restlessness and our loves, including our quest for happiness, we will discover that Augustine is prescient for our contemporary context. For Augustine believed "that the moral judgments we form on the basis of our passions reveal to us objective features of a morally ordered universe."[72] It is not that one always has to start with existential issues of the heart to open the door to the head. Yet, in an age that prioritizes personal lived experience, aiming at the existential features of personhood and human desire—which are important and inescapable aspects of our existence—engages people in a way that, to recall Hunter's expression, has "mass." It is more likely to move them. Moreover, it confronts secular narratives where they are most vulnerable and where their adherents will likely feel the most pressure. For while late moderns are passionate about their moral and aesthetic ideals, they lack a narrative that grounds and adequately sustains them.

Minimizing the social imaginary and the inner, affective aspects of personhood, along with the inner connectivity between the two, is a recipe for an apologetics in post-Christendom that may win small victories but will miss the mark in responding effectively to the growing tide of "nothing in particulars."[73] So far this chapter has imagined which concerns Augustine might call our attention to if he were at our apologetic table today. Previewing the central role Augustine will have in expanding our apologetic vision in later chapters, we have begun to gesture at how he might help us respond to these challenges.

---

72. In the original context of this quotation, James Peters (*Logic of the Heart*, 20) contrasts David Hume's failure to imagine such a world as plausible with an Augustinian vision of the universe. Here Peters uses "passions" to refer to feelings generally. John Cavadini (*Visioning Augustine*, 110–37) elects to use "passions" more narrowly to refer to lust and uses "emotions" when referring to feelings in general.

73. Burge, *The Nones*, 2, 97–102.

## The Need for the Whole *City of God*

For illustrative purposes, in this section we will engage with two recent works outside the dominant streams of apologetics that take seriously the social imaginary. Yet, to be fully Augustinian in apologetic method, we will argue that both will need to go further. For while one could go further in critiquing the idolatries inherent within our current *zeitgeist*, the other never engages the question of how Christianity might be offered as the fulfillment of the creaturely longings that have become disordered in our current culture. Thus, while each is beneficial in its own way, we see the potential for some version of each to be applied in tandem for a fully Augustinian vision.

In *The Rise and Triumph of the Modern Self*, author Carl Trueman makes clear his purpose: "My aim is to explain how and why a certain notion of the self has come to dominate the culture of the West, why this self finds its most obvious manifestation in the transformation of sexual mores, and what the wider implications of this transformation are and may well be in the future."[74] In the introduction he explains what the book is not and describes pointedly the limits of his undertaking: "My task here is limited: to demonstrate how many of the ideas now informing both the conscious thinking and the instinctive intuitions of Western men and women have deep historical roots in a coherent genealogy that helps explain why society thinks and behaves the way it does."[75] Trueman does not attempt a significant discovery of points of agreement between the modern person and Christianity, nor does he offer insight into how the modern self might afford openings to a Christian apologetic. Instead, he views his work as a "prolegomenon" for future discussion necessary for Christians to have surrounding culture.[76]

The church's response is left mainly for later discussions precipitated by his book, but he does anticipate some possible, rather bleak, futures as they relate to sexual morality, gay marriage, transgenderism, and religious freedom.[77] He offers some prudent, albeit "unscientific" (his word), predictions about where all of this may lead. Then he finishes the book with three brief suggestions that should propel the church forward into the future. First, "the church should reflect long and hard on *the connection between aesthetics and her core beliefs or practices.*"[78] The church should beware of the negative effect of absolutizing aesthetics and instead prioritize the biblical narrative, which rests on "the being of God and his act of creation." Second, if the church is "first and foremost doctrinal, then . . . *she*

---

74. Trueman, *Rise and Triumph of the Modern Self*, 31.
75. Trueman, *Rise and Triumph of the Modern Self*, 29.
76. Trueman, *Rise and Triumph of the Modern Self*, 31.
77. Trueman, *Rise and Triumph of the Modern Self*, 393–402.
78. Trueman, *Rise and Triumph of the Modern Self*, 402.

*must be a community.*"[79] The church, as a strong community, should shape moral consciousness, socially construct selves, and provide a place to belong. Third, "*Protestants need to recover both natural law and a high view of the physical body.*" Trueman concedes that natural law will not likely persuade the outside world to change its opinions, but his concern "is not primarily for the outside world but for the church herself. She needs to be able to teach her people coherently about moral principles."[80] His advice to the church is primarily antithetical to the prevailing culture.

Admittedly, his aim is not primarily constructive; rather, his goal is predominantly to engage with the question, How did we get here? But since he does give advice on how the church can move forward, we wish he would have also offered more outwardly focused ways for engaging the world outside the church. How do we persuade non-Christians in such a culture that the gospel is really good news? Nothing in his predictions about the future or his advice to the church suggests that we can find points of agreement in order to demonstrate how the church's gospel message heals the soul in search of therapy, helps individuals in their quest for an identity, and might resonate in the heart of the one desiring to live an authentic life. Readers who are looking for advice on how to reason *with* the "modern self" must turn elsewhere. If Trueman hasn't largely given up on persuading those outside the church, at the very least he has largely left the question of how to do that for others to consider.

The second book is Justin Ariel Bailey's *Reimagining Apologetics*. Bailey's aim is more explicitly focused on apologetics. It is a constructive project inspired in some measure by the cultural analysis of Charles Taylor and designed to build an apologetics of hope.

Bailey's apologetic "assumes the active presence of the God in whom all live and move and have their being."[81] God is here and is "all that you can honestly wish Him to be, and infinitely more."[82] In his "divine generosity," God makes "space for the authentic human search."[83] With this in mind, the apologist can tap into the specific and contextual human desires for beauty and demonstrate how the Christian faith fulfills those desires within its expansive story. In the conclusion to his book, Bailey explains his approach:

> But for the beauty of the Christian faith to be felt, we must first explore what a person *would* find resonant, what *would* strike them as beautiful, and what *would*

---

79. Trueman, *Rise and Triumph of the Modern Self*, 404.
80. Trueman, *Rise and Triumph of the Modern Self*, 405.
81. Bailey, *Reimagining Apologetics*, 233.
82. MacDonald, *God's Words to His Children*, 116, quoted in Bailey, *Reimagining Apologetics*, 233.
83. Bailey, *Reimagining Apologetics*, 233.

capture their imagination. Then we must inquire in what way the gospel might speak to those desires, reorienting them, or creating a larger context in which they might be transfigured.[84]

Bailey's project is a fulfillment project, grounded in hope and the imagination, that looks for points of agreement and then expands on those connections by demonstrating the power of the gospel to transform desires and satisfy them in beautiful ways.

Bailey avoids condemning the culture or pointing out how the culture has failed to fulfill our deepest longings, a negative approach that he refers to as "the apologetics of despair."[85] In contrast, his methodology does not attempt to push atheism or other worldviews to the point where they are exposed to be hopelessly unlivable and inconsistent. He contrasts these two kinds of apologetics:

> But rather than seeking to surface the weaknesses of a rival worldview, I want to move in the opposite direction. I want to explore aesthetic sensibilities and to situate desire within a broader theodramatic context. I want to water the best imaginative impulses and to provide them a more fertile, transcendent ground.[86]

Bailey admits that for some skeptics the critical approach "may be necessary in order to clear the way for hope." He even affirms the possible usefulness of the negative strategy: "Despair can expose pretensions of objectivity, deflate narratives of enlightened maturity, and undermine humanistic confidence."[87] Yet, Bailey's apologetic focuses not on condemning cultural ills but rather on building upon creational goods. Antithesis is not the first or second step in his preferred approach, nor does it take a central role in the book. He writes, "Instead of starting with our existential angst caused by our finitude and fallenness, hope moves forward on the conviction of the original goodness of creation and human creativity."[88] Practically, his readers will need to turn elsewhere to develop the ability to expose the existential failures of a skeptic and critique the inconsistencies in their way of being in the world.

Keeping in mind the earlier comparison between Virgil's and Walt Disney's respective influences in their respective cultures, a brief example can help highlight the differences between the two apologetic instincts exemplified in Bailey and Trueman, to attempt to reason *with* (Bailey) and *against* (Trueman) the grain of our present culture. Consider a lyric that echoes throughout the Disney

---

84. Bailey, *Reimagining Apologetics*, 231.
85. Bailey, *Reimagining Apologetics*, 11.
86. Bailey, *Reimagining Apologetics*, 11.
87. Bailey, *Reimagining Apologetics*, 11.
88. Bailey, *Reimagining Apologetics*, 12.

movie *Frozen 2*: "You feel what you feel, and those feelings are real." The movie is a popular expression of the fragility and anxiety, along with the hopes and dreams, of late modernism. The characters spend much of the film grasping for something real and enduring, emphasizing the importance of feelings and holding out love as the only thing that lasts—as epitomized in Olaf's deathbed confession that he has found "one thing that's permanent . . . love." In response to the *zeitgeist* to which the film belongs, someone adopting Trueman's approach would likely focus on the emotivist's problematic use of feelings: "Not feelings! Truth!"[89]

Bailey's approach, on the other hand, would ask us to consider how feelings might lead someone to the truth. For after all, feelings are indeed "real." Emotions are an aspect of what it means to be human and are not themselves the problem. The problem, Augustine would remind us, is disordered loves.[90] We desire to find true love and happiness, but we paradoxically run from the source in whom we can find it. But if in our approach we focus on mocking the narcissism or inconsistencies of the song that a community's social imaginary has been dancing to for most of their lives, don't expect them to even consider changing tunes. The longing to see love as eternal (see the doctrine of the Trinity) and to acknowledge the restlessness of our feelings (see the Psalms or *Confessions*) means that, while these cultural expressions aren't within the right plotline or aimed properly, they are nonetheless subplots that can be taken up and put within the true story line, which reorders our loves properly and fits with the grain of the universe.

Nevertheless, Trueman's account can be used to jolt the person into seeing the problems in their thinking and way of life. When we challenge others to see that what seems like common sense hasn't always been common, it alerts them to the tenuous, if not contradictory, nature of many of their assumptions. The story they are assuming is often quite parochial and untested. It is unlikely to last or to end well. When we confront others with these problems and the inconsistency and even despair inherent in their position, the door can open for them to consider trying on Christianity—intellectually and existentially—in earnest. As we will see later, this balance is modeled by Augustine in *The City of God*, the first *apologia* of this kind, critiquing the very underpinnings of society

89. In the final chapter of his recently published *Strange New World* (169–87), an abridged and modified version of *The Rise and Triumph of the Modern Self*, Trueman has incorporated some positive observations concerning expressive individualism alongside his critique, while also signaling the emotional rehabilitation that Christianity offers. We find these remarks to be more friendly to Augustine's strategy for persuasion in *Confessions* and *The City of God* that we will explore in more detail in part 2 of this work.

90. See Augustine, *The City of God* 14. Augustine routinely appeals to the feelings of restlessness and the human desire for happiness as he seeks to persuade people of the truth of Christianity.

at large and then offering a constructive narrative as the fulfillment of his culture's deepest aspirations. As will become more apparent in chapter 5 as we map out Augustine's method, his apologetic employs antitheses and agreement. Independently, each can be useful. But to be fully Augustinian we need both working together.

### Where Are the Church's Leaders?

This chapter has raised practical and philosophical problems with some of the most popular approaches to apologetics. By neglecting the cultural contingency of how people instinctively imagine the world to be, the most popular apologetic pedagogies have given sparse attention to the resources and skills needed for effective contextual persuasion. This has left many ministers trained in these approaches flat-footed, attempting to engage with a rapidly changing West but using methods developed within and for a different context. This problem is compounded by reductionistic anthropologies operating within the dominant methods.

Humans are creatures who seek understanding, believe without absolute proof, and long to love and be loved. As Augustine writes as he appeals to the pagans concerning the universal desire for peace in *The City of God*, "No one's vice is so completely contrary to nature that it destroys even the last vestiges of nature."[91] These universal aspects of human nature, however, take different forms throughout history and across cultures. People think, believe, and love, and such actions will be accompanied by value, moral, teleological, and aesthetic judgments, though how people act and judge will be shaped by particular fallen social imaginaries. The less Christians examine and understand these particular expressions, the less weighty our persuasion will be. Moreover, because such cultural expressions are formed in a fallen yet still structurally good world, unbelievers will seek to rebel against the created order without being able to fully dislodge the givens of their created nature. Thus, the apologist must be prepared to challenge distortions and appeal to human longings manifested through cultural expressions.

Yet, one might ask, Why has the discipline of apologetics been susceptible to the specific problems surveyed in this chapter and in large measure slow to come to grips with and adjust to the changing cultural terrain?

The issues we have described in this chapter are interconnected, but they are also related to another fundamental problem yet to be explored: contemporary apologetics has been largely separated from the life, leadership, and

---

91. Augustine, *The City of God* 19.12.

theology of the local church. On the one hand, pastors and missionaries are underrepresented in the conversations about apologetic method and are no longer leaders in setting the agenda for apologetic training. On the other hand, leading apologists who provide models and exemplify the discipline have largely worked vocationally outside, or on the margins of, the church.[92]

This is not to say that the field does not need philosophers who hold academic posts and are able to zoom in and break things down to their smallest component parts as well as zoom out in order to genealogically trace the philosophical lineage that led to our present age. The precision and specialization they bring to the apologetic table is invaluable. Alvin Plantinga, to name a splendid example from analytic philosophy, is a gift to the world and the church.[93] And by this point it should be clear that this book owes a particular debt to the philosopher Charles Taylor. May both Plantinga's and Taylor's tribes increase! We need academic philosophers of all stripes to join in. The anti-intellectual strain of the church neglects such philosophical treasures to their own poverty. This isn't a question of whether the church and its leaders need to be intellectually serious or whether academics are valuable in the church's mission; the answer to those questions is an emphatic yes! The question is, "Who will lead, and what will be the primary location from which a Christian apologetic emerges?"

Our training and vocational context form us to see certain things and miss other things.[94] As the saying goes, if all you have is a hammer, everything looks like a nail. Different academic specialties and vocational contexts shape how one approaches issues. For instance, while both the academy and the church are concerned with questions related to God and suffering, the specific questions and the ways one is educated to respond are often different. The demands of pastoral care offered in times of pain and heartache cannot help but form the

---

92. Consider the ministries or posts of today's leading apologists. With a few notable exceptions, their primary vocational contexts are parachurch ministries or schools.

93. It is worth noting, however, that Plantinga himself acknowledges that previous pastor-theologians were influential in inspiring his challenge to modern foundationalism and his development of a distinctly Christian, rather than allegedly neutral, account of rationality (for a condensed summary of his approach, see Plantinga, *Knowledge and Christian Belief*). And though this will be more relevant to our next chapter, we'd be remiss not to add that Plantinga's account connects reason to our affections, and more broadly to human telos, in a way that resembles Augustine. In the words of James Peters, "Plantinga shares with both Augustine and Pascal the conviction that the question of what it is rational to believe is bound up with our conception not only of the proper function of reason in human life, but of the purpose, design, or meaning of human life itself." *Logic of the Heart*, 41.

94. Some of the material in this conclusion has been adapted from Chatraw, "The Pastor Theologian as Apologist," in *Becoming a Pastor Theologian: New Possibilities for Church Leadership*, ed. Todd A. Wilson and Gerald Hiestand (Downers Grove, IL: IVP Academic, 2016), 173–84. Used with permission.

apologetic approach to the questions of evil and suffering. The apologist and apologetic methods that emerge from these contexts will often be attentive to different concerns and have distinct textures.

If apologetics is formed within and for the church, it has a greater potential to be viewed as an integrative discipline that includes the theoretical but focuses practically on specific people and how best to persuade them.[95] Accordingly, apologetics not only calls for a team approach, with academics of all types serving as an essential part of the church, but also needs leadership from pastors, missionaries, and ecclesial theologians who are trained in the integration and application of multiple disciplines. Leaders are needed who are compelled to zoom out to see the big theological picture and make connections and who are trained to put insights from various disciplines into practice as they do ministry amid the contingencies of our evolving culture.

Those called into ecclesial ministry are called to learn to persuade within a given context's particular expressions of unbelief and skepticism. Such a context almost always represents the broader concerns of a community (in comparison to the narrower culture of academic departments) and is informed by the ongoing lived realities that aren't well represented by one-off interactions on the debate stage or conference circuit. Those ministering in the church simply can't afford to settle for approaches or arguments aimed at an imagined abstract or universal person. The primary concerns and questions of faithful apologetic ministry engage the specifics of the social imaginary of the typical person in their city and local congregation in a way that keeps the apologist's feet on the ground and their eyes on the hearts of their community. The faithfulness (doctrinal accountability within an orthodox confession) and fruitfulness (effectiveness within a given context) of an approach are tested weekly within the life of the church.

Faithful apologetics, similar to faithful theology, should be ecclesial. Like theology, apologetics is integrally connected to the life and health of the church; both should be done with the aim of worship and applied in support of missions, evangelism, and discipleship. Apologetics—again, like theology—is to be primarily formed in the life of the church rather than chiseled out within the academy and then given to the church to apply. And for most of the history of the

---

95. In contrast to this understanding of apologetics, Craig asserts in *Reasonable Faith* that "apologetics is primarily a theoretical discipline . . . that tries to answer the question, 'What rational warrant can be given for the Christian faith?'" Therefore, answering questions like "Why are there so many hypocrites in the church?" is, for Craig, more appropriate for "courses or books on evangelism" (15). Our concern is that this narrower understanding of the discipline could end up disconnecting the questions of goodness and beauty from questions of truth in a way that takes us further from a more realistic view of how humans actually reason and are persuaded.

church, contracting out apologetic leadership was never an option. Apologetics was done from ecclesial contexts and was led by pastors. While the academy should come alongside the church, it cannot without harm replace the church as the epicenter for the formation of apologists and the direction setter for the discipline.

Why haven't pastors and missionaries taken up a leadership role in apologetics?[96] Certainly, modern specialization, along with the contracting out of theology and training from the church to the academy and to parachurch ministries, has played an important role in this shift. Furthermore, modern expectations and pressures on pastors have left many with little time to reflect theologically and philosophically about their ministry.

Three additional points help answer this question.

First, many pastors and missionaries have problems with how apologetics has been done, and thus, they have been hesitant to pick up the apologetic mantle. As in my (Mark's) story at the beginning of the chapter, many pastors were sold on apologetics until they attempted to use the methods they learned in ecclesial and missional settings. Their ineffectiveness in connecting with the people in the pews and on the streets left them looking to other means of ministry.

Second, "apologist" is seen by many as the identity of philosophers, not exegetes or theologians or even missionaries. Most pastors are primarily trained in biblical studies or theology, and missionaries have much of the same training but with the added emphasis on cross-cultural ministry. Both pastors and missionaries have taken maybe one token class on philosophy. They are not philosophers and thus don't view themselves as apologists either; that title is typically reserved for analytic philosophers who teach such courses and typically write the textbooks.[97] Rather than seeing apologetics as involving multiple disciplines in a way that calls people of different gifts and specialties to sail the ship together, often these apologists have defined the discipline narrowly and then "welcomed" everyone else on board as long as they follow the captain's rules. It is no wonder that pastors and missionaries have often gone looking for another boat. Pastor-theologians, those who have been able to carve out a large amount of time for in-depth reflection, thus often find themselves paradoxically fashioning themselves after the likes of Augustine and Irenaeus but giving little attention to the importance of their own self-identity as the church's apologists.

---

96. Certainly, there are some wonderful contemporary exceptions, such as N. T. Wright (formerly the Anglican bishop of Durham) and Timothy Keller (formerly the senior pastor at Redeemer Presbyterian Church in New York City). Yet, even Wright and Keller are typically only, at best, on the periphery of methodological discussions in most apologetic circles.

97. Additionally, by necessity today some evangelists and youth speakers are left to fill the role of apologist.

Third, apologetics is seen by some as theologically light. It was B. B. War-field who said that "apologetics has been treated very much like a step-child in the theological household."[98] Many of the most theologically engaged pastors have too often imbibed a general attitude akin to the one Warfield describes. For many, "apologist" signals either a glibness that ignores theological nuance in favor of easy answers or an excessive wandering away from the Bible itself. "Apologist," then, becomes a dirty word or the butt of a joke. A recent acquaintance's jesting captures this attitude: "What do you call an amateur theologian? An apologist."

Though that joke might get some laughs around a table of theologians today, Augustine, along with the rest of the church fathers, wouldn't get it. Allowing Augustine to speak into contemporary apologetics might just change the way pastors and missionary church planters see the discipline and imagine their place in it. As he utilized philosophy and the diversity of his training, Augustine's pastoral vocation, theology formed within the church, and reading of the Scriptures drove his apologetics and his method. These factors, combined (as we saw in chapter 1) with his unique personal and contextual situation and its surprising analogues for our context today, lead us to welcome Augustine back to the table for more than a critique. For in apologetics, as in anything else, demolition is easy. Building is much harder. In constructing an apologetic for and within the church, we will need all the help we can get.

## An Apologetic Re-enchantment: From Dallas to South Bend

Years after my time in Norman Geisler's apologetic course, I visited the University of Notre Dame, seeking to become a theology student in their PhD program (while in my midforties, which was almost unheard of in Notre Dame's program). John Cavadini, who was then the chair of the department, explained to me their pedagogical approach with a simple phrase: "faith seeking understanding." Admittedly, when I heard him lecture, some of his teaching made me nervous. The shadow of those early days in Dallas still loomed large. Would my defense of my faith come crashing down if I reimagined it in a different way? Yet, his passion for Augustine's way opened my mind to new possibilities.

Since then, I have explored those possibilities. I have dug into Augustine's pastoral approach to apologetics and found him doing apologetics on the ground where real people live. For instance, as Charles Mathewes has emphasized, even the great and arduous *City of God* was *not* written "for an essentially 'religious' audience, composed of priests and monks; he wrote it for a lay one, embedded

98. Warfield, *Selected Shorter Writings*, 93.

in 'the world.'"[99] Moreover, the greatest influences in his theological formation and ministry were not the Neoplatonist philosophers (though they did certainly influence him) but Scripture, Christ, and the church.[100] He understood the power of the social imaginary, even before Charles Taylor coined the term, and the power of living in the Bible's redemptive story; he persuaded people as holistic beings appealing to their longing for happiness, peace, and love; he demonstrated a nimbleness in adjusting his approach according to his audience and their real challenges, questions, and longings; and he ingeniously critiqued the corrupting errors in society and affirmed the good, the true, and the beautiful wherever he encountered it. As we turn to the second part of this book, we do so with the hope of hearing Augustine's voice afresh, to listen for how he might instruct the church to build an apologetic for today.

99. Mathewes, "Another City," 103.

100. Brian Stock puts it well when he says that by the time Augustine wrote *Confessions*, the Scriptures had become the dominant influence on and authority in his life: "The life of Christ thus becomes his point of reference for evaluating Platonist doctrines. For, in his view, the incarnation personalized truth as no abstract philosophy could." *Augustine the Reader*, 66.

PART 2

# An Augustinian
# Vision for Today

# 3

# A Renewed Posture

"I don't think it insignificant that the deeper I have dug into Christianity with a thirst for the truth, the more difficult it has become to have faith. In fact, for me, it has become impossible." This is the public confession of Rhett McLaughlin, cohost of the popular YouTube show *Good Mythical Morning* and the podcast *Ear Biscuits*. Rhett (he and his cohost are popularly known by their first names, "Rhett and Link") grew up attending a Bible-believing church in the middle of the Bible Belt.[1] He was raised to believe that "Jesus is the only way to heaven when you die," and for him "Jesus was as real as he could be without physically manifesting his presence." In high school and college, he was bothered by what he describes as a natural skepticism but could "plaster" over his doubts by listening to Christian apologists. After attending college, Rhett served on staff with Campus Crusade for Christ (now Cru). Part of his ministry was to combat the arguments of the New Testament scholar and well-known critic of Christianity Bart Ehrman. Rhett *was* an apologist. Yet, at this point Rhett began to feel the weight of his doubts. And here's the kicker: as Rhett sees it now, the professional apologists were part of the problem.

Rhett's deconversion testimony comes across as an intellectual journey in which the scientific, archaeological, and historical support for his faith unraveled even though he put in quite a bit of time digging through popular apologetic works. In college he went on a journey from being a young-earth creationist to being a somewhat conflicted theistic evolutionist. Along the way he concluded

---

1. Rhett's deconversion story is available at "Rhett's Spiritual Deconstruction," Ear Biscuits (YouTube channel), February 9, 2020, video, 1:44:50, https://youtu.be/1qbna6t1bzw. Unless otherwise indicated, the quotations in this section come from this video.

that the arguments for a historical Adam didn't hold water and that, basically, those who held to a historical Adam and Eve did so because they "knew they needed them for Christian doctrine." But a "non-historical" Adam proved problematic for Rhett, since he saw the Bible as presenting Adam and Eve as real individuals. The house of cards was beginning to fall. Soon he came to believe that much of the evidence for the historicity of the Old Testament rested on arguments from silence, and he eventually found that Bart Ehrman's takes on the New Testament and Jesus proved more persuasive than books he had read by popular apologists. He began to think that the Bible made more sense as merely a collection of human writings. At a decisive point, he asked himself the question that would lead to his deconversion: "If I didn't want to believe X (people are going to hell, or God would command genocide), then why would I?" He would soon begin to allow himself to think, "Why am I still doing this?"

So Rhett, in his own words, "jumped ship." He describes the vulnerability of his leap into the unknown like this:

> You see, I kind of saw Christianity as a boat in a very stormy sea. It's stable. There's a lot of other people on it. It's got a destination. You're gonna get through this. It gives you something to hold on to. It gives you stability. It gives you meaning. It gives you direction, and it gives you community. And when I jumped ship, I didn't jump to another boat. . . . I jumped into a sea of uncertainty.

In a later episode Rhett explains that he actually jumped off the illusion of certainty into "the sea of nothingness."[2] And in the most recent update, Rhett speaks of his evolving spiritual journey.[3] What remains clear is that after a long search he found that Christianity and its defenders failed to provide the answers and evidential support he was looking for. The apologists had been big on promises, but—at least in his view—they couldn't actually deliver.

Rhett was angry at the Christian thinkers "who had written books saying that evolution didn't have any evidence" and "the people who had written systematic theology books who basically made it seem like this was all pretty simple." Still, he did not have a particular "personal tragedy story." Initially, he swung into atheism, but that was replaced by an agnosticism with "openness and curiosity." He lost his appetite for certainty. He has come to think that belief in God is very reasonable and that the universe is meaningful and has a

---

2. "Rhett's Spiritual Deconstruction—One Year Later," Ear Biscuits (YouTube channel), February 21, 2021, video, 1:27:33, https://youtu.be/CnYG6x-aOTk. This quotation comes from his one-year-later account. All other quotations are from his original deconstruction story.

3. "Rhett Bought a Bible—Two Years Later," Ear Biscuits (YouTube channel), March 6, 2022, video, 1:35:43, https://youtu.be/jQGwPQHlTjs.

purpose, which he finds comforting, but he doesn't know anything about the God who is "behind all of this." His focus has shifted from transcendent realities to the immanent. He now worries not about what happens after you die but about "what happens while you live." Channeling, perhaps unaware of the historical pedigree, a Montaignian skepticism in response to his recognition of competing possible world-and-life-views, Rhett confesses to ignorance on the questions of transcendence, and he sets out to live within an immanent frame: "The only thing I know that I got is this life."[4] Yet, he insists that he is still open to revelation, is not a naturalist, and is willing to change his mind. He describes himself as a "hopeful agnostic."

Public deconversion stories like Rhett's have become highly publicized the past several years. Well-known pastors, contemporary Christian music artists, and other public Christians are leaving the faith "out loud." Many of these coming-of-age stories include gut-wrenching accounts of how, both intellectually and morally, the Christian faith was no longer sustainable. Christianity seemed neither true nor good to them anymore.

While Rhett's story is representative of this growing phenomenon, our intention here is not to engage the ins and outs of his own account or offer a full-orbed critique. We actually share some of his concerns about how theology and apologetics are too often practiced. Reading through many of the apologetic manuals written over the past twenty years, as we did when we wrote an apologetics textbook several years ago, we noticed a disconnect between how apologetics is often taught and the ability of the trainees to help people like Rhett in practical ways.

Rhett, like so many others with a similar story, appears to have defaulted into a posture that was unwittingly programmed to destruct the faith under certain conditions, even though that posture was passed on to him and was confirmed by apologists and other Christians as protecting the faith. Rhett is correct to find Christianity wanting if he is operating on the premise that simply looking at historical evidence and making logical calculations *demands* rational assent to the faith. While he never says this outright, he seems to have approached the faith, in practice, with an Enlightenment-style rather than premodern, Augustinian-like rationality.[5] For example, when Bart Ehrman introduced Rhett to the world of critical scholarship, it felt very distant from his Christian roots, so in defense Rhett marshaled some of the biggest names in popular apologetics. Evidence

---

4. As we saw with Pascal at the end of chap. 1, as we retrieve Augustine's help to engage this mindset, this will not be the first time someone enlists Augustine's help in diagnosing the malaise that results from the modern pursuit of immanent contentment. See Storey and Storey, *Why We Are Restless*, 10–98.

5. This is along the lines of the contrast made in Peters, *Logic of the Heart*, 60–82.

that demanded a positive verdict was pitted against evidence that demanded a negative verdict. But were these approaches very different? Certainly, the conclusions were diametrically opposed, but perhaps their postures were not always so.[6]

Science, history, and logic are friends of our faith; Rhett wasn't wrong to look there. We're not suggesting fideism was the route he should have traveled. Yet, the hardened skeptics and brash believers, who are both attempting just to let the science or the history or the logic lead them to the truth, have overreached. Neither the "assured" results of critical scholarship nor the "proofs" of Christian apologists have produced the kind of results many have hoped for. Even if you personally find certain arguments and evidence persuasive, what happens when they aren't so for the person you are trying to help? And what should you do when Christendom has receded and with it the willingness of most to even bother following your favorite chain of reasoning? Do you just keep rehearsing the same kind of arguments in the same sort of way, not worrying about the "mass"[7] of the argument for those you are trying to help? If not, what other option is available?

In this example, Augustine would have us starting with where Rhett is at and likely asking him some questions. Is leaping into "nothingness" viable? Is it even possible? Augustine would expose the problem of such an idea. The question, for Augustine, is not *if* you will have faith but *what* you will believe in, not *if* you will hope but *what* is trustworthy to hope in, not *if* you will worship but *whom* or *what* you will worship. When it comes to living, there is no opting out for "nothingness." This, of course, would be not the end but the beginning of a journey that Augustine would suggest we learn to take with the skeptics we wish to persuade.

For now, we are not asking what the specifics of an Augustinian approach are; we will discuss method in more detail in chapter 5. Instead, in this chapter our focus is on how Augustine's basic insights concerning human nature might influence the posture exemplified and offered by apologists. We will see that Augustine offers an option for seeking the answers to the big questions of life that is an alternative to the reductive rationalism that peaked during the Enlightenment and the "you do you" approaches of much of today's popular culture.

---

6. See, e.g., Wallace, "Gospel according to Bart": "It seems that Bart's black-and-white mentality as a fundamentalist has hardly been affected as he slogged through the years and trials of life and learning, even when he came out on the other side of the theological spectrum. He still sees things without sufficient nuancing, he overstates his case, and he is entrenched in the security that his own views are right. Bart Ehrman is one of the most brilliant and creative textual critics I have ever known, and yet his biases are so strong that, at times, he cannot even acknowledge them" (349).

7. Recall our reference in the previous chapter to the concept of "mass" as used by Graeme Hunter.

Augustine would have us rekindle the embers of an ancient way, learning to see that the search for truth is as much a quest to find true peace and love as it is a quest to discover the right data.

## Seeking Truth with Augustine

Augustine's own story recounted in *Confessions* helps us with two questions relevant to the posture of the apologist: (1) What is our nature as humans? (2) How do we know? Augustine's own reconstruction story provides us with a different posture from the one cultivated in the lives of so many young Christians today.[8]

*Confessions* is Augustine's mature recollection of his restless journey to faith. When he reflects on his own intellectual journey, focusing especially on his attraction to the allegedly rational claims of Manicheism, he does so from the perspective of one who now realizes that his search actually emanated from a fragmented and disordered heart. He has come to understand that his intellectual questions cannot be separated from his loves and longings; his reasoning is a part of his quest for love.

In some respects, young Augustine's problems with Christianity will sound strikingly similar to Rhett's. Yet, when Augustine recounts his intellectual journey, he is in a different place from the one Rhett describes in his most recent podcasts. Rhett seems, at least for now, to still inhabit a kind of skepticism and at times to be *almost* settled into a hopeful agnosticism. Yet, he acknowledges that he senses a need for a spiritual community, truth, and meaning. He candidly admits that if he does turn from his ambiguity, he will look back to a tradition he is familiar with. In his latest interview, he explains he even purchased a new Bible with critical notes. At present, however, he appears to be bouncing back and forth between a narrow rationalism and a reflexive skepticism. At times he speaks with great confidence about science and biblical critical scholarship—as if they are monolithic fields rendering unified and certain conclusions—undermining traditional Christian beliefs. But at other times, while his spiritual impulses and quest for meaning leave him grasping for

---

8. In addition to Rhett's story, Bart Ehrman's own story reflects this posture. In *Jesus, Interrupted*, Ehrman tells his own coming-of-age story, which begins with him as a young Christian at the fundamentalist Moody Bible Institute driven by "a religious desire for certainty" and then proceeds to his time at Princeton, where he faces two options he describes in binary terms: "My choice was either to hold on to views that I had come to realize were in error or to follow where I believed the truth was leading me. In the end, it was no choice. If something was true, it was true; if not, not" (xi). Here he is referring to his doctrine of Scripture, but this quest for the "truth" more generally led him eventually to become an agnostic with atheist leanings.

something solid to hold on to, his skepticism seems to hollow out the religious options that could provide what he is seeking.

By the time we meet the middle-aged Augustine writing his *Confessions*, he has fully returned to the faith with a realistic perspective on his youthful reductive thinking. He is more aware of his own fallenness and finitude and more conscious of his integrated nature as a loving being who believes and thinks most truly within a storied, ecclesial community. His own return to the Christian tradition and his maturation as a Christian bishop have opened his eyes to the interconnectedness of what a human is and how they come to know—and it is only by this new posture and the experiences that followed that he has discovered a mature confidence in the faith.

Recall that as a young man whose imagination was absorbed by a distorting rationalism, Augustine left his mother's version of catholic Christianity and committed himself to Manicheism. Yet, eventually, as he devoted his mental energies to finding "some definite proofs," he found himself dissatisfied with the Manichees. He discovered that some philosophers outside the world of the Manichees held "more probable views" on the natural world and the way our senses relate to that world. With the failure of the Manichean worldview to deliver on its own rationalistic promises, he decided to leave this religion and take the position of "doubting everything." Thus he entered a brief "period of uncertainty."[9]

At the end of book 5 of *Confessions*, Augustine moves at a rapid literary pace through various levels of certainty: from the "defensible" and "intellectually respectable" claims of the catholic Christian faith to the lack of "definite proofs" of the rationalistic Manichees to the "more probable views" of various philosophers to the "doubting everything" of the skeptical Academics. He admits later that he had "longed to become as certain of those things I could not see as I was seven and three makes ten."[10] Disappointingly, with this posture he had not reached the definitive conclusion he desired. He came to realize that in addition to certainty he had always been searching for something more from a philosophy. He was more than a mere logic processor; he needed a cure for his disoriented, disintegrated wretchedness. "I flatly refused to entrust the cure of my soul's sickness to philosophers who were strangers to the saving name of Christ."[11] So, in his uncertainty, he decided to return to the universal church of his childhood to see whether some kind of insight into the way things really are would occur to him.[12]

---

9. Augustine, *Confessions* 5.14.25.

10. Augustine, *Confessions* 6.4.6.

11. Augustine, *Confessions* 5.14.25.

12. Augustine, *Confessions* 5.14.25: "I resolved therefore to live as a catechumen in the Catholic Church, which was what my parents had wished for me, until some kind of certainty dawned by which I might direct my steps aright."

He would return to the church until he either found what he was looking for or became convinced that the search was not worth the trouble.

Looking back on his story, anachronistically we could say that Augustine is following the spirit of Pascal's advice, "You want to find faith and you do not know the road. You want to be cured of unbelief and you ask for the remedy: learn from those who were once bound like you and who now wager all they have. These are people who know the road you wish to follow, who have been cured of the affliction of which you wish to be cured: follow the way by which they began. They behaved as if they did believe, taking holy water, having masses said, and so on."[13] In reality, of course, it only could have been Pascal looking back to Augustine's thought for inspiration. And it isn't quite accurate to say Augustine behaved as he "did believe"—for he was not yet a participant in the sacraments. Yet, it is an apt description of something like what Augustine appears to have been doing before his conversion and what he, in *Confessions*, implicitly invites his readers to follow him in. By entering the church as a catechumen during this period of uncertainty, he opened up his life and mind to the wisdom of the church to see if it was true.

During Augustine's time of reconsideration within the church's tradition, he began to recognize even more clearly the cracks in the Manichean promise of absolute proof and unqualified certainty. He started to realize that everyone believes in something; for life's metaquestions there's no such thing as pure rationalism that has no trust in something or someone else. At one time Augustine had been emboldened to leave "authority" behind to pursue truth through this quasi rationality, but he came to realize he had been naive. He had simply exchanged one authority for another. He discovered that everyone puts their trust in some authority. We see this, for example, when he explains to his friend Honoratus, who is still entrenched in Manicheism, that true understanding relies on belief: "There is no right way of entering into the true religion without believing things that all who live rightly and become worthy of it will understand and see for themselves *later on*, and without some submission to

---

13. Pascal, *Pensées*, 124–25. Graeme Hunter clarifies how this advice fits into the logic of Pascal's argument: "The main part of this longish and much-discussed fragment sketches a kind of dialogue in which Pascal attempts to persuade a generic unbeliever to live his life as if Christianity were true. This unbeliever, who is committed to reason, discovers in the course of the dialogue that his religious scepticism is not as reasonable as he had imagined, but only something that mimics reason. He comes to see that his rejection of religion was in fact *caused* in him by his passions. He is shown that, to change his way of thinking, he needs to weaken the passions that misdirect him and put other more reasonable passions in their place. Pascal proposes a therapy to help him make that transition." *Pascal the Philosopher*, 104.

a certain weight of authority."[14] Believing comes before understanding. There's no other way.

The Manichees were hypocrites because they asked people to enter their community by trusting in the enlightenment that they promised. Ironically, they promised a path of pure reason to those who would first *believe* in them. Augustine had tried that on. Such a position, he found, couldn't cope with reality. It lacked a fittedness, being too snug for the larger reality he experienced on a daily basis.

The Manichees promised to solve the mysteries of the universe through science and reason. But eventually Augustine realized that this was an overreach. They actually suppressed probing questions. In truth, the catholic church was more honest because it admitted to mystery. Augustine explained why he came to prefer catholic doctrine: "I came to see that in commanding that certain things must be believed without demonstration the Church was a good deal more moderate and very much less deceitful than those parties who rashly promised knowledge and derided credulity, but then went on to demand belief in a whole host of fabulous and absurd myths which certainly could not be demonstrated."[15] Rather than explain things, the Manichees ignored holes in their logic and suppressed honest questions.

## A Reasonable View of Rationality

Augustine had longed for certainty—the kind that could be known through naked rationality and sensory proof apart from faith in an authority. But he came to understand that believing, healing, loving, and knowing are intimately connected. As Augustine himself puts it, his soul "could be healed only by believing, yet it shirked the cure for fear of believing what was false. It struggled in your [God's] hands, though it is you who have prepared the healing remedies of faith and spread them over the ills of the world, enduing them with marvelous potency."[16]

Augustine began to realize that faith in unproven assumptions or personally unobserved claims was absolutely necessary for functioning in everyday life. Why would the discovery of the most important, life-changing truths be any different?

> So it was, Lord, that you began little by little to work on my heart with your most gentle and merciful hand, and dispose it to reflect how innumerable were the

---

14. Augustine, *Advantage of Believing* 9.21 (emphasis added).
15. Augustine, *Confessions* 6.5.7.
16. Augustine, *Confessions* 6.4.6.

things I believed and held to be true though I had neither seen them nor been present when they happened. How many truths there were of this kind, such as events of world history, or facts about places and cities I had never seen; how many were the statements I believed on the testimony of friends, or physicians, or various other people; and, indeed, unless we did believe them we should be unable to do anything in this life.[17]

Augustine did not, at this time, simply turn from unbelief to belief or from skepticism to unquestionable certainty or from the autonomy of his own logic to belief in the authority of the church or Scripture.

Moreover, coming back to the church did not have the emotional neutrality of flipping on a light switch. Faith seeking understanding can be traumatic, especially when a seeker feels the pressure of death always looming in the shadows (as is signaled by the frequent mention of death in *Confessions*). Even with the drastic differences in life expectancy between Augustine's time and our time, our shared human condition means that the awareness of our own future death still carries an emotional weight that connects us to Augustine's existential concerns.[18] In other words, Augustine's quest for the truth was not a purely cerebral project. Nor should it be today. Augustine understood how much was at stake. He pressed into faith's most difficult questions, grappling with the heavy emotional and intellectual challenges of developing an intentional faith.[19]

Augustine came to see how a quest for truth involved his whole person. Seeking truth engaged his believing as he admitted that everyone lives within the norms of some narrative and no one can make their way through this world without accepting the testimony of others. The quest for truth absorbed his thinking as he reasoned through various options, considered the implications of certain conclusions, and discovered the limits of humanity's rational capacities. Coming to know God involved his loving as he explored his fear and guilt, confessed his twisted longings, and followed his deepest desires to the possibilities of hope.

In an important work, James Peters demonstrates how, for Augustine, loving, believing, and thinking are interrelated in the formation of our knowledge of God, the world we inhabit, and ourselves: "Central to Augustine's theory of reason and faith is his conviction that our reasoning about how to live well as humans ought to be directed and molded by our needs and desires as feeling agents who are fundamentally, and above all else, lovers."[20] The way we reason

---

17. Augustine, *Confessions* 6.5.7.
18. Becker, *Denial of Death*.
19. See, e.g., Augustine, *Confessions* 7.5.7.
20. Peters, *Logic of the Heart*, 60.

is bound up in what we love. For the Augustinian apologist, "'*credo ut intellegam*' [believe to understand] is the spiritual equivalent of '*amo ut intellegam*' [love to understand]."[21]

As we noted in chapter 2, people are not *simply* logic processors or believing animals. Rather, they are lovers who are seeking someone to love them and to give their love to. But humans are also believers and thinkers.[22] It is the importance of love in Augustine's anthropology, not a neat separation of believing from desiring, that leads him to prioritize faith for the sake of a more reasonable rationality.[23]

It is important not to misunderstand this point. Augustine does not recommend fideism or reject rational thinking. Rather, he puts forward a way that is properly rational. It is rational to believe that we are much more than brains and that there are limits both to how far our cognitive powers can take us and to how much control they can give us. He does not suggest that we should ignore or break free from rational thought; instead, he offers us a realistic rationality that humbly accepts its own limits and lets go of a false belief that through a type of technological precision we can achieve guaranteed right beliefs.

For Augustine, in order to know God a person needs to have the right type of posture. Therefore, an Augustinian apologist's instinctive move is to find ways to persuade others to shift their posture from one of pride to one of humility.[24] This posture is in accord with who they are as lovers and seekers. The first paragraph of *Confessions* frames the posture required of a seeker of the truth:

21. Peters, *Logic of the Heart*, 159. We know the truth through love, as Augustine makes clear: "Love knows it. O eternal Truth, true Love, and beloved Eternity, you are my God, and for you I sigh day and night." *Confessions* 7.10.16.

22. Carol Harrison notes, "In *City of God* we found that, acknowledging the will's incapacity rationally to deliberate, choose, and act upon the good, Augustine broke with classical moral philosophy in attributing the desires and passions, which it relegated to the body and viewed merely as disturbances, to the will itself and gave them a positive role in directing the fallen will towards the good. Love, operating through the passions, therefore takes the place of reason in directing man's will towards God. As Augustine comments in *City of God* 11, 'For we are justified in calling a man good not because he knows what is good, but because he loves the good' (11.28). Of course, no one can love the good unless he in some sense knows it ([*The Trinity*] 10.1.1)—and we have seen that Augustine held there were certain truths which are both innate to man's mind and made known to him through God's revelation of Himself in Scripture. But it is love which both increases this knowledge ([*Homilies on the Gospel of John*] 96.4) and enables man to act upon it and use it rightly." Harrison, *Augustine*, 95–96.

23. Peters, *Logic of the Heart*, 60.

24. One could use Alan Jacobs's *How to Think* or C. S. Lewis's *The Abolition of Man* in this vein. Neither work is making the case for Christianity; rather, both are appealing to a way of inhabiting the world that will lead to virtuous people who are better able to discern wisdom and truth, thus establishing postures that could open one to persuasion and the possibility of conversion.

Great are you, O Lord, and exceedingly worthy of praise; your power is immense, and your wisdom beyond reckoning. And so we humans, who are due part of your creation, long to praise you—we who carry our mortality about with us, carry the evidence of our sin and with it the proof that you thwart the proud. Yet these humans, due part of your creation as they are, still do long to praise you. You stir us so that praising you may bring us joy, because you have made us and drawn us to yourself, and our heart is unquiet until it rests in you.[25]

This paragraph provokes such probing questions as, Who am I restlessly longing for? Who is stirring me to seek? What am I made for? and, What is the source of my true delight? The opening paragraph of *Confessions* raises readers' awareness of their nature as fallen mortals, their frustrations as a consequence of their pride, the infinite difference between their Creator and them as creatures, and the scarcity of their knowledge in comparison to the vastness of God's wisdom. For Augustine, our posture impacts our final destination. Prideful reasoning will ultimately lead in the wrong direction.

## Questioning and Seeking

Essential to the right posture is accepting that seeking the truth is a lifelong process that is never finished in this life and is attained only in the life to come. We are never completely at rest here and now. Augustine "envisions human life as a journey of faith." Accordingly, one way to discover a proper confidence is to accept mystery as part of faith, since we are finite and fallen creatures. Peters explains that "in its ideal form, human life is a journey beginning in faith (*fides*) and ending in that fully completed state of understanding that Augustine calls wisdom (*sapientia*). In Augustine's view, the starting point, faith, and the ultimate *telos*, wisdom, serve as the ideal alpha and omega stages of Christian discipleship."[26] Augustine stated the point in its most classical form: "Faith seeks, understanding finds; whence the prophet says, 'Unless you believe, you shall not understand.'"[27] The completed state of understanding is never reached in this life. In this life faith continues to seek understanding; it is on a continuing quest. Again, faith is seeking understanding not just for better arguments or more evidence, though these will be involved, but for a more mature apprehension of the source of beauty and love.

In *Confessions*, seeking often takes the form of questions. Early in book 1, after an opening doxology and his most famous sentence, "You stir us so that praising

25. Augustine, *Confessions* 1.1.1.
26. Peters, *Logic of the Heart*, 64.
27. Augustine, *The Trinity* 15.2.2.

you may bring us joy, because you have made us and drawn us to yourself, and our heart is unquiet until it rests in you," Augustine launches into several pages of questions, beginning with questions related to seeking, preaching (Scripture), praising (doxology), believing, understanding, and knowing:

> Grant me to know and understand, Lord, which comes first: to call upon you or to praise you? To know you or to call upon you? Must we know you before we can call upon you? Anyone who invokes what is still unknown may be making a mistake. Or should you be invoked first, so that we may then come to know you? But how can people call upon someone in whom they do not yet believe? And how can they believe without a preacher? But scripture tells us that those who seek the Lord will praise him, for as they seek they find him, and on finding him they will praise him. Let me seek you, then, Lord, even while I am calling upon you, and call upon you even as I believe in you; for to us you have indeed been preached. My faith calls upon you, Lord, this faith which is your gift to me, which you have breathed into me through the humanity of your Son and the ministry of your preacher.[28]

Augustine's is a faith gifted by God's grace, grounded in Scripture, and drawn to the happiness of praise, continuously seeking deeper understanding. And with understanding comes knowing. And with knowing come more questions, better questions. His faith seeks understanding of the one it seeks, a knowing that brings about joyful praise . . . and more questions . . . and more seeking and more praising. As Charles Mathewes observes, Augustine's questioning is not primarily seeking mere technological answers to his questions, a "certain, final 'unquestionable' faith" or a skeptical undoing of all we thought could be known.[29] Rather, Augustine journeys hopefully, in faith and agony, toward deeper understanding and knowledge of the one he loves and longs for. He continues his questioning quest throughout the pages of *Confessions*. He keeps on asking, seeking, and knocking, drawn along by God's grace and driven forward by his longing for love.

This process continues throughout the book until he concludes his extended restless quest with the reality check that the fullness of rest will not be achieved until "we too may rest in you, in the Sabbath of eternal life."[30] For some, this might sound discouraging; we will never be fully at rest until the repose of the next life. Contrariwise, this is actually a hopeful orienting point, reminding the *quest*-ioner that the journey is not pointless. Learning to ask the right questions can lead one toward home, toward eternal rest in God—each person's true north.

28. Augustine, *Confessions* 1.1.1.
29. Mathewes, "Liberation of Questioning," 544.
30. Augustine, *Confessions* 13.36.51.

The final few paragraphs of *Confessions* are not a conclusion, as we might expect. Actually, as Charles Mathewes observes, the final sentences of the book situate us in a future-oriented life of searching, longing, and being: "Let us rather ask of you [God], seek in you, knock at your door. Only so will we receive, only so find, and only so will the door be opened to us."[31] That is, as lovers seeking understanding, we continue our quest for God with open-ended expectation. Mathewes notes the somewhat odd final word of the book: "*aperietur*, 'will be' or 'shall be opened.'"[32] This "conclusion" has an awareness that the ultimate resolution to the questioning search will not be fully realized until we rest in eternal repose in God, until we receive the true wisdom we were made for and we long for.

Augustine is not setting out to offer proof of God's existence as the necessary foundation for faith—though, as we will see, he places value in persuading others of the reasonableness of the faith. Augustine's focus is on reasoning our way from or with faith. God reveals enough for our journey but not all the knowledge we shall have when we reach our full and final happiness in God. So we trust God's word to us without comprehending now all that we would like to know.[33]

## Faith, Reason, and Desire

Given that we have emphasized love as the center of Augustine's integrated anthropology, how does the classic statement on the priority of faith ("faith seeking understanding") relate to a doxological understanding of humans?

Neither thinking nor believing are emotionally detached affairs. Ironically, it seems that fear of being duped by common human experiences and longings compels the Cartesian pursuit of epistemological control. In this case, an emotion—namely, fear—pushes a person to control the pursuit of truth by way of committing only to things that fit into a narrow box of "indubitable conclusions" as well as bracketing off anything that seems subjective and neglecting the full range of human experience. The problem is that when this is done, it sidelines what is most fundamental to our humanity and misconceives our rationality as something disconnected from our morality, aesthetics, and affections. There is no hard proof for visions of love, beauty, goodness, hope, wonder, and sacrifice. They cannot be studied under the lens of a microscope or broken into small component parts to be tested in an experiment, but when they are bracketed off from our quests for truth or explained away and reduced to simply biological

---

31. Augustine, *Confessions* 13.38.53.
32. Mathewes, "Liberation of Questioning," 539.
33. Peters, *Logic of the Heart*, 64–66.

features of the human machine, the most common and most essential features of our lives as humans are put to the side. This narrow posture a priori rules out important "evidence" from consideration from the start.

Moreover, not only do people who have inherited a reductionistic posture toward the quest for truth actually fail to keep affections and fears out of the believing or reasoning process, but—like all people—they don't avoid the risk of potentially being duped. In fact, for them it is worse. Taking epistemological wagers is an inescapable part of being human, and they wager on a parochial view of rationality. They wrongly imagine they have isolated their logic and have made a decision in reference to God apart from emotions. Yet because of mounting evidence, a wager on this kind of epistemology—in which we make our big decisions in life by way of some type of rational-choice theory—looks increasingly like a bad bet. Allegedly disinterested skeptics, who position themselves as neutral observers, should not take pride in their so-called objective search for the truth or feel superior to those who fully engage their desires in the pursuit of God. To the extent that certain skeptics fall prey to this reductionism, they are displaying an "irrational" conception of rationality. Various recent studies have drawn together neurological, social, and psychological research to conclude, as Jonathan Haidt has put it, that "human rationality depends critically on sophisticated emotionality. It is only because our emotional brains work so well that our reasoning can work at all."[34] In a similar vein, Iain McGilchrist's wide-ranging work combining both neurological research and historical analysis leads him to say that "feeling is not just an add-on, a flavoured coating for thought: it is at the heart of our being, and reason emanates from that central core of the emotions, in an attempt to limit and direct *them*, rather than the other way about."[35]

Here is the Augustinian point: it is reasonable to give up the illusory and irrational ideal of adopting a dispassionate posture or neutral framework for deciding life's big questions. The perseverance to continue the quest to find true joy, the humility to accept our creaturely contingency, and the courage to seek out a higher authority that can be trusted over oneself are far from neutral. And yet, for an Augustinian, these desires, aimed by the mysterious work of the Spirit, form the posture necessary to guide one on the path to ultimate truth.

For the rational mind to truly know and believe God without loving him is, for Augustine, nonsensical. Again, Peters provides clarity:

> What Augustine refers to as reason is not reason thought of as a mere blind machine, indifferently processing data, but reason as seeking an end and thus being passionate and desiring. . . . Augustinian reasoning is not a neutral technological

34. Haidt, *Happiness Hypothesis*, 13.
35. McGilchrist, *Master and His Emissary*, 185.

process but is an ethical and teleological activity. As Augustine states, reason by its very nature seeks to know and thus possess and enjoy the good. . . . The Augustinian rational person employs reason neither to master nature nor simply to see why things are as they are, but to become the sort of person whose internal order enables him or her, by God's grace, to find his or her proper place in the order of creation.[36]

However, it would be wrong to read Augustine as advocating an irrational leap of faith. Augustine can also say that in one sense, reason precedes faith:

And so, the Prophet stated quite reasonably, *Unless you believe, you will not understand* (Is 7:9 LXX). There he undoubtedly distinguished these two and gave the counsel that we should believe first in order that we may be able to understand whatever we believe. Hence it was reasonably commanded that faith should precede reason. For, if this command is not reasonable it is, therefore, unreasonable. Heaven forbid! If, then, it is reasonable that faith precede reason with respect to certain great truths that cannot yet be grasped, however slight the reason is that persuades us to this, it undoubtedly also comes before faith.[37]

Augustine, perhaps recalling the days when he "resolved to live as a catechumen in the Catholic Church . . . until some kind of certainty dawned by which I might direct my steps aright," understood that the use of reason was part of his return to the realm of the church and Scripture to seek the truth. He reasoned that belief in the church and the Scriptures' authority might just provide the framework in which he could discover the right kind of understanding. But how do we know whether this authority should be trusted? Peters answers this question, demonstrating that, for Augustine, epistemology and anthropology are bound up together:

For Augustine, the remedy for both kinds of disorder comes to us not by means of our own devices, but only through God's grace. Faith in God serves as the medicine of the soul by which these unhealthy forms of affection are transformed into genuine love. To the question, "Which ultimate authority is it reasonable to trust?" Augustine responds that it is reasonable to trust as one's highest authority only the authority of the One who is the True Physician. The rationality of belief in God, then, which is essentially the rationality of trusting in the proper authority, is, quite astonishingly for a modern reader, a matter of the rationality of choosing the right physician. Hence the Augustinian canons for justified religious

36. Peters, *Logic of the Heart*, 70–72.
37. Augustine, *Letter* 120.3.

belief, far from being merely a matter of epistemology, are bound up with such questions as, "What are people for" and even "Why are people so unhappy?"[38]

*Confessions* is, among many other things, an apologetic aimed at showing that the Christian God is the authority that should be trusted. It is a testimonial defense of Augustine's faith and an appeal to love the God he cherishes, believe in the God he trusts, and seek understanding of the God he knows. It is an invitation to the honest struggles of discovering the type of people we humans actually are—so that we can find Christ as the key that unlocks the healing we need and the happiness we long for.

To these ends, in *Confessions* Augustine does not set out to straightforwardly "prove" God's existence through isolated syllogistic reasoning and certainly not by bracketing off the affections. Instead, he reasons as he narrates, inviting his readers to trust in and love the right authority by providing cogent explanations of Christian teaching about humans and the world they find themselves in. And in the midst of a pluralism in which many other competing explanations and remedies are on offer, he seeks to open their eyes to the therapeutic possibilities of grace.

In chapter 5 we will look more closely at just how he went about doing this in both *Confessions* and *The City of God* as well as how we might apply his approach to our world today. But for the present chapter, our focus is not on the specifics of apologetic technique but on posture. In this regard, *Confessions* has the potential for showing us a different way. For as Augustine recounts his journey so far, he appears more like a seasoned traveler than a muscular boxer. He models for us how to invite modern skeptics and deconstructers to consider, or reconsider, the faith. He offers us another option, one that avoids strutting into the arena with an epistemological swagger or dancing around the ring, looking to land an apologetic knockout punch. Rather, Augustine is apologist-as-fellow-traveler, taking other pilgrims along and journeying side by side with them. He knows the dangers and pitfalls, is honest about the dead-end paths he has taken, and admits that he has gotten lost more than a few times along the way. Yet, the invitation is to join him on a journey to the home we all long for, a yearning that no place or experience in this world will finally satisfy.[39]

---

38. Peters, *Logic of the Heart*, 74–75.

39. Here we are gesturing to the key Augustinian insight at the core of C. S. Lewis's famous argument from desire: "If I find in myself a desire which no experience in this world can satisfy, the most probable explanation is that I was made for another world." *Mere Christianity*, 120. On the importance of Augustine in shaping the theological context for Lewis's argument, see McGrath, *Intellectual World of C. S. Lewis*, 107.

## Epistemic Humility: Genesis 1–3 as a Test Case

As we already mentioned, ever aware of his own fallibility, Augustine learned to be content with different degrees of confidence. Through his intellectual, spiritual, and pastoral journey, he came to realize the hermeneutical and epistemological implications of his limited and sin-tainted perspective. His expositions of Genesis 1–3 serve as a test case that illustrates his learned posture of epistemic humility.[40]

### Genesis 1

First of all, Augustine demonstrates humility in his literal interpretation of Genesis 1. In *Revisions*, Augustine defines what he means by "literal" in the title of his earlier work, *The Literal Interpretation of Genesis*: he is "not concerned with allegorical meanings but with the proper significance of actual facts."[41] Yet, lest our understanding of "literal" or "the proper significance of actual facts" be obscured by modern young-earth-and-old-earth debates, it should be clear that he does not intend "literalistic" to mean that the actual historical origins of creation are recorded in Genesis in ways that match our modern literal standards. For Augustine, the literal contains the allegorical, and perhaps surprisingly for moderns, "it is the figurative meaning that is assumed and the historical that needs to be established."[42] For Augustine, the literal and historical are not to be equated with a simplistic, flat reading of the text; a full literal interpretation means looking to the underlying historical events and to allegorical readings of the narrative.

Specifically, in relation to the "days" of Genesis 1, Augustine allows for mystery and warns against a rash interpretation. For him, a close reading of the text betrays the fact that the word "day" is used in various ways and light is created days before the luminaries. This makes it difficult for him to know what actually happened. He posits an instantaneous creation that included a material creation and a functional creation, but he remains open to various ways of reading the text. Indeed, Genesis 1 is historical, but many of the details of how creation actually happened are difficult to discern.

When it comes to the authorial intent, Augustine believes it was possible for Moses to have multiple meanings in mind. Augustine also admits that while he wants to know the mind of Moses, he often does not know Moses's meaning for sure and is open to various interpretations. Gavin Ortlund explains that

---

40. In this section we are following Ortlund, *Retrieving Augustine's Doctrine of Creation*.
41. Augustine, *Revisions* 2.24.
42. Ortlund, *Retrieving Augustine's Doctrine of Creation*, 114.

Augustine's desire to know Moses's intended meaning did not always, or even often, produce a clear understanding of what that intended meaning was:

> Augustine's openness to multiple interpretations does not result from a lack of interest in Moses' intention but his uncertainty as to what it was. It is instructive that in such situations Augustine is willing, sometimes more so than contemporary interpreters of the Bible, to navigate in terms of probabilities. . . . He is willing to say not only, "I don't know," but also "Here are three possible views; I think number two is right, but it might be number three."[43]

Thus Augustine is open to a multiplicity of meanings and interpretations other than his preferred meaning. In addition, he is comfortable with the ambiguities of the text even as he seeks out the most probable interpretations. The same can be said of his perspective on the events in Genesis 2–3.

### Genesis 2–3

Was there an actual garden of Eden, a real tree of the knowledge of good and evil, an authentic talking snake, or were all of these mere symbols? "Reading Genesis 2–3 literally means for Augustine interpreting these chapters as referring to historical events, not as taking all the images and language in a literalistic way."[44] Augustine strives to retain the historicity of these events when possible, unless the reading would render the text absurd. Again, the historical sense does not preclude the figurative and prophetic meanings of the text but rather could actually contain them. Ortlund identifies "Augustine's dual concerns with respect to the early chapters of Genesis: on the one hand, he wants to maintain their historicity; on the other, he wants to interpret them with literary and apologetic sensitivity."[45]

Augustine accepts the possibility that he might be wrong with regard to the literality of the passage, but he trusts in the authority and faithfulness of Scripture. He asserts, "Certainly, if the bodily things mentioned here could not in any way at all be taken in a bodily sense that accorded with truth, what other course would we have but to understand them as spoken figuratively, rather than impiously to find fault with holy scripture?"[46] Augustine prefers the literal and historical interpretation of Genesis 2–3, but he acknowledges the merely figurative interpretation of the text as possible for orthodox Christians. In his humble approach he demonstrates a flexibility that allows him to stay committed

---

43. Ortlund, *Retrieving Augustine's Doctrine of Creation*, 143.
44. Ortlund, *Retrieving Augustine's Doctrine of Creation*, 206.
45. Ortlund, *Retrieving Augustine's Doctrine of Creation*, 209.
46. Augustine, *The Literal Meaning of Genesis* 8.1.4.

to the truthfulness of the sacred text while remaining open to discovering interpretations more proper than his own.[47] Augustine's epistemic humility and interpretive dexterity, demonstrated in his comments on the early chapters of Genesis, model for the contemporary apologist a way to navigate the diverse readings of Genesis 1–3 and the divisive creation debates. A humble, nimble posture is vital to apologetics, especially here but in general as well.

For Augustine, the text of Genesis is infallible, but the problem is that its interpreters are fallible.[48] Augustine anticipates unnecessary problems being precipitated by insistence on dogmatic interpretations of Genesis that may later be contradicted by scientific discoveries. He warns that to offer an interpretation that undermines the truthfulness of the text displays a kind of interpretive rashness; wise interpretation calls for "hermeneutical patience."[49] A rash, proud interpreter can close off what might turn out to be the most faithful readings of the text and therefore create unnecessary apologetic difficulties for the whole church.

This humble posture, with its aim toward charity, is modeled for us in *Confessions* book 12. Augustine displays a generous attitude toward those who assert the truthfulness of the text yet differ on its interpretation. In the context of the early chapters of Genesis, Augustine writes:

> But as for those who feed on your [God's] truth in the wide pastures of charity, let me be united with them in you, and in you find my delight in company with them. Let us approach the words of your book together, and there seek your will as expressed through the will of your servant, by whose pen you have dispensed your words to us.[50]

He admits that exploring minds will produce a variety of interpretations of the Genesis creation narratives and that we must therefore guard against dogmatism on issues that are not certain. It's not that Augustine does not know anything with higher degrees of confidence. He is confident of many things in the text, such as the fact that God created the heavens and the earth, but about other things he is not so sure, such as *how* God created the heavens and the earth. That is unclear but could be made clearer by discoveries in nature.

47. Ortlund emphasizes Augustine's dexterity and flexibility as an interpreter of Genesis 1–3. *Retrieving Augustine's Doctrine of Creation*, 70, 83, 93, 107, 133, 195, 198, 199, 205, 207, 221, 239, 246.

48. "Nonetheless, those who uphold an infallible text must always remember that they only read and use it fallibly. This is a hallmark of Augustine's approach to Scripture: his dual emphasis on both the infallibility of the text and the fallibility of its interpreters." Ortlund, *Retrieving Augustine's Doctrine of Creation*, 90.

49. Ortlund, *Retrieving Augustine's Doctrine of Creation*, 94.

50. Augustine, *Confessions* 12.23.32.

Make no mistake about it: Augustine is not laissez-faire in his approach to reading Scripture. He keeps on asking and seeking with the hope of finding. He never stops questing and questioning, but he does so in faith, with a humble posture and with the ultimate telos of loving God and others.

In Augustine's reading of Genesis 1–3, the bishop situates us between a prideful, rationalistic, technological kind of certainty and a falsely humble, skeptical denial that we can know anything at all. He refocuses our attention on reading the text in the *ecclesia*, a loving community genuinely open to considering the interpretations of others. Such an interpretive community, Augustine anticipates, would take his insights seriously. He envisions a reading community whose ultimate hermeneutical canons are loving God and loving others. Truth is discovered for the purpose of rest and love, and knowledge is gained for the goal of knowing God and one's self.

What if Rhett McLaughlin's approach to reading Genesis 1–3 had been formed in the kind of ecclesial interpretive community that Augustine envisioned? What if the nones who have left the church had been shown and had experienced a different reading posture, one that took the Scriptures seriously as God's authoritative revelation but was open to fresh discoveries and ancient readings? Perhaps such a posture would have connected with their natural intellectual curiosities and opened the door for them to see the richness of the sacred text? Augustine knew what it meant to leave the church, and he also understood what kind of interpretive community it would take to keep others from doing the same. Or, perhaps better, he understood what kind of community would be needed to heal the seeker and keep them on the journey home.

## No Neutrality While Plundering the Egyptians

Augustine's generous posture of reading Genesis 1–3 should not lead us to conclude that he did not draw any hard lines in the sand. Several times above we mentioned Augustine's commitment to the authority of Scripture. Perhaps his commitment to think within the categories of Scripture is nowhere better illustrated than in his (re)imagination of his own life (*Confessions*) and of world history (*The City of God*). His thought world was held captive to Scripture. Thus he contemplates ultimately only two types of realms in life: heavenly and earthly. Augustine is clear that a person is in either the city of God or the city of man. These are two different locations (perhaps better, two different pathways) from which we love, believe, and reason. For him, when it comes to the heavenly city and the earthly city, it is a clear either-or, not both-and.

In *The City of God*, Augustine contrasts these two cities.[51] The most significant difference between the city of man and the city of God is discovered in what they love. Augustine writes, "Two loves, then, have made two cities. Love of self, even to the point of contempt for God, made the earthly city; and love of God, even to the point of contempt for self, made the heavenly city."[52] These cities *are* what they love.[53]

According to Augustine, these two cities intersect but can be clearly distinguished. He explains that "in this world, in fact, these two cities remain intermixed and intermingled with each other until they are finally separated at the last judgment."[54] The two cities relate to one another but cannot be collapsed into a single entity. Further, Augustine imagines no neutral secular space between them.[55] Though at times they may possess shared values like "no civil war, no domestic violence, public civility, a common and orderly use of temporal goods,"[56] they inhabit no neutral secular space where they operate without reference to the essence of what they really are. They are distinct. The city of man originated in pride, while the city of God was birthed in humility. The earthly city is self-centered, wrapped up in itself; it is self-dependent and glories in itself. The heavenly city is oriented toward God and others; it depends on God and directs praise to him. One is a city of pride and selfishness; the other is a city of humility and love.

What does this mean for apologetics? Anthropologically, in *The City*, as we already saw in *Confessions*, reasoning is connected to love and telos. A person reasons with their visions of the good and the beautiful directed toward the earthy city or the heavenly city. As we've seen, Augustinian apologetics embraces logic, history, and evidence. And it doesn't insist that a person first adopt a Christian worldview or posit the Trinity before they can use reason or consider evidence. Yet Augustinian apologetics does recognize that one's posture—one's desires and visions of the good life—will invariably impact how one reasons and will impact the ways arguments are crafted and appeals are made.

---

51. Augustine does not always equate the city of God with the church, because there are some in the (institutional) church who are not true members of the church or the city of God and there are some in the earthly city who are predestined to membership in the true church and the city of God. Yet, sometimes Augustine speaks of the city of God as if it were equivalent to the church.

52. Augustine, *The City of God* 14.28.

53. See J. Smith, *You Are What You Love*. Some of the content of this section first appeared in Allen, "City of God," 8–11.

54. Augustine, *The City of God* 2.35.

55. See James Wetzel's view contrasted with that of Robert Markus in Wetzel, *Augustine's City of God*, 3–5. "What I am willing to claim is that it is no accident that the most fruitful new forays into that massive [*City of God*] text tend not to read a neutral secularity into the space of 'mingled cities'" (5).

56. Wetzel, *Augustine's City of God*, 3.

Even though Augustine possesses an unflinching commitment to an either-or construct with respect to the city of God and the city of man, he does not make what we might describe today as the genetic fallacy; that is, he doesn't reject everything in a philosophical system or cultural framework because it did not originate in the Scriptures. The fact that a school of philosophy or religion did not place itself under the authority of Scripture, ground itself in trinitarian theology, and center itself on the incarnation of Jesus Christ did not mean that it contained nothing useful or true. An apologist may tap into aspects of another non-Christian worldview not just for rhetorical and persuasive connections but because they contain wisdom. For Augustine, though all claims must be subjected to Scripture, all truth is God's truth.

Augustine's relationship with Platonism[57] illustrates well how he related positively and negatively toward worldviews that were different from Christianity at basic and substantial points. Augustine appreciated Platonism's contribution to his faith, but he also came to see its great deficiency. Augustine regarded pride as Platonism's supreme inadequacy because this philosophy denied that the Word or Logos became flesh. Platonism regarded the incarnation as repugnant. Thus, when Augustine wrote *Confessions*, he was reading Platonism through scriptural eyes. He used what was helpful and discarded what was harmful. The Christian Augustine—who "thoroughly absorbed, 'digested,' and transformed"[58] Platonism, converting it beyond his Milan mentors—explains how Platonism functioned in supporting his faith:

> And I had come to you from the Gentiles. I set my heart upon the gold which at your bidding your people had brought out of Egypt, because wherever it was, it belonged to you. So you told the Athenians through your apostle that in you we live and move and have our being, and that indeed some of their own authorities had said this, and unquestionably those books I read came from there. I disregarded the idols of the Egyptians, to which they paid homage with gold that belonged to you, for they perverted the truth of God into a lie, worshiping a creature and serving it rather than the creator.[59]

57. We primarily use the broad terms "Platonic," "Platonists," and "Platonism" to refer to Plato's philosophical tradition, as does Augustine in *Confessions* and *The City of God*. Yet we recognize that "when Augustine speaks of Plato, the Platonists and Platonism, he seems to be referring less to the doctrines of Plato himself and more to those that were derived from his thought over the centuries and that [scholars] now place under the umbrella of Neoplatonism." Boniface Ramsey, notes to Augustine, *The City of God* 8.4 (p. 245n18). Augustine himself acknowledges the preference of Neoplatonists to identify themselves simply as Platonists: "The most distinguished philosophers of more recent times, who chose to follow Plato, did not want to be called either Peripatetics or Academics, but simply Platonists." This included specifically those whom scholars today would identify as Neoplatonists. Augustine continues, "Of these, the most notable are the Greeks Plotinus, Iamblichus, and Porphyry." *The City of God* 8.12.
58. Brown, *Augustine of Hippo*, 59.
59. Augustine, *Confessions* 7.9.15.

Some champions of today's "worldview" thinking too quickly dismiss ideas or thinkers simply because they are "secular" (though this error is not necessarily representative of the best of this kind of thinking). Augustine would not let us get away with such a reactionary mistake. He sees the value of learning from sources within his cultural thought world but outside the Scriptures and Christian tradition if they help him gain insight into truth. For example, many Neoplatonic philosophers overly disdained the material and therefore denied the incarnation of Jesus Christ, which is central to Augustine's conception of Jesus's mediation. Because of the incarnation, Augustine identifies humility as a central virtue in the Christian way of inhabiting the world. In the Platonic philosophers Augustine read nothing of Christ's humble embodiment.[60] Yet, although Augustine rejects their paganism and pride, he discovered in their writings and teachings truth that opened his fourth-century Greco-Roman eyes and mind to Scripture's way of conceiving of the world, and he used that understanding for apologetic purposes in *Confessions*.

In his day, Platonism had real culture-shaping influence within elite circles and, consequently, over popular society. Some in the church, often traced back to Tertullian (b. AD 160) of Augustine's North Africa, stood in a tradition more negative toward the integration of Greek philosophy and biblical Christianity as well as any appropriation of Platonic philosophy. This thinking is captured in Tertullian's famous question, "What has Athens to do with Jerusalem?" Like most of the church fathers, Augustine saw things quite differently. He was among the Christians in Milan who benefited from Platonism. Along with them, he plundered the Egyptians for metaphysical gold but energetically rejected the dross of idolatry. Unlike the Israelites who idolized the Egyptian gold, Augustine took away the good without bowing to the whole system. When the Greeks embraced a theological truth such as "In him we live and move and have our being" (Acts 17:28), a Christian could, as the apostle Paul did, use the truth without indulging in the idolatrous worship of Zeus. God used aspects of the Platonic framework to open Augustine's mind to theological riches of the biblical text.

Again, the point here is that Augustine claims that God used Platonism as a bridge back to the catholic faith for him. Using Paul's interaction with the philosophers on Mars Hill (Acts 17:22–34) and the Israelites' exodus from Egypt with booty (Exod. 12:33–42), Augustine models for his congregants a critical appropriation of cultural currents in order to help them live out their faith in their everyday existence. By finding points of agreement and pointing out areas of difference, Augustine used Platonism to help his congregants make sense of their late fourth-century and early fifth-century questions, longings, and pressures.

---

60. Augustine, *Confessions* 7.9.13.

In an instructive chapter, John Cavadini illustrates Augustine's dialectical use of Platonism:

> Platonism, as Augustine portrays it, is an enabler of Empire, selling us out to the tender mercies of *imperium* and the lust for domination which creates it. In that sense, Platonism is an ideology of empire, pitting a distorted and static contemplative vision against the forward-looking prophetic spirit that in every age has seen through the arrogance of all the kingdoms of the world.[61]

Yet Cavadini brings this conclusion to his article into perspective with a final footnote:

> The Platonic vision of God is indeed a vision of the fatherland to which we tend, but it is a vision at a great distance, and distorted as by the cataract of intellectual vision, a dim obscurity of the imagination. See *civ Dei* [*The City of God*] 10.29, to the Platonists: "You see after a fashion, although at a distance, and with clouded vision, the country in which we should abide; but you do not hold fast to the way that leads to it."[62]

Even though Platonism fails to take us to the promised land, it is born out of our human longing for home. Augustine critiques Platonism but also leverages it for Christian instruction and culturally aware persuasion. In plundering the Platonists, he shows us how to avoid making the genetic mistake in our apologetic approach today. Often we fail to make persuasive connections because we are absolutists and obscurantists in our condemnation of worldly systems, failing to admit the relative good, beauty, and truth and missing the buried structures within worldviews outside of Christianity. Our rhetoric falls flat because we do not hear the late-modern longings for the fatherland.

We see this same posture as Augustine preaches in critique of the pagans gathering for festivals just outside his church. "Nobody in fact," he instructs the congregation, "can live any style of life without those three sentiments of the soul; of believing, hoping, loving."[63] While he demolishes the idolatry of the pagans, he builds upon the creational studs. Faith, hope, and love are inescapable features of our structure as humans—features of our humanity waiting to be built upon apologetically. The question is not *whether* we will be characterized by such a "style

61. Cavadini, "Ideology and Solidarity," 110.
62. Cavadini, "Ideology and Solidarity," 110n10.
63. Augustine, *Sermon* 198. He makes the same point at the end of book 18 of *The City of God*: "But their temporal lives are directed by different faiths, different hopes, and different loves, until at last they are separated by the final judgment and each receives its own end, of which there is no end."

of life" but toward *who* or *what* it ultimately makes the most emotional, moral, and rational sense to direct our faith, hope, and love. Sometimes it's tempting (and pleases our Christian base) to simply try to burn rivals to the ground rather than explore what might be apologetically salvageable in their beliefs, excavating to expose foundational posts still standing amid the debris, pointing beyond themselves to the triune God. Augustine wisely models for us how to do the latter.

## The Church as an Apologetic

Of course, a pastor's role is not simply to lead individuals but to lead and form ecclesial communities that live out this posture. Augustine pastored people. His primary vocational identity was as a pastor of a congregation. This seems obvious, but it is often missed. He was not a professor in a university (as vital as that vocation is!) or the leader of an apologetic brand only loosely, if at all, connected to a parish. Augustine's apologetic posture can never be legitimately separated from his pastoral ministry over a flock.

This brings to the fore an opportunity to address an ongoing problem with Western apologetic enterprises. With the rise of large apologetic ministries, online resources, and leading apologetic celebrities, there is a troubling absence in apologetics: namely, the church. This problem fits in with the analysis of contemporary apologetics offered in chapter 2. Today's anemic ecclesiology in apologetics is directly related to the reductionistic anthropology that would, as we've seen, also be in Augustine's sights. For if humans are reduced to mainly thinking beings, then the local church might easily be sidelined and left on the margins of apologetics. Why not just assemble the brightest Christian academics and have them make their apologetic argument for the world to see online or in packed arenas and then train others to do likewise?

Many of today's apologists have entered the scene after training for one-on-one debate matches, ready to force their opponent to tap out using logical proofs. The practice of the discipline has too often assumed that the apologist's job is to be the strongman, outmaneuvering opponents within the ring of abstract and ahistorical reasoning—with aesthetics and the affections off-limits. This is not only a problem of metaphor and imagination; it is, as we've seen, also a failure to think rationally about the limits of reason and reason's relationship to visions of the good and beautiful. But to go further, it also is in danger of skimming over the communal nature of how humans think.

All thinking, as Alan Jacobs contends, "is necessarily, thoroughly, and wonderfully social."[64] No one actually thinks for themselves. We can't escape the

---

64. Jacobs, *How to Think*, 37.

relational nature and thus historical nature of our rationality. We will always be thinking in response to others, reasoning within and against the categories of others, trusting together in an authority, and aiming our thoughts toward or away from conceptions of the good that we inherit. If someone imagines otherwise, they haven't escaped thinking with others; they have only avoided acknowledging this reality. As Jacobs emphasizes, the question is not *if* we will think with others but *who* we will think with and *how* we will do so.

Given a holistic anthropology and the communal way humans think, Augustine offers us a vision for persuasion that we can use to invite others to accompany us on a journey along a new path with a new community. In actuality, the culture outside the church has long been effectively catechizing holistically and communally, persuading along the lines of a logic of the heart by using coming-of-age stories and modern myths of freedom to convey promises of control and power. If we saunter into the ring with *just* our individualistic epistemology and logical evidences, fighting against the host of pagan liturgies and "secular" communal rituals, we shouldn't be surprised if we not only fail to persuade but also watch as more of our teammates tap out.[65] For it could be that before we have even stepped into the arena, we have ceded the match by accepting reductionistic terms.

Since we are more than just individual thinking beings—we are also doxological creatures who believe and think in community—we humans are persuaded in regard to life's most important questions by reasoning within a social imaginary that traffics in a community's stories, practices, and symbols. Enter the *ecclesia*. The church is meant to invite others into a better way—countering the disenchanted, naturalistic narratives and the nihilistic or pseudospiritual consumeristic practices of our age—with a rival social imaginary and a more capacious rationality, offered through the lens of the biblical story, our cruciform lives together, and gospel-shaped communal practices.[66] The social imaginary formed by the church is meant to provide the context from which a variety of different kinds of apologetic arguments are heard and that the Augustinian apologist invites the unbeliever to "taste and see" (Ps. 34:8).

For Augustine, the church is like an apologetic hospital for the blind and broken. It catechizes the seeker of truth, not just to help them discover the right beliefs or creedal affirmations—though it should surely do that—but also to shape the seeker into a way of loving, believing, and understanding. For Augustine the church is God's means for providing the "healing for the eyes of

---

65. See J. Smith, *Desiring the Kingdom*.

66. Though we disagree with aspects of his proposal, a somewhat similar point is made by Stanley Hauerwas: "In fact, the God we worship and the world God created cannot be truthfully known without the cross, which is why the knowledge of God and ecclesiology—or the politics called church—are interdependent." *With the Grain of the Universe*, 17.

our hearts." "An ointment for believing," according to Augustine, is administered by way of the communal practices of God's people: "It is for this that the holy mysteries are celebrated, for this that the word of God is preached, to this that the Church's moral exhortations are directed."[67] Augustine understands the church as a healing community that puts back together fragmented souls and redirects disordered loves and longings toward the love of God and others. Treating the eyes of the heart is a vital part of seeing.

The church is to be a community of pilgrims on a journey home; the journey together is part of the healing process. As we have seen in this chapter, it is a Scripture-interpreting community where we hold loosely our own private interpretations and open ourselves to hearing the perspectives of others. Of course, the church should have an uncompromising commitment to Scripture and its interpretation within the framework of catholic orthodoxy, but it should also seek fresh readings of Scripture that are open to and learn from hermeneutical, historical, and scientific advances that take us deeper into the text of Scripture. The church recognizes that all truth is God's truth, even if it is discovered outside the *ecclesia*, and may be plundered for the church's own intellectual maturation, cultural engagement, and relevant persuasion. Augustine encountered this reorienting idea first in Ambrose and the church in Milan, and he develops it more fully in the midst of the epochal shift taking place during his own ministry in Hippo. The church, in Augustine's ideal vision, can live in tension, nuance, and, oftentimes, ambiguities as it makes its way upward and onward on its pilgrimage to the heavenly city. Epistemic humility, the posture so important for the apologist, is attained by participating in the local church.

Augustine reinterprets the details of his life as he reflects on his own search for truth and love. Through a scripturally saturated imagination he sees his own life in ever new ways, both where he has been and where he is going. This happens for him primarily as he shepherds God's flock. In his own reflections on his life outside and inside the church, he models for his congregation how the story of Scripture and its lived narrative in the church can refashion their lives as they walk along the pilgrim way. The church helps the seeker of truth trace the hand of God in their life as a part of their pilgrimage homeward. Here, seeking lovers believe in order to understand. Affections are redirected, beliefs are reframed, and understanding grows. Consequently, the church is an apologetic community that plays a formative role in instilling the primary apologetic virtue of humility.

Imagine for a moment that Rhett, or the increasing number of nones that his story represents, had grown up in a church with this humble Augustinian pastoral wisdom. Would he have rejected the central claims of Christianity?

---

67. Augustine, *Sermon* 88.

Acknowledging that some have accused him of simply rejecting a narrow type of southern American evangelical Christianity, Rhett has actually somewhat agreed with that assessment because that is what he grew up with and what he knows. Even though he resolutely claims that he has rejected not only this expression of Christianity but also the most central Christian beliefs about Jesus's deity and resurrection, we have to wonder, had he not grown up in an ecclesial context that, by his own account, appears to have been marked by epistemological overreach, would it have been different? Maybe not. But who knows?

If the rising number leaving the faith had been nurtured in a church context that viewed humans as lovers who believe in order to understand, would less of them have jumped ship into the cold waters of uncertainty? Would as many be bouncing from one tribal interpretive community to the next if they had been shepherded within a community that had adopted an Augustinian posture, with its more generous and more expansive catholic fences? Would it have been different for many of the nones if they had fed within the wider pastures of ecclesial interpretive orthodoxy? Would such a hard break from the faith of their upbringing have felt so necessary if they had learned how to (re)trace the work of God in the details of their life and to reorient their journey homeward through an imagination saturated with Scripture? There might still be time to find out.

As we move deeper into post-Christendom and feel more acutely the malaise that hangs over our modern world, people are looking for healing and hope. In their search, at least some who remain haunted by the name of Christ, as Augustine was, will take another look inside the church. Perhaps in God's providence they will be surprised to find the wider halls of a humbler orthodoxy and an apologetic hospital whose leaders are skilled at applying the balm of Christ.[68]

---

68. For a book that is aimed at this audience and follows the Augustine way, see Chatraw and Carson, *Surprised by Doubt*.

# 4

# An Ecclesial Pilgrimage of Hope

Apologetics can be a lonely calling.

In an article in *The Worldview Bulletin*, Tyson James writes about this common experience among apologists, and as the global chapters director for Reasonable Faith, a role that has him supervising more than two hundred chapters, he is in a position to know.[1] James explains that the apologists he oversees express feelings of isolation "because those around them think these things [apologetics, or at least their approach to the discipline] abstruse or uninteresting (or, in the worst cases, un-Christian)." Thus, while they testify that apologetics has personally set them free, they "suffer the privation of solitary confinement."[2]

The rest of the article takes aim at offering a remedy for this loneliness: "As a healthy venue for the expression of this coping mechanism, *fellowship*, then, constitutes a treatment."[3] Augustine would be supportive. After all, *Confessions* itself, in the words of Peter Brown, is "an act of therapy" that could be cathartically performed only within the right kind of community.[4]

Yet, as James focuses on the specifics of what he envisions, the article makes a noteworthy move, pointing to parachurch ministries as the solution. When the church and its clergy are mentioned, they are implicitly characterized as largely not *getting it* and thus ending up as sources of frustration and further

1. Tyson James, "Christian Apologists in Community: The Necessity of Fellowship for the Front Line," *Worldview Bulletin*, October 21, 2021, https://worldviewbulletin.substack.com/p/christian-apologists-in-community.
2. James, "Christian Apologists in Community."
3. James, "Christian Apologists in Community."
4. Brown, *Augustine of Hippo*, 158.

isolation for the apologist. In chapter 2 we suggested that this shouldn't be surprising: when approaches to apologetics and apologists themselves are primarily formed outside the church, unhealthy tensions will often arise between the apologist and the church.

But isn't this lack of receptivity at least partly the result of pastors and churches being anti-intellectual? This certainly is part of the problem, and it needs to be addressed. Yet, a church's rejection of one form of intellectualism doesn't necessarily entail a rejection of intellectualism per se. Many churches are intuitively suspicious of reductionistic versions of rationality that lead to brain-on-a-stick or experientially sterile versions of Christianity.

Although anti-intellectualism is part of the problem, we must learn, as when attempting to convince nonbelievers, to persuade the actual believers (anti-intellectual or not) in front of us, not the people we'd like to be in front of us. Those who have been presenting themselves as offering the church the solution for persuading others find themselves in an awkward position. For over the past few decades they have been leading the largest apologetic parachurch ministries in the West as well as sitting at the reins of the Bible-college and seminary apologetics courses, which train thousands of church leaders, while also often lamenting the difficultly in persuading churches to get on board and welcome their apologetic vision. This tension alone might give one reason to pause. What might explain this disconnect? Before we too quickly bypass the church or explain away the disconnect (for there are undoubtedly many contributing factors), Augustine would ask contemporary apologists to start by looking self-critically at the possible planks in their own eyes.

Is it possible that some of the blame for the lack of receptivity by churches and the personal loneliness among apologists is bound up with the approach and posture taken in these training programs? Consider that while James acknowledges that the laity and clergy who aren't receptive to their approach to apologetics are a source of this isolation, he notes, "It's no coincidence that a disproportionate number of our chapter directors—and, I believe, Christian apologists in general—are military veterans (or come from similar high-risk environments, such as law enforcement or fire and rescue). The similarities are obvious. Apologetics, in practice, is often ideologically adversarial. Like serving in the military, being a good apologist requires exorbitant amounts of training, reconnaissance, precision, adaptation, courage, and a sense of urgency."[5]

---

5. James, "Christian Apologists in Community." We have no doubt about the high level of training and discipline required to be effective soldiers and police officers. However, we would note that this also holds true for effectiveness in many vocations. Wouldn't we say similar things about the rigorous and disciplined training needed to be a model medical doctor or concert musician or builder or entrepreneur? Of course, one difference is that in these fields, one doesn't typically have

High-risk occupations such as these are needed in a fallen world, but are the job description and required skills of an apologist closer to those of, say, a sniper or a police officer than to those of a pastor or a missionary? The former require the threat, if not use, of physical force rather than the tools needed to discuss the big questions of life and the posture to wisely guide others through their unbelief and doubt to trust in Christ. And if ministers—whose weekly tasks should entail caring for souls, responding to doubt, and persuading people in the pews and on the streets to believe the gospel—require tools and occupational teloi that are similar to those of the faithful apologist, why are people from high-risk vocations attracted to apologetics in such high numbers while leaders lament a frustrating lack of interest from pastors and missionaries?

This short article declines to ask such questions or consider whether apologists need to be more self-reflective about their loneliness and their relation to the church, peeling back the layers to see whether their emotional distress could be a sign that deeper problems lurk under the surface. Instead, it offers a straightforward solution: parachurch "brand" ministries.

We aren't suggesting that parachurch ministries are inconsequential; many of them play an important role in supporting the church. And needless to say, bringing leaders together to talk shop is a worthwhile endeavor; if this were all that was meant by the article, and if the centrality of the church were evident in the discipline, then our concern could easily be dismissed as being overly critical. However, the way the article skims over the church mirrors the lack of ecclesiological reflection and commitment in apologetics circles more generally.[6] In practice parachurch ministries have too often replaced the parish as the primary formative context for apologists.[7]

At the end of the previous chapter, we noted the importance of the church as a community whose corporate life functions as an apologetic. In this chapter we will see how healthy churches—routinely listening to and acting out the story of Scripture together through hearing the Word, confessing the faith, singing spiritual songs, and partaking of the sacraments, thus aiming their lives in love

---

to worry about being shot at. But then again, we don't know many apologists in North America who experience being shot at as a regular hazard of their occupation.

6. In the article Acts 2:42 ("They devoted themselves to the apostles' teaching and fellowship, to the breaking of bread and the prayers") is even recast and applied to a gathering of apologists to hear a famous speaker during a large conference once a year.

7. We are not, of course, saying that all churches are healthy and therefore that to relocate the center of apologetics to the church would automatically solve the problems. However, the church is God's plan A, and there is no plan B. We can't simply sidestep the church. If this were a book about the problems of churches in general, we'd have much to say about the issues, including the instrumental instincts, the functional teloi, and the celebrity cultures built within many churches today that unfortunately mirror the logic and vices of much of our late-modern world. Yet, a problem for much of contemporary apologetics is that ecclesiology is barely, if at all, on the radar screen.

toward the King and his kingdom—should be the incubators for nurturing apologists who possess both virtue and skill.

Augustine would have apologists today return to the parish, not as saviors but as fellow travelers. For Augustine did not form himself into an apologist. It was within the church[8] and its scriptural narrative that he pressed forward—with disarming honesty, critically engaging his own false gods and *libido dominandi*—into the reality of the way his own sin and the fallen world around him had malformed him. He inhabited the biblical story in the life of the church, allowing it to critique his own life and to offer him a new, more capacious way of seeing and inhabiting the world. In *Confessions* he prayerfully and confessionally recounts his journey out loud, from the public confession of his own checkered past to his ongoing struggles as a bishop. He offers a story not of personal glory but of his prodigal wanderings in order to repeatedly shine the spotlight on the glory of a Father who ran out to meet him.

We will see that the internal work on display in *Confessions* prepared Augustine to write the most important apologetic work of its time. Before Augustine composed *The City of God*, with its penetrating societal critique and apologetically aimed redemptive narrative, he first journeyed into his own soul—critiquing his own idolatries and learning to map the story of grace onto his own life. In short, *Confessions* led him to *The City*.

Augustine will thus call us to unite what our modern training models have pulled asunder: spiritual formation and apologetics. While today these are often taught out of different departments on our campuses, for Augustinian apologetics they are wedded within the same course. It was Augustine's spiritual and theological formation within the *ecclesia* that gave him both the diagnostic skill and the cruciform posture needed to offer the church and the world his more expansive, public vision of Christianity's counternarrative, spanning from creation to consummation.

### Creation: A Radically Positive Metaphysics

In contrast to the caricature of Augustine as hostile to physical creation, it does not take long for the reader of *The City of God* to encounter Augustine's view of the fundamental goodness and beauty of creation.

---

8. A book-length treatment would be necessary if we were to outline a thick account of Augustine's ecclesiology and how it might map onto contemporary biblical and ecumenical discussions. Needless to say, such a treatment is beyond the scope of this project. Further, one does not have to embrace all of Augustine's ecclesiology or what he might have meant by "catholicity" to see how, in the spirit of Augustine, striving to overcome the current disunity that plagues Christians is a part of our apologetic calling (John 17:20–23).

For Augustine, creation is profoundly good. By means of his Word, the good God made the good creation.[9] Evil was not somehow baked into creation so that good could ultimately triumph over it. Augustine confronts the likes of Origen who held such views:

> There are some who were unwilling to accept with good and simple faith such a good and simple reason for creating the world—that the good God might create good things, and there might be, below God, things that are not what God is but are still good, and are things that only a good God would create.[10]

Gerard O'Daly explains, "What Augustine objects to in this [Origen's] theory is the way in which it seems to contradict the unequivocal scriptural insistence on the goodness of the created universe. This goodness is not vitiated by the presence of sinful souls."[11] No mixture of good and evil existed at creation. Creation, including bodies and matter, was pure goodness from the beginning.[12]

Though the presence of threats like "fire, cold, wild beasts and the like"[13] might lead some to deny that God created all things purely good or to claim that creation is no longer good, Augustine insists on the persistence of the goodness and beauty of creation. Truly these heretics, as Augustine calls them, lack a scripturally formed imagination. Augustine asserts,

> These heretics do not notice how flourishing such things are in their rightful places and in their own natures, or with what ordered beauty they are arranged, or how much they contribute, each according to its own share of beauty, to the whole scheme of things, as if to the common wellbeing of all, or how much they actually work to our own benefit, if only we make appropriate and intelligent use of them.[14]

When we fail to see the usefulness of created things, this obscurity is due to our lack of discovery, not a failure on the part of creation. When creation's usefulness is hard to find, this only serves as an "antidote to pride." "For there is no nature whatsoever that is evil; in fact, 'evil' is nothing but a term for the privation of good."[15]

Even before his conversion to the Christian faith, Augustine demonstrated an irrepressible passion for beautiful things and a curiosity for discovering beauty's

---

9. "Augustine deliberately echoes Plato's reason (*Timaeus* 29e): 'that good things might be made by a good God' (11.21)." O'Daly, *Augustine's City of God*, 143.

10. Augustine, *The City of God* 11.23.

11. O'Daly, *Augustine's City of God*, 142.

12. Augustine, *The City of God* 11.21, 23.

13. Augustine, *The City of God* 11.22.

14. Augustine, *The City of God* 11.22.

15. Augustine, *The City of God* 11.22.

meaning. He would ask his friends, "Do we love anything save what is beautiful, then? And what is beautiful, then? Indeed, what is beauty? What is it that entices and attracts us in the things we love? Surely if beauty and loveliness of form were not present in them, they could not possibly appeal to us."[16] At that time, he had written several books on beauty, but he had lost those books by the time he wrote *Confessions*.[17] Yet he recalls that according to his preconversion reflections, beauty was a quality inherent within all material objects.[18] Yet, his prideful faith in his own mind's ability to figure out the nature of good and evil in the world apart from God's revelation in the church and Scripture hindered him from realizing the true source of the beauty he longed for. He pridefully trusted too greatly in the supremacy of his own intellect and gave too much credit to evil as a substantial component in the world.[19] This created a distorting and irritating noise in his mind that inhibited him from hearing God's beautiful music within creation:

> The materialistic images on which I was speculating set up a din in the ears of my heart, ears which were straining to catch your inner melody, O gentle Truth. I was thinking about the beautiful and the harmonious, and longing to stand and hear you, that my joy might be perfect at the sound of the Bridegroom's voice, but I could not, because I was carried off outside myself by the clamor of my errors, and I fell low, dragged down by the weight of my pride. No joy and gladness from you reached my ears, nor did my bones exult, for they had not yet been humbled.[20]

This problematic posture toward creation cut him off from goodness and beauty's true purpose. It was only in the church and through Scripture that he would learn to reason with the grain of the universe and with his deepest and truest longings. This doesn't deny that the truth embedded in these creational longings and experienced outside the church was significant in leading to his conversion. Truth, as Augustine acknowledged, could be found throughout God's creation, even among the pagans. But pagan reasoning alone could not lead to saving knowledge of God. Pagan reasoning would lead to Christ only if it were humbled and made open to the revelation of Christ. Only then would

---

16. Augustine, *Confessions* 4.13.20.

17. Augustine, *Confessions* 4.13.20, 4.14.21, 4.15.27.

18. Augustine, *Confessions* 4.13.20.

19. Augustine, *Confessions* 4.15.24. James J. O'Donnell explains that, here, Augustine's self-criticism "is twofold: that he did not know that evil was not itself a substance, and that he thought that the human mind itself was the *summum bonum*. The problems thus posed are all-encompassing: the nature of God, the nature of created being." *Commentary Books 1–7*, 255.

20. Augustine, *Confessions* 4.15.27.

the philosopher discover the true philosophy and be brought to Christ, the true meaning and source of beauty.

Augustine's introspective journey in *Confessions* was not simply an academic pursuit to find answers to abstract questions; it was a quest driven by the longings of his soul for the good, true, and beautiful. As he tried on the teaching of the church as a catechumen, he began to discover the spiritual and intellectual resources with which he could address his attraction to and curiosity about the material world's inherent beauty. His own mind, apart from the Word, proved insufficient. Within the church and her Scriptures, he could hear more clearly the truth that God, who is ultimate beauty and goodness, had created the universe essentially good and beautiful. Each part of creation is good and beautiful, and all the parts taken together are exceedingly good and beautiful. In the last book of *Confessions*, with a heart still seeking but more at peace, Augustine comments on God's creative activity depicted in the first chapters of Genesis:

> And you looked upon all the things you have made, O God, and lo, they are exceedingly good; we too look upon them, and even in our eyes they are exceedingly good. . . . Severally good, they are exceedingly good all together. Every beautiful body conveys the same message, for a body consisting of beautiful limbs is far more beautiful than its component parts individually, because though each one has its own loveliness, it is only through their exquisite coordination that the whole organism attains its perfection.[21]

Further, God not only created all things beautiful but also sustains their goodness by his own infinitely good and beautiful being: "Through him we see that everything is good which in any degree has being, because it derives from him who has being in no degree at all, but is simply *He is*."[22] To exist is to possess some inherent goodness.

Creation has a divinely given telos. The goodness and beauty of creation reflect God's own goodness and beauty and should be loved, not for and of themselves but as a means toward turning our hearts to the love and praise of God. The goodness, beauty, and truth of creation, combined with our longing for them, are signposts pointing toward the Creator's ultimate goodness, beauty, and truth. Thus, creational goods are not loved for themselves or praised because of themselves but rather exist to warm our hearts to the love of God and bring us to praise of God:

> If sensuous beauty delights you, praise God for the beauty of corporeal things, and channel the love you feel for them onto their Maker, lest the things that please

21. Augustine, *Confessions* 13.28.43.
22. Augustine, *Confessions* 13.31.46.

you lead you to displease him. If kinship with other souls appeals to you, let them be loved in God, because they too are changeable and gain stability only when fixed in him; otherwise they would go their way and be lost. Let them be loved in him, and carry off to God as many of them as possible with you.[23]

The apologist's longings are to be rightly directed and scripturally nurtured in the church so that they love rightly and teach others to do the same. Through the means of grace the apologist is trained to instinctively look beyond mere creation in order to cast their longing gaze on God and thus learn to attend to the world and God's image bearers with insight and wisdom. To discern in any given situation what is best to say and how to say it, the apologist should be attuned to what the person or people are seeking within creation and how they are seeking it, in order to reason with them in a way that looks beyond the created to the Creator. This requires spiritual and practical insight that comes from a transformation not only in apologetic methodology but also within the apologist.[24] The church has been given as a spiritual hospital for this kind of holistic healing.

What relevance does Augustine's radically positive metaphysics have for methodology? Augustine encourages people to long more for the good and beautiful—not less.[25] If we settle for apologetic appeals that rest on logic alone or assume unbelievers have no appetite for the good, we risk serving up stale arguments. Since all creation, including the human creature, possesses a nature that is structurally good (albeit perverted by evil, as we will see in the next section), the apologist can reason from and appeal to a skeptic's longings for the good and beautiful. Thus, as Curtis Chang says, we can follow Augustine in seeking "to breathe more life into [human desires]" and "to encourage signs of true life in his opponents."[26]

In book 19 of The City of God, Augustine states emphatically, "It is not possible for there to be a nature in which there is no good. Not even the nature of the devil himself is evil, insofar as it is a nature. It is perversity that makes it evil." Thus, the apologist, in cooperation with the Holy Spirit, should persuasively inflame the skeptic's desires for the good and beautiful and make an appeal that those "better goods" are to be found in God. For as Augustine claims, those humans "who make the right use of such goods, which are meant to serve the

---

23. Augustine, Confessions 4.12.18.
24. Stanley Hauerwas says something similar of Barth's project in Church Dogmatics: "Barth was attempting to show that Christian speech about God requires a transformation not only of speech itself but of the speaker." With the Grain of the Universe, 176.
25. Chang, Engaging Unbelief, 88.
26. Chang, Engaging Unbelief, 87–88.

peace of mortals, will receive fuller and better goods . . . in an eternal life meant for the enjoyment of God and of one's neighbor in God."[27]

Since creation, including us humans and the world around us, was originally designed as good and maintains its structural beauty, multiple aspects of this creation still serve as sources for apologetic appeal, ways by which we can call people back home to creational structures. Rowan Williams notes that "our ability to make judgments about beauty, our instinctive appeal to a standard of ideal harmony, is one of Augustine's most familiar grounds for asserting an innate God-directedness in the mind."[28] Such positive arguments for God hold promise for us today as we work with the grain of those beautiful minds created to be directed toward the God of beauty.

This way of making an appeal is contrasted with the violent and nihilistic spirit of our age. As we are bombarded with fearmongering at almost every political turn, and as even "Christian" leaders rally their bases by similar methods, a functional Hobbesian ontology is at work. The result is that public persuasion routinely plasters over human desires for love, peace, and beauty and opts instead to appeal to fear and anger. In contrast, John Milbank asserts the ontological priority of peace over conflict in Augustine's thought:

> The non-antagonist, peaceful mode of life of the city of God is grounded in a particular, historical and "mythical" narrative, and in an ontology which explicates the beliefs implicit in this narrative. It is in fact the ontological priority of peace over conflict (which is arguably the key theme of his entire thought) that is the principle undergirding Augustine's critique. However, this principle is firmly anchored in a narrative, a practice, and a dogmatic faith, not in an abstracted universal reason.[29]

Following Augustine, Milbank claims that "more than is usually recognized, Christianity implies a unique and distinctive structural logic for human society. And this is what ecclesiology is really all about."[30] The place that God has given us in which to offer this alternative structural logic for society is the church, the location where the Christian's apologetic rationale and methodology should be formed. It is from within this counter-community centered on the love and fear of God, in contrast to communities centered on the love of vainglory and fear of people, where the apologist learns to persuade by inflaming the desires

27. Augustine, *The City of God* 19.13.
28. See Augustine, *Confessions* 7.17.23. Williams, *On Augustine*, 62.
29. Milbank, *Theology and Social Theory*, 392.
30. Milbank, *Theology and Social Theory*, 410.

for peace, happiness, and beauty, which point beyond creation to the God the human heart was made for.[31]

## Fall: Beauty and Order Misdirected by Evil

Humans are wonderful and wretched.

We are wonderful because we are created and sustained by God's own good and beautiful being. Even after the fall we retain our structural goodness and beauty. We are wonderful still. Yet, according to Augustine, we are also wretched. Out of our pride we have chosen self-love over love of God, arrogant empire-building over humble sacrifice and service, and worship of creation as god instead of worship of the good Creator. Our loves are disordered, bent inward on themselves.

In *The City of God*, Augustine diagnoses the diseased heart of the Roman Empire and its accompanying cultural practices. To critique the empire, he employs the construct we introduced in chapter 3: the city of God (the heavenly city) and the city of man (the earthly city). These cities are two distinct entities, though they are intermingled and interrelated during the *saeculum*, the present age. The heavenly city is marked by love for God and humble service of others. The earthly city is characterized by love of self and the desire to dominate others.[32] Using this construct, he unmasks the wretchedness of Rome's contemporary manifestation of the earthly city.

In some sense, the Roman Empire is the foil that demonstrates what sin looks like in public processes and practices. Rome displays what the fallenness of the soul looks like in the collective life as well as how the individual's inner world may be shaped by the way people organize themselves. By using the metaphor of the city, Augustine demonstrates that what occurs in social life cannot be separated from the inner life of the individual. He does not separate private life from public life but instead demonstrates that the real difference in the public square is not between public and private but "between political virtue and

---

31. This point is not meant to undercut the substantive goodness and beauty of this present world and age but rather is intended to acknowledge creation's supreme functions now: (1) pointing away from itself to the God who upholds its present existence and (2) directing our vision forward to the full redemption of all things.

32. Simplistically, we may equate the Roman Empire with the city of man and the church with the city of God, but Augustine is at times versatile in his usage. For instance, while he sometimes identifies the church with the city of God, he also can distinguish between the two. See, e.g., Augustine, *The City of God* 16.2. This versatility could be due to his different meanings of the word "church," sometimes using it in the mystical sense and other times referring to the visible institution.

political vice."[33] In important ways the public and private worlds cannot and should not be disentangled.

With force and clarity Augustine exposes Rome's public sins and the consequences of their wretchedness for its citizens. In what follows we will attempt to lay out in only a few short paragraphs an argument that spans about nine hundred pages of text in English translations of *The City of God*. To begin with, Roman society's public practices and sacrifices supported a mythos that led people away from the true God and to false gods that could never satisfy their truest human longings.[34] Thus, Roman civic and religious life was structured toward the wrong vision of the good life. Rome's religious and civic structures aimed at the wrong teloi.

What were those teloi? Two of the most profound were the desire to dominate and the longing for glory. Rome, which for Augustine was the latest manifestation of "a city whose founding is coincident with the fall, not creation,"[35] embraced the values and mythology of victory, power, and acquisition: *libido dominandi*. What began for the Romans as a quest for liberty degenerated into an obsession for domination. At times, another telos could check the obsession with domination: glory. Practically speaking, a self-interest that seeks its own glory in the advancement of the glory of the earthly city can actually hold back other, worse vices: "For the sake of this one vice—that is, the love of praise— these men suppressed the love of riches and many other vices."[36] The desire for glory, not in itself a true virtue, could function productively to temper the lust to dominate. Thus, organized public life, including what is honored and celebrated, shapes and reinforces citizens' imagination and desires toward, at worst, a desire to dominate and, less bad, a love of glory—a self-interested glory that often appears on the surface to be a virtue.

So are these Roman "virtues" of any value? Yes. O'Daly summarizes Augustine's point: "It is better, and more beneficial, that the citizens of the earthly city possess those virtues than that they do not (5.19). . . . Yet even the beginnings of Christian holiness are superior to Roman glory (5.19)."[37] These Roman virtues, or, as some have termed them, "splendid vices," are better than your run-of-the-mill vices, but they aren't true virtues. Thus, the empire ultimately misshapes

33. Rowan Williams emphasizes that at a certain level, "*De civitate* [*The City of God*] is not at all a work of political theory in the usual sense, but sketches for a theological anthropology and a corporate spirituality." *On Augustine*, 111.

34. J. Smith, *Awaiting the King*, 26–30.

35. J. Smith, *Awaiting the King*, 27.

36. Augustine, *The City of God* 5.13. Augustine adds, "But let it also be agreed that those who are not citizens of the eternal city . . . are more useful to the earthly city when they at least have the kind of virtue that serves human glory than when they do not" (5.19).

37. O'Daly, *Augustine's City of God*, 99.

people, wrongly forming them in twisted virtues, directing them toward lesser loves, and fulfilling their lower desires. It disorders its citizens' loves toward the elevation of themselves and other created things over the Creator. Citizens of the empire use things and people for the wrong purposes.

Can a country with such wrong purposes ever achieve lasting and substantial peace? The answer is an uncompromising no. Rome can never achieve for its people true peace and meaningful harmony, because it offers idolatrous teloi. Williams captures Augustine's point: "In short, while it may be empirically an intelligibly unified body, it is constantly undermining its own communal character, since its common goals are not and cannot be those abiding values which answer to the truest human needs."[38] A society will be restlessly divisive as long as its purposes, practices, and processes are not directed toward loving God.

The Roman Empire—for Augustine the latest version of the city of man— will never be a true commonwealth, and retrospectively, we know that it will be replaced by another and then another. By contrast, the city of God is truly an eternal city, uniting its people more substantially in their love for God and being destined for eternal peace in a heavenly dominion.

The earthly city originated in the prideful and self-centered fall in the garden. While retaining their own essential goodness in a beautiful land, those of the earthly city desired inferior things rather than the supreme good, who is God. They defected from the ultimate good and directed their will toward lesser things. They perversely loved their own power and their own good rather than directing their will toward the origin of all power and goodness. "They defect from that which has supreme existence and defect to that which has lesser existence."[39] And because they retain their essential goodness, they realize, with a painful restlessness, the depth of their own wretchedness and misery.[40]

How can Augustine sustain such a piercing critique of the Roman Empire? He has deeply inhabited and analyzed both cities. He received a Roman education and imbibed the Roman way of life. He traveled its downward, disintegrated path toward success. He felt the malaise caused by the existential pressure points within the empire's vision of the good life. More importantly, he has been reeducated and reformed within the church. He has turned his questions toward the Christian Scriptures and directed his longings toward the God of the church and its Scriptures. In the Christian community, he looks into his own soul, reimagining what it means to be human and how people should use the goods of this world for higher purposes.

---

38. Williams, *On Augustine*, 113.
39. Augustine, *The City of God* 12.8.
40. Augustine, *The City of God* 12.4–9.

Before his conversion, Augustine famously struggled with the classic problem of evil: if God is perfectly good and all-powerful, then evil cannot exist; but it does exist. Manichean dualism and materialism seemed to help him deal with this problem. Matter is evil; spirit is good. God is good but not all-powerful; evil is equally powerful. This good-versus-evil drama played out in microcosm in the human: the body is evil, but the soul is good. Eventually, Augustine adopted the Manichean construct, but after some time he began to experience intellectual dissatisfaction with the Manichees' answer to the problem of evil. As a catechumen in the church, he began to see that creation and being were good and that evil is no substance at all. To not be good is to not exist; to exist is to be good. Scripture taught that sin and evil entered the world through the choice of Adam. But what is evil and what is its cause? Freed from his Manichean materialism, he came to believe that to subsist is good. Evil, then, is not a substance; it is nonexistence. It is nothing. Created things are good. Evil is a lack. To explain its cause is to attempt to know something that cannot be known. "No one, therefore, should look for an efficient cause for an evil will. For it is not an efficient but a deficient cause, because the evil will itself is not an effect but rather a defect."[41] These reflections helped him understand and articulate a Christian response to the problem of evil.

Yet, all this did not deny that evil was wretched and caused real pain, suffering, and loss. *Confessions* honestly records the agonies Augustine felt and the prayers he said on his journey through the Roman world as a wonderful and wretched being. He struggled with pursuing his own glory and prestige as he moved within elite circles. It is all laid bare for readers: his desire to conquer, to live among the elite, to be praised and honored, and to use things and people for his own advancement. The social dimension is also apparent in these pages: his parents, his teachers, and his friends played their part in making him a true Roman. But his longing for true beauty and the hauntings of his lingering human goodness (enlivened, of course, by God's grace) caused enough pain and disappointment within him to open his heart and mind to another way. With intimations of Eden mysteriously imprinted on his soul, he kept looking for something better than empire, a society formed and sustained by values that transcended fear, domination, and prideful glory. *Confessions* is his testimony to his own journey through the empire's allurements as well as his guide, for others, to a better path.

The church was that path. Under its care he was resocialized and re-storied by her mythos and practices. As we will demonstrate in the next two sections, Augustine found redemption through a divine Mediator and hope for happiness in

41. Augustine, *The City of God* 12.7.

the hereafter. In the church he discovered the way of humility and was redirected toward loving God and loving others. Creation was not something to possess and exploit for his own pleasure and glory; rather, it existed as a signpost pointing to God and his grace. The church's humiliation held out more promise than the empire's domination, and the church's suffering enriched his life more than all the wealth of Rome. This community formed him in a way that unmasked his sin and equipped him to see through Roman glory. Though imperfectly, the church guided him to direct his love toward God and others. Scripture reading, prayer, and confession in the community freed him to reimagine and repurpose his life. He learned to live with the grain of God's goodness and beauty in creation in order to serve as a signpost pointing others to God and the truly good life in him.

In *Confessions* Augustine shares his honest exploration of his own wretchedness within the church's theology and community. Doing this as an act of pastoral service provided an illustration of apologetics and also gave him the resources to critique the underpinnings of the Roman Empire and to diagnose its malaise. But to take the Augustine way means to do more than unmask the corrupt motives and diagnose the disorders of a particular society; it means to lay bare one's own corruption and open one's own heart to the balm of Christ. And it is only this personal turn inward, in which one learns to see one's idols and turn to Christ to find forgiveness and healing, that prepares the apologist to critique the ills and diversions of our age with the right ethos and Logos.

### Redemption: Incarnation, the Cross, and Resurrection

Following Augustine, Williams defines redemption in Jesus Christ as an "attunement." In our sin we are out of tune with our created selves because we, as finite creatures, are in disharmony with the infinite Creator and source of our being. He writes,

> Consequently, for us to be delivered from evil is to be fully attuned to the order we did not and could not make, an attunement that happens in the life of grace as experienced in the baptized community; and this grace is made available to us because of God's act to restore broken harmony in the earthly presence of Jesus Christ and all that flows from this. God enacts his being in the history of Jesus so as to heal our diseased desires and renew our delight.[42]

The redemption of Jesus Christ attunes us to creational goodness and beauty and, ultimately and most importantly, to the source of all creation. The earthly

42. Williams, *On Augustine*, 104–5.

presence and historical actions of Jesus Christ restore broken harmony and enact God's gracious healing in our lives.

According to his own testimony, before his conversion, Augustine's creational goodness had been perverted, and he had defected from the source of all true beauty. Pride and self-interest had fragmented his life and distanced him from true knowledge and wisdom. He habitually misused creational abundance, and his loves were bent back toward himself. But Jesus Christ, the divine Doctor and Teacher, opened up Augustine's life to new therapeutic possibilities and truly wise perspectives.

In books 7 and 10 of *Confessions*, Augustine explains how Jesus Christ, as Mediator, gave him the wisdom he sought and the healing he longed for.[43] Augustine recounts this for himself but also for the church he shepherded so that the congregants would gain the diagnostic acumen and healing tools they needed to recognize and recover from their wounds.

In book 7, the postconversion Augustine looks back on his preconversion self, recounting how his lack of humility had dulled his heart and mind to Jesus's wisdom and healing as God in the flesh: "For the Word became flesh so that your [God's] Wisdom, through whom you created all things, might become for us the milk adapted to our infancy. Not yet was I humble enough to grasp the humble Jesus as my God, nor did I know what his weakness had to teach."[44] Yet, the incarnate Word "heals [the creature's] swollen pride" and "nourishes their love."[45] Augustine's humbled memory, one that has been shaped by the humility of the incarnate Christ, allows him to reflect on his former life from the perspective of the wisdom and healing of Jesus Christ. Lewis Ayres notes the important place of memory in Christ's redemptive work: "The reformation of the memory through the work of grace now becomes central to the work of God."[46] The wisdom of Jesus Christ equips Augustine to reflect on the real events and thought processes of his former life in a way that brings about healing. Book 7 illustrates the relationship of memory to wisdom and healing, which Augustine emphasizes in book 10.

---

43. Augustine, *Confessions* 3.4.8, 5.14.25. From his youth Augustine never gave up believing that wisdom and healing were found in the name of Jesus Christ; he just did not know how to find them. It is important to note here that Augustine never wrote a work devoted to incarnation or Christology. He did Christology with an occasion-oriented approach in response to pastoral needs. Fitzgerald, "Jesus Christ," 111–13.

44. Augustine, *Confessions* 7.18.24. See Harrison, *Augustine*, 24; Kolbet, *Augustine and the Cure of Souls*, 142.

45. Augustine, *Confessions* 7.18.24.

46. Ayres, "Christianity as Contemplative Practice," 194.

At the end of book 10, Augustine is in a different place than he was in book 7. He has been humbled by the incarnation and death of Christ. Yet, he confesses his ongoing need for Christ to teach him and heal him:

> You know how stupid and weak I am: teach me and heal me. Your only Son, in whom are hidden all treasures of wisdom and knowledge, has redeemed me with his blood. Let not the proud disparage me, for I am mindful of my ransom. I eat it, I drink it, I dispense it to others, and as a poor man I long to be filled with it among those who are fed and feasted. And then do those who seek him praise the Lord.[47]

God uses our memory to apply the redemptive work of Jesus Christ in a way that teaches us wisdom and heals our inner world. These interconnected themes of redemption, wisdom, and healing are pervasive throughout the Augustinian corpus. So much more could be said, but two major application points related to Augustine's apologetic demand our attention.

First, Jesus Christ, teacher of the wisdom of God, gave Augustine new diagnostic tools to analyze his past life and critique his present thinking and affections. "From a time not far removed from his baptism, Augustine sees Christ as the wisdom of God, and he applies the couplet knowledge-wisdom (*scientia-sapientia*) to Christ in a way that makes the practice of worship a means to wisdom. Christ is both wisdom and the way to wisdom."[48] Through Jesus Christ we know, and through him we become wise. The mystery of his conception, the lowliness of his incarnation, and the suffering of his cross give us the insight to assess our own inner world. But more than that, Christ, our Mediator, shapes the way we see the outer world. This happens within the worship, life, and teaching of the church. For Augustine, Jesus Christ is "the condition, the author and the method of all his thinking, . . . the source and method for his philosophical and theological thinking"[49]—and, we would add, his apologetic thinking. Christ functions "as the interior teacher (*magister interior*), the knowledge and wisdom of God (*scientia et sapientia dei*) in Augustine's illuminationist approach to knowledge."[50] Christ was not just someone Augustine looked to but rather the one he looked through to see himself and the world around him. Christ healed his sight and opened his eyes to a point of view in which humility was the key to knowledge. Redemption in Jesus Christ is ocular; it changes the way we see. Christ and his body form apologetic diagnosticians with the

---

47. Augustine, *Confessions* 10.43.70.
48. Fitzgerald, "Jesus Christ," 118.
49. Drobner, "Overview of Recent Research," 27–28.
50. Drobner, "Overview of Recent Research," 28.

wisdom and knowledge to see themselves, with ever-increasing insight, as they have been, as they are, as they should be, and as they will be.

Second, Jesus Christ, the doctor and healing of God, began in Augustine a therapeutic process of soul cure.[51] The wisdom of God heals wounded people, administering his treatments in a way that fits humanity's sickness and restores them to their original goodness. "In this way, 'Wisdom adapted its healing art to our wounds by taking on a human being' and becoming 'itself both the physician (*medicus*) and the medicine (*medicina*).'"[52] Jesus Christ, the Wisdom of God, is the doctor and the treatment. The blood of Christ heals the sin-sick person, applying the balm of forgiveness and binding up the wounds with the healing love of God. The crucified Christ is the cure of "disordered loves hardened by habit." This "cure comes in the context of the Christian community's teaching and preaching of scripture."[53] We have heard it said that hurt people hurt people. But the wounds of Jesus Christ are healing wounds that transform hurt people into healers. "By incarnation, death and resurrection, the Word creates a relation between himself and the human race that brings all human experience within the scope of healing and restoration."[54] Through word, sacrament, and rightly ordered love, the church becomes a place of healing. Christ's redemption and redemptive community heal our sin disease, reordering our loves toward God and people and restoring us to creational goodness. *Confessions* testifies to the healing power of Christ through his church and directs others to these therapeutic resources. The church is a healing community that is itself in need of the healing of Christ as it awaits its future redemption.[55]

There is an essential feedback loop in this narrative: the Wisdom of Jesus Christ heals us, and this healing makes us wise, which allows us to heal further, which in turn deepens our wisdom, and so on. Thus, knowledge and healing are mutually reinforcing and are constantly building on the gains of the other. The church is a place that embodies this redemptive wisdom and healing of God as it increases in his people. Here the eyes of the heart are both opened and healed, forming apologists with holistic and therapeutic diagnostic capacities.

Augustine uses the same redemptive diagnostic tools and therapeutic resources in *The City of God* that he uses in *Confessions*. The personal remembrances and reflections of *Confessions* have prepared him to critique Roman culture and tell a better story of social healing. Book 10 of *The City of God*

---

51. It was a healing process that was never completed in this life. "His death was the cessation of a lifelong convalescence." Kolbet, *Augustine and the Cure of Souls*, 163.

52. Kolbet, *Augustine and the Cure of Souls*, 142, quoting Augustine, *Teaching Christianity* 1.14.13.

53. Kolbet, *Augustine and the Cure of Souls*, 142.

54. Williams, "Augustine's Christology," 181.

55. Kolbet, *Augustine and the Cure of Souls*, 205.

contains the main diagnostic tool and the source of public therapy: Jesus Christ, the Mediator.

Book 10 culminates the first "half" of *The City of God*. In particular, it concludes a discussion begun in book 8 that critiques Platonic theology.[56] The incarnation and death of Jesus Christ provide a point from which Augustine can critique Platonism. Or perhaps better, they are a lens through which he can see the inconsistencies and inadequacies of Platonic theology. Crucially, Platonism lacks the wisdom and healing found in the Mediator.

In 10.28–29, Augustine demonstrates that the Platonists cut themselves off from wisdom and healing because they reject the lowliness of the incarnation and cross of Jesus Christ. John Cavadini explains that Porphyry recognizes the human need for grace but rejects its source because this conflicts "with his own Platonic teaching about bodies, which makes the Word's humble acceptance of a body appear too humiliating for philosophical wisdom to accept ([*The City of God*] 10:29)." Further, the philosophers' unwillingness to glorify God and give thanks to him for the grace revealed in Jesus Christ enables them to maintain their claim to be "wise."[57] But "by refusing to accept the 'medicine'" that even simple, humble Christians accept, "the Platonist philosophers 'are not healed; rather, they fall into a still more grievous affliction.'"[58] Augustine recognizes this struggle within Platonism because, as we saw in book 7 of *Confessions*, he recalls his own pride, which previously cut him off from the wisdom of the Word. After using 1 Corinthians 1:19–25 to demonstrate that Christ will "destroy the wisdom of the wise" (v. 19) and that he is "the power of God and the wisdom of God" (v. 24) as opposed to the foolish wisdom of the philosophers, Augustine states clearly, "This is what the Platonists despise as foolish and weak, as if they were wise and strong on their own. But, in fact, this is the grace which heals the weak, who do not proudly boast of their false happiness but rather humbly confess their true misery."[59] The wisdom and healing Augustine has received through the humility of the Mediator equips him to critique larger cultural narratives, such as the Platonism of his day.

In the structure of *The City of God*, Jesus Christ, as the wise and healing Mediator, also serves as the hinge to the second "half" of Augustine's massive work. Books 11–22 cover the narrative expanse of Scripture from creation to the new heaven and new earth. Providing a theological bridge from the first "half" to the second "half," Augustine states in 11.2 that the Mediator is the truth and the way to God: "And in order that, by faith, the mind might walk more

---

56. Cavadini, *Visioning Augustine*, 246.
57. Cavadini, *Visioning Augustine*, 251–52.
58. Cavadini, *Visioning Augustine*, 252; Augustine, *The City of God* 10.29.
59. Augustine, *The City of God* 10.28.

confidently toward the truth, the truth itself, God, the Son of God, having assumed humanity without ceasing to be God, established and founded this same faith, so that man might have a path to man's God through the man who was God." Scripture is the authority upon which Augustine will build his narrative journey in the second half of *The City of God*. This authority is established by the Mediator, who is the primary link between books 1–10 and 11–22. Augustine continues in 11.2, "This mediator spoke first through the prophets, then through himself, and later through the apostles, telling us as much as he judged sufficient. He also established the Scriptures which are called canonical. These Scriptures have preeminent authority, and we put our trust in them concerning those matters of which it is not expedient for us to be ignorant but which we are incapable of knowing on our own." After the paragraph containing this explanation of the Mediator's relationship to Scripture, Augustine commences his exposition of the biblical narrative. In this narrative, Augustine presents a vision of the heavenly city, the just society, redeemed by the blood of the Lamb, grounded in the love of God and neighbor and united around creation's good and beautiful telos. It is a narrative that lays out a wise and healing path for the flock under Augustine's care and for society at large, if they will but travel on the Way to God.

The Mediator has given Augustine a lens by which he can reobserve the world. The incarnation and crucifixion of Jesus Christ provide a perspective for critiquing important movements and influences of his day. The divine-human Teacher and Doctor illuminates the errors in false ways of conceiving of the world, and he sheds light on the goodness, beauty, and truth of a redeemed creation.

C. S. Lewis famously said, "I believe in Christianity as I believe that the sun has risen, not only because I see it but because by it, I see everything else."[60] We might say something similar about Augustine's perspective on Jesus Christ as the wisdom and healing of God. Augustine does not just look at Jesus Christ—which, of course, he does—but also sees through him. As he looks at Jesus Christ's wisdom and healing, this divine-human teacher and doctor enables him to see himself and the world in a new light. Jesus Christ opens his eyes to false paths and dead-end journeys and places his feet on a new road. As Augustine travels down this way, it is Jesus Christ who directs the bishop's gaze hopefully toward a renewed vision of home.

---

60. Lewis, *Weight of Glory*, 140.

## Restoration: Eschatological Realism

In this life wisdom is never total, and healing is never complete. We are on a pilgrimage toward home. The wisdom of Christ is the pavement we travel on during this lifelong journey of healing.

> Furthermore, we are still on the way, a way however not from place to place, but one traveled by the affections. And it was being blocked, as by a barricade of thorn bushes, by the malice of our past sins. So what greater generosity and compassion could he show, after deliberately making himself the pavement under our feet along which we could return home, than to forgive us all our sins once we had turned back to him, and by being crucified for us to root out the ban blocking our return that had been so firmly fixed in place?[61]

Augustine's eschatological perspective—that complete healing and full happiness will ultimately occur in the new heaven and new earth—gives him a kind of realism toward how much progress Christians can expect in this life. This hope of future restoration and this realistic view of his own spiritual progress is reflected in *Confessions* and *The City of God*.

*Confessions* is unique in ancient literature because of its raw personal honesty. Augustine reflects openly about his twisted past. Peter Brown explains how this is in contrast to other biographies in the ancient world: "In so many ancient and medieval biographies . . . we meet heroes described in terms of their essential, ideal qualities. It is almost as if they had no past: even their childhood is described only in terms of omens of the future 'peak' of their life. . . . We meet them full face: it is as if they had sloughed off, in their past, all that did not point directly to the image of perfection to which they conformed."[62] Not so with Augustine; even his youth is a realm for spiritual examination and confession. Sarah Ruden also comments on Augustine's unusual honesty and how he modifies a common pagan literary genre: "Both his mind and 'inward ear' are freely exercised . . . for the world's benefit; here, he is squarely in pagan literary territory. But unlike pagan writers, he demurs in alarm from any pretense to comprehensive understanding or a rounded or even privileged view: he repeats that he is no better off spiritually than the *parvuli*, the simple-minded 'little children' of the church—and he can be (in fact, has been) much worse off because of arrogance and self-satisfaction separating him from God."[63]

The spiritual realism expressed in *Confessions* is due in large part to the fact that Augustine conceives of his conversion as a road on which he travels toward

61. Augustine, *Teaching Christianity* 1.17.16.
62. Brown, *Augustine of Hippo*, 167.
63. Ruden, in Augustine, *Confessions*, xxiii.

home, though he is not home yet. All things have not yet been restored to their
creational goodness and beauty. It is his eschatology that gives him a spiritual
realism and frees him, in contrast to the tales of personal glory in the ancient
world, to display his scars and ongoing failures.[64]

*The City of God* itself is a unique literary work because of the epochal shift that
precipitated its writing and the way the scriptural narrative shapes its content
and structure. Although "the structuring idea of the *City of God* was not . . . a
new one in Christian tradition or Augustine's thought,"[65] no other Christian
apologetic is quite like it; its scope and approach are ambitious and innovative.[66]
This great work presents an unusually thorough and penetrating critique of the
Greco-Roman world. With "cultured pagan noblemen of Rome [beginning]
to make their presence felt, as refugees, in the *salons* of Carthage,"[67] Augustine
feels compelled to defend Christianity against a strong movement to return to
Rome's pagan religious, philosophical, and literary tradition. Augustine, inhabiting "great books,"[68] offers an internal critique of the failure of Rome's gods
to bring earthly happiness (books 2–5) and eternal happiness (books 6–10).

Augustine's scriptural narrative in books 11–22—grounded in, centered on,
and completed by the Mediator—demonstrates the culmination "to which evil
leads in doing its harm" as well as the culmination "in which good is brought
to its full realization."[69] That is, the biblical story makes clear that the telos of
the earthly city is eternal harm, and the telos of the heavenly city is eternal
blessedness. This gives Augustine a vantage point from which he can critique
the current social order: Where does it lead? Does its path take us to the fulfillment of our heart's desire or to deepest disappointment? Are we on a path to
the fullness of God or to a vacuous emptiness? Is it a bridge to eternal life or

---

64. James K. A. Smith describes this as a gift that Augustine has left us: "One of the gifts
Augustine offers is a spirituality for realists. Conversion is not a 'solution.' Conversion is not a
magical transport home, some kind of Floo powder to heaven. Conversion doesn't pluck you off
the road; it just changes how you travel." *On the Road with Saint Augustine*, 15.

65. Harrison, *Augustine*, 197.

66. "Thus, while Augustine undoubtedly borrows themes and arguments from the earlier
apologists and related literature, no one of his precursors has either a dominant or a profound
influence on his apologetic concerns and strategies." O'Daly, *Augustine's City of God*, 52.

67. Brown, *Augustine of Hippo*, 298; cf. O'Daly, *Augustine's City of God*, 27–34. "Augustine tells
us that he felt compelled to answer the complaints of Pagan sophisticates who were missing their
gods and blaspheming against 'the true God' (*deum verum*) more than usual ([*Revisions*] 2.43.1)."
Wetzel, *Augustine's City of God*, 2.

68. "It seems as if Augustine were demolishing a paganism that existed only in libraries. In fact
Augustine believed, quite rightly, that he could best reach the last pagans through their libraries."
Brown, *Augustine of Hippo*, 303.

69. Augustine, *The City of God* 19.1.

a dead end? Does it restore us to creational goodness and beauty or plunge us into confusion and despair?

Augustine's eschatology also supports a public polemic that is capable of avoiding the problem of overrealized expectations and underrealized hopes. Augustine's apologetic both critiques the reigning social imaginary and works for the good of its inhabitants. It imagines for the people of the heavenly city a way of inhabiting the world that is sustained by the heartbeat of the church and shaped by the grand scriptural narrative. These pilgrims journey through the world, happy in hope while being sanctified by the struggles of intermingling with the earthly city. The city of God's eschatological hope gives it a place to stand, a plateau from which to critique Roman culture. Peace and justice are coming. We live realistically, in love of God and neighbor, with hope in the happiness that is to come.

As James K. A. Smith has demonstrated from Augustine's critique of Varro in *The City of God*, this eschatological realism gives us perspective on today's political mythologies, public rites, and cultural idols. A society's liturgies form its citizens' loves.[70] The church counterforms us and re-aims our hearts toward the kingdom that is to come, equipping us with the diagnostic tools to see into a society's idolatry and forming us into a source of healing and hope for our neighbors.[71]

An overrealized eschatology—or, in Augustine's parlance, to "live ahead of time"[72]—may cause one of two problems. It can lead to a retreat into an enclosed Christian society in order to avoid the struggle of engaging with the world or to remain "pure." Or it can inhibit the ability to critique contemporary cultural and social ambitions that are "unrealizable in this world," as happened with the many Christians who lost the critical distance from Rome's quest for temporal peace and justice.[73]

To the latter point, an overrealized eschatology runs the risk of secularizing *shalom*. Too little "not yet" in our eschatology makes the "already" susceptible to being seduced by secular humanist visions of the good life. Gradually shaped by secular liturgies that ground present-day happiness exclusively in the immanent and find pain and sacrifice antithetical to joy, even so-called "Christian" visions of peace, justice, and happiness risk tacitly pushing some of the Scriptures'

70. In other words, the earthly city's mythology is bound up in its religious or liturgical practices in such a way that it requires Augustine to deconstruct the myth and the practices. See J. Smith, *Awaiting the King*, 26.

71. J. Smith, *Awaiting the King*, 213.

72. This is a phrase from Augustine, *Letter* 189.5. James K. A. Smith puts this phrase in today's theological language: "Don't think we can 'live ahead of time' is Augustine's way of saying: don't fall for the temptation of a realized eschatology." *Awaiting the King*, 199.

73. Harrison, *Augustine*, 207.

emphases and depictions of God to the margins. For example, while in *A Secular Age* Charles Taylor rightly critiques what he refers to as the anthropological shift and warns of the dangers of a kind of overrealized eschatology, we wonder whether he is at times still swayed by both.[74] For he eschews traditional descriptions of God, such as a God of wrath, when he sees them undermining human flourishing.[75] Have the distinctions for Taylor between the different teloi of the city of God and the city of man begun to collapse, thus at times surrendering his critical and diagnostic distance to the present?

The danger is that the city of God on pilgrimage and God himself are both refashioned into the image of the parochial gods of our own age. In contrast, maintaining Augustine's eschatological realism positions the contemporary apologist to accept the tensions inherent in the "already-not-yet" of the New Testament and maintain doctrines that are perceived as hard in certain cultural milieus, which enables the church to counter shallow and unstable visions of flourishing in a fallen world with a more realistic, imaginative, and nuanced picture. Even though, as we will see in the next chapter, Taylor offers important contributions to our retrieval of Augustinian apologetics, we worry that in this case Taylor provides an example of an error that Augustine, with his eschatological vantage point, would warn us against.

Augustine's realistic posture allows him to confront Rome's overreach as well as the overly optimistic zealots who immanentize the eschaton. According to Augustine, even the best of Christian high hopes, like "rightly ordered love" of God and neighbor, are "unattainable" in this life.[76] With the sack of Rome, Augustine works out an apologetic response that keeps a critical distance from the empire while offering a realistic hope for happiness and healing. His approach can help us avoid the apologetic problems that accompany an over-realized eschatology.

This is an apologetic fashioned in the church. "It is in the formative worship of the church—rehearsing the biblical drama whose *telos* is the eschaton—that we learn both the norms for flourishing *and* how to wait."[77] For Augustinian apologetics, the church itself is an apologetic community forming apologists as it explains and embodies the story of creation, fall, redemption, and restoration.

74. For both his warnings and his dismissal of traditional doctrines, see Taylor, *A Secular Age*, 221–69, 639–75, 728–44.

75. See Michael Horton's critique of *A Secular Age* in "Enduring Power," 23–38. See chap. 5 below for our positive appropriation of Taylor.

76. Harrison, *Augustine*, 211.

77. J. Smith, *Awaiting the King*, 89.

## Conclusion: The Apologetic Pilgrimage

We began this chapter with the observation that many apologists in our age are experiencing psychological fatigue as a result of attempting to enter the apologetic trenches in isolation. We suggested that Tyson James diagnoses a real problem but settles for a partial solution that glosses over the needed prescription. As beneficial as parachurch ministries can be, we must learn to build churches as field hospitals and headquarters for apologetic witness rather than treat them as territories full of land mines to be maneuvered around. Furthermore, since the loneliness James describes as a problem for apologists is actually part of a wider malaise that reaches well beyond the walls of the church, it is of apologetic importance that treatment is offered by local parishes.

The growing discontentment and restlessness within our society often confounds the overrealized secular eschatology of those within a consumeristic, therapeutic kingdom. For when people hail self-actualization and technological progress as messiahs but salvation never arrives, a nagging doubt can quickly spiral into a hopeless despair. Thus, even though people can point to wide-ranging encouraging stats, from lower infant mortality rates to rising GDP, angst and depression are on the rise. And even when these negative symptoms are skimmed over and one manages to divert attention from these realities in daily experience, society's artists and storytellers continue to offer sobering reminders of our sickness.

Apple's hit series *The Morning Show*, for example, takes us behind the curtain of what it feels like to have climbed the ladder, not to the seat of power in Augustine's Roman Empire but to one of the positions of fame and influence in contemporary America: the pinnacle of entertainment and media. One might interpret *The Morning Show* as offering a modern secular version of an Augustinian-style cultural and anthropological analysis, sans divine grace.

Reece Witherspoon plays an upstart anchorwoman, Bradley Jackson, with aspirations to change the world. Owing to her tenacious personality and a good bit of luck, all of a sudden she finds herself hosting the morning show on one of the major national television networks in New York City. As a small-town girl from a broken home, she embodies the kind of rags-to-riches story Americans love to tell. She has arrived. Admired by millions, she spends her days with the rich and famous and is ready to use her platform to make a real difference. Yet, reality soon sets in.

Her own dysfunctional past contributes to self-destructive patterns of behavior that do not magically change with her new circumstances. Underneath the glitz and glamour of her new job, she finds herself in a world where no one is satisfied, a world of narcissism and backstabbing, a polis that promises

Eden but is closer to hell on earth. She is absorbed into a community that, in Augustinian terms, has in practice deified fame, power, and money—for in these things the community imagined a kind of immanent salvation. And yet, just about everyone in the show, including Jackson, is either on the verge of a panic attack or vainly pursuing diversions to hide from their own misery.

We can only imagine how our time-traveling bishop would see in these modern pictures a portrait of his ancient self. With a sigh, he might recall the scene he wrote of long ago, when he, on the fast track to worldly fame himself and en route to deliver a speech to the emperor, bemoaned his plight: "My heart was issuing furnace-blasts anxiety over this assignment, and seething with the fever of the obsessive thoughts disintegrating me from within, as I passed down a street in Milan and noticed a destitute beggar." The beggar, Augustine would recall, was a drunk finding an illusory joy at the bottom of a bottle, while Augustine and his friends, with all their achievements and pride in hand, were in even worse shape, living with "the many sufferings of our insanity." The drunk would be sober by morning, but Augustine would remain sozzled by his delusions, with no relief in sight.

While outsiders would have seen Augustine as liberated and free to enjoy the pleasures of life, we can imagine him saying he was trapped in the same dazzling prison as the characters in *The Morning Show*: "My longings sharply prodded me to drag along a load of my own unhappiness that was heaped up higher with the exhaustion of dragging it."[78] Like *Confessions*, Augustine would tell us, *The Morning Show* portrays a world of false gods who are brutal taskmasters, making promises but then always demanding more. Offering a mirage, they trick humans into meeting their demands while hollowing our capacity to truly flourish. In contrast with the picturesque, skyline luxury apartments overlooking the city and the European villas opening up to vineyards, the pictures from the inside are of characters trapped in darkness, pain, and loneliness. Having turned in on themselves, they are a long way from true joy. Surprisingly, even Augustine's view of fallen nature is given voice in the show. As one character enthusiastically declares to Jackson in a climactic scene of the first season, "Human nature: it's surprisingly universal, and it's universally disappointing."[79]

And yet, the show, like *Confessions*, offers a more nuanced picture of human nature than cursory interpretations might suggest. In an interview shown after the credits of one of the episodes, Witherspoon reflects on what the series is attempting to depict. In a line that sounds as though it could have been penned

---

78. Augustine, *Confessions* 6.9. In this section, the quotations from *Confessions* are from Sarah Ruden's translation.

79. *The Morning Show*, season 1, episode 10, "The Interview," aired December 20, 2019, Apple TV+.

by Augustine himself, she explains, "As human beings we are fallible; we are capable of horrible things." But, she adds, "we are capable of wonderful things." At moments, the series even gestures toward the possibility of grace. Jackson's cohost, played by Jennifer Aniston, says the show is attempting to address "the big question. . . . Is there redemption for anyone? Is there forgiveness?"[80]

*The Morning Show* reminds us that we live in a world where, even in its more "secular" pockets, people still know of guilt and loneliness and deeply feel their own unhappiness while also longing for redemption, forgiveness, and even something like grace. But, as depicted by the cohost's interrogatives, no clear source for hope is on offer. Given the writers' dark depiction of human nature, could redemption really come from ourselves? Forgiveness is, at times, held out as an ideal, but the explanation for *why* and the resources for *how* are left almost entirely unexplored. No source or logic for grace is on offer.

In our time, such are the apologetic openings.

Enter the church as a community living out the drama of the gospel and thereby serving as a hospital for the restoration of broken and rebellious image bearers. In an age that Philip Rieff has memorably described as "the triumph of the therapeutic"—when questions about how to feel better now have replaced questions of eternal salvation—Augustine would have us reconsider how far those questions are actually apart.[81] For the eternal One came down into our world, taking on flesh and our infirmities to pay for sin, defeat evil, and heal our diseased souls. Linking these questions of eternal salvation and human flourishing means seeing mourning and happiness, meekness and flourishing, not as opposites but as entailments of becoming whole in a fallen world. But in making these connections we will be in good company, for this paradox is a key move in Jesus's most famous sermon, the Sermon on the Mount.[82]

Augustine would remind us that, as the city of God on pilgrimage, we are an apologetic people who are experiencing the cure and thus turning from pride to humility and from love of self to love of God and others. At the same time, the bishop is realistic about what we can expect in this life: our pilgrimage is not marked by perfection in virtue but by forgiveness,[83] though true forgiveness does leave its marks.

---

80. *The Morning Show*, season 2, episode 7, "Inside the Episode: La Amara Vita," aired October 29, 2021, Apple TV+.

81. See Rieff, *Triumph of the Therapeutic*. That is, as we will see in the next chapter, the West sees feeling better as the human telos but feels the pinch: as souls who were made for God, the secular options offer weak medicine. They only mask our deepest malady for a time.

82. See Pennington, *Sermon on the Mount*.

83. Augustine, *The City of God* 14.28, 19.27.

Consider the closing remarks Augustine makes to his congregation after a sermon that pagans were allowed to hear and that was filled with apologetic appeals along a therapeutic plane. After the pagans have been dismissed, Augustine exhorts the congregation:

> I've already said to you yesterday, brothers and sisters, and I say it again now and am always begging you to win over those who haven't yet believed, by leading good lives—otherwise you too, I fear, will have believed to no purpose. I beseech you all, in the same way as you take pleasure in the word of God, so to express that pleasure in the lives you lead. Let God's word please you not only in your ears but in your hearts too; not only in your hearts but also in your lives, so that you may be God's household, acceptable in his eyes and *fit for every good work* (2 Tm 2:21). I haven't the slightest doubt, brothers and sisters, that if you all live in a manner worthy of God, the time will very soon come when none of those who have not yet believed will remain in unbelief.[84]

Apologists, indeed, are called to give answers and use words to persuade, a calling to which Augustine committed his life. The next, and the longest, chapter in this book is dedicated to tracing out an Augustinian approach to apologetics with the skills and resources Augustine developed in the church as he prayed for, preached to, and pastored his congregation. But verbal appeals, as Augustine himself understood, are to be done from the context of a city on pilgrimage to meet the true King:

> Let these be the answers—and others, if more fruitful and suitable ones can be found—that the redeemed family of the Lord Christ and the pilgrim city of Christ the king make to their enemies. Remember, however, that among those very enemies are hidden some who will become citizens, and do not think it fruitless to bear their enmity until they come to confess the faith.[85]

The church's calling is to be a living apologetic while suffering affliction, as all people must in this life. Yet, through our affliction, God is at work to reorder our loves[86]—as we, "the pilgrim city of Christ the king," listen to the Scriptures, sing praises to his name, and partake in the sacraments.

Along this road we corporately become the people who have the quality necessary for fulfilling the apostle Peter's apologetic command: hope. Peter's apologetic imperative, the only time the word *apologia* is used in the Scriptures, is contingent on a people who, amid the persecutions and miseries of this life,

---

84. Augustine, *Sermon* 360B.
85. Augustine, *The City of God* 1.35.
86. See Augustine, *Confessions* 7.12.

have learned to hope ("Always be ready to make your defense to anyone who demands from you an accounting for the hope that is in you," 1 Pet. 3:15). And it is through this embodied hope that we find a chastened, though nonetheless true, happiness in a fallen world:

> Nevertheless, if anyone uses this life in such a way that he directs it to that other life as the end which he loves with ardent intensity and for which he hopes with unwavering faithfulness, it is not absurd to call him happy even now, although happy in that hope rather than in this reality. Without that hope, in fact, this reality is only a false happiness and a great misery. For it does not make use of the true goods of the soul, because no wisdom is true wisdom if it does not direct its intention—in everything that it discerns with prudence, bears with fortitude, constrains with temperance, and distributes with justice—to the end where God will be all in all in assured eternity and perfect peace.[87]

Today the church remains, having outlasted its rivals from the ancient world, as God's apologetic community, called to persuade others of this true happiness in hope and to raise up apologists who know how to use the things of the world—both joys and pains, beauty and beastliness, design and disorder—refracted through the light of the cross and resurrection to display the manifold wisdom of God. With this in mind, we now turn to our final chapter to learn from Augustine what this might look like today as we seek to apply his wisdom in response to new rivals and challenges.

---

87. Augustine, *The City of God* 19.20.

# 5

# A Therapeutic Approach

"I believe in hope. I believe in believe."

The words of coach Ted Lasso epitomize the spirit of the surprising hit television show that premiered during the COVID-19 pandemic. Ted, played by Jason Sudeikis, is a formerly successful college football coach who now finds himself, like a fish out of water, on the other side of the pond, at the helm of a British football (yes, soccer) club in the English Premier League. Riffing off Mark Twain, Sudeikis describes the show as being like life itself—"a comedy, drama, and tragedy" all rolled into one. Surprising initial critics, the show has become a cultural phenomenon, garnering praise from a variety of different corners and piling up awards, including a record-breaking twenty Emmy nominations for its first season.

Coach Lasso is a cool, modern version of Mister Rogers. Unlike *Mister Rogers' Neighborhood*, the show is geared toward adults. But like Rogers, Lasso embodies a kindness and empathy that people still aspire to, even if they find themselves unable to mirror his attitude as they are tossed to and fro by the ups and downs of life. Lasso's optimistic humor in the midst of mocking criticism and the grief of broken relationships is part of the show's charm. In one episode he's asked whether he believes in ghosts, to which he replies matter-of-factly that he does, "but more importantly, I think they need to believe in themselves."

Sudeikis explains one of the show's assumptions and aims: "One of the themes is that evil exists—bullies, toxic masculinity, malignant narcissists—and we can't just destroy them. It's about how you deal with those things. That's where the positivity and some of the lessons come in—it's about what we have control over."[1]

Though religion is only referenced in passing, the overwhelming success of *Ted Lasso* says something about faith in our commercialized and fragmented "secular" West. People intuitively accept that evil exists. They are looking for ways to cope. They desire peace. They long for hope. And they still believe . . . in something. In this chapter, we'd like to introduce Ted, or at least those attempting to engage his audience with the gospel, to Saint Augustine. For while apologists are having trouble finding an effective voice in a culture that religiously streams episodes of *Ted Lasso*, our ancient bishop seems to have seen him coming from sixteen centuries away.

### Today's Pagans

In a sweeping look at our current religious landscape, with her book *Strange Rites*, Tara Isabella Burton helps us better understand our apologetic terrain from the ground level. The religiously unaffiliated, the "nones," as they have been labeled, are the fastest-growing demographic in America, comprising a quarter of the population and almost 40 percent of those born after 1990. And yet, despite what the label might suggest, Burton reveals that this group is anything but nonreligious. Burton's thesis, however, extends far beyond nones to tell "the story of the religious sensibility of a whole generation."[2] Westerners, as it turns out, aren't actually shunning religion in the Durkheimian sense.[3] They are instead "remixing" religion—creating their "own bespoke religions, mixing and matching spiritual and aesthetic and experiential and philosophical traditions."[4] As Augustine arrives on our scene, he will be unsurprised to find humans, epitomized in late modernity by characters like Lasso, still searching for peace, hope, and a way to deal with anxiety and disorder.

---

1. Jeremy Egner, "'Ted Lasso' Is Back, but No Longer an Underdog," *New York Times*, updated September 24, 2021, https://www.nytimes.com/2021/07/14/arts/television/ted-lasso-jason -sudeikis.html.

2. Burton, *Strange Rites*, 9.

3. Also see Holland, *Dominion*, whose thesis is more specific: Not only are Westerners still religious, but they are still in many significant ways living off Christian sentiments, though these tacit Christian assumptions have mutated in various ways. Or, for an earlier book that makes the case that even a modern, in spite of seeking to be nonreligious, still in his or her "deepest being . . . retains a memory of it," even if only in the "depths of the unconscious," see Eliade, *The Sacred and the Profane*, 213. All of this sits well within the Augustinian understanding of humans as fundamentally worshiping beings.

4. Burton, *Strange Rites*, 10.

While metaphysical atheism remains an option for the masses in ways it wasn't before our post-Enlightenment world, the polls tell us it is a path that the vast majority, even in the "secular" West, are disinclined to take. Those who do, ironically, often still exercise faith in modern science for a kind of salvation or a sacralized view of humanity while also smuggling in religious values.[5] Most Westerners still leave room for a higher power, even if this spiritual force resembles more closely the god of moral therapeutic deism than the God of the Bible.[6] For while Christianity no longer operates as the standard default option, people still find it difficult to shake the longing for the "fullness" that has been historically connected to religion.[7] The result has been an explosion of different commercialized ways of making sense of our lives and finding peace and happiness. They are "commercialized" in the sense that in our market economy everything is "for sale" and commonsense logic works by way of the narrative of profit and consumption. This is a kind of consumerized spiritual syncretism. These are the new pagans, who, like the pagans in Augustine's day, seek ultimate fulfillment in the present through trusting in many different kinds of immanent "gods."[8]

Yet, neither the progressive new pagans nor the atheists who fashion themselves as champions of Enlightenment values can quite find a home in the neighborhood of Augustine's pagans. For his pagans, as we've already seen in chapter 1, reveled nostalgically in the glorious reign of the Roman gods and, in contrast to modern pagans, lived before Christendom. Though Christ and his legacy—whether they fully realize it or not—continue to haunt these new pagans, especially in their moral intuitions,[9] they reject institutionalized religion in favor of their own personalized mixture of "gods" and rituals.[10] While

---

5. Burton, *Strange Rites*, 245. Also see C. Smith, *Atheist Overreach*, for how supposedly purely secular accounts continue to "overreach" and smuggle in religious, and particularly Christian, ideas.

6. On "moral therapeutic deism," see C. Smith and Denton, *Soul Searching*, which studied thirteen- to seventeen-year-olds and found that the majority of American teens see God as "something like a combination Divine Butler and Cosmic Therapist: he is always on call, takes care of any problems that arise, [and] professionally helps his people to feel better about themselves" (165).

7. "Fullness" is Charles Taylor's preferred term for what is lacking in those cut off from transcendence. See *A Secular Age*, 677.

8. Their looking to other gods stands in contrast to looking to a transcendent God who enters our present, fallen world to redeem and reorder lives around himself. The thesis of S. Smith, *Pagans and Christians*, is that T. S. Eliot was basically right when he said, in the first half of the twentieth century, "I believe that the choice before us is between the formation of a new Christian culture, and the acceptance of a pagan one."

9. See C. Smith, "Does Naturalism Warrant a Moral Belief?," 292–317.

10. See Hart, *Atheist Delusions*: "Even the most ardent secularists among us generally cling to notions of human rights, economic and social justice, providence for the indigent, legal equality, or basic human dignity that pre-Christian Western culture would have found not so much foolish as unintelligible. It is simply the case that we distant children of the pagans would not be able

Burton's following summary could be revised slightly to include atheists who reject intuitional spirituality while religiously trusting in the omnicompetence of "science" and mysteriously believing in the sacredness of certain human values,[11] her description still captures something of the ethos of a growing population:

> Today's Remixed reject authority, institution, creed, and moral universalism. They value intuition, personal feeling, and experiences. They demand to rewrite their own scripts about how the universe, and human beings, operate. Shaped by the twin forces of a creative-communicative Internet and consumer capitalism, today's Remixed don't want to receive doctrine, to assent automatically to a creed. They want to choose—and more often than not, *purchase*—the spiritual path that feels more authentic, more meaningful, to them. They prioritize intuitional spirituality over institutional religion. And they want, when available institutional options fail to suit their needs, the freedom to mix and match, to create their own daily rituals and practices and belief systems.[12]

These are our new pagans. We must learn to persuade them.

But what is there to learn?

## The Problem of Nontransferability

A contemporary apologist might reply to the question, "What is there to learn?" with the following answer: "We must simply do what we have always done. Teach skeptics and unbelievers how to think. We must reason with them." Indeed, we should reason with them. But *how* should we reason with them?

Critical-thinking skills do not automatically lead to Christianity. Just read Voltaire. Or ask Richard Dawkins. Is it just poor critical-thinking skills or a refusal to look at the evidence that causes atheist intellectuals to disbelieve in God? Clearly there's more to reasoning and persuasion than just logic. As we saw in chapter 2, the philosopher Alasdair MacIntyre sums up why basic logic is

---

to believe in any of these things—they would never have occurred to us—had our ancestors not once believed that God is love, that charity is the foundation of all virtues, that all of us are equal before the eyes of God, that to fail to feed the hungry or care for the suffering is to sin against Christ, and that Christ laid down his life for the least of his brethren" (32–33).

11. See, e.g., Steven Smith's critical engagement with the committed naturalist Ronald Dworkin's invocation of the "sacred" and "religion without God" to ground objective morality, meaning, and purpose in human life. Smith concludes, "Dworkin's religion would seem to be of the immanent variety." Smith also observes that the popular atheist Sam Harris makes a move somewhat similar to that of Dworkin in resorting to such terms as "spiritual, mystical, contemplative, and transcendent" to describe another dimension of reality (*Pagans and Christians*, 232–57). As we will see later in this chapter, even atheists like Steven Pinker continue to invoke the "sacred."

12. Burton, *Strange Rites*, 10.

not enough to solve larger metaphysical or moral conflicts: "Observance of the laws of logic is only a necessary and not a sufficient condition for rationality." Instead of logic alone, it is "what has to be added to observance of the laws of logic" that justifies notions of rationality.[13]

So, yes, we need logic. But logic is not enough. When we are talking about the big truths and major commitments of life, it is what is added to basic logic that does some heavy lifting. And the differences in what we add on—both the evidence we choose to value and the social imaginary we embrace—result in different frameworks of rationality that cannot be overcome simply by lining up more data. This challenge of the nontransferability of competing rationalities— the problem of proceeding in the face of disagreements when the fundamental disagreement is over the rational framework itself—is one that many apologists have attempted either to ignore or to defeat with straw-man arguments. Yet, it is a real problem that we must face.

In his 1987 Gifford Lecture on natural theology, Alasdair MacIntyre offers a taxonomy of rational inquiry spanning the past two hundred years, which we will apply to help us see more clearly the nature of the challenge of nontransferability and modern paganism in apologetics. MacIntyre begins his address by pointing out a feature of the history of the Gifford Lectures that would disappoint Lord Gifford and his colleagues. Established over a hundred years ago, the lecture series set out to enlist star academics to "promote and diffuse the study of Natural Theology in the widest sense of the term—in other words, the knowledge of God."[14] Unfortunately, however, says MacIntyre, the series has failed "to secure more than minimal agreement within philosophy upon how it is rational to proceed in respect of the formation and criticism of beliefs."[15] But this isn't simply a problem specific to the Gifford Lectures. The lectures are illustrative of a problem that plagues contemporary philosophy:

> It is not of course that philosophers of each particular contending school and party do not supplement the inadequate resources of a shared minimum rationality by schemes of argument which enable them to transcend the limitations of that shared minimum. Scientific materialists, Heideggerians, possible-worlds theorists, phenomenologists, Wittgensteinians, and a host of others all do so; but there exists no generally agreed way of resolving the issues which divide the protagonists of these alternative and incompatible standpoints.[16]

13. MacIntyre, *Whose Justice?*, 4.
14. "The Gifford Lectures: Over 100 Years of Lectures on Natural Theology," Gifford Lectures, accessed August 1, 2022, http://www.giffordlectures.org.
15. MacIntyre, *Three Rival Versions of Moral Enquiry*, 12.
16. MacIntyre, *Three Rival Versions of Moral Enquiry*, 12.

MacIntyre identifies several factors that account for this incommensurability. First, people don't agree about the point at which one should begin to justify belief. Second, disagreement exists concerning what factors are most important in justifying one set of beliefs over another. Third, there are "limited resources provided for reasoning about the justification of beliefs."[17] In view of these issues and illustrative of them, MacIntyre maps out the major rival forms of rationality of the past two hundred years in the West. The dominant approach in the nineteenth century was held by encyclopedists, who "were committed to the notion of a single, unitary rationality."[18] This was rarely an explicitly stated philosophy; for the most part, it was simply an assumption about how knowledge acquisition worked universally, "one which every educated person can without too much difficulty be brought to agree in acknowledging."[19] In other words, "all rational persons conceptualize data in one and the same way" and would "report the same data, the same facts."[20]

The encyclopedists understood the human story as directed by the progress of reason: they "saw their whole mode of life, including their conceptions of rationality and of science, as part of a history of inevitable progress, judged by a standard of progress which had itself emerged from that history. . . . That the history of rationality and science might itself *be* a history of ruptures and discontinuities was for them an unthinkable thought."[21] Rather than historically dependent realities, a unitary reason led to "timeless truth" expressed by universal and noncontingent principles. Kavin Rowe captures the ethos of the encyclopedists:

> In short, to be reasonable is to be an encyclopaedist. . . . Truth is thus "what is independent of standpoint [and] can be discovered or confirmed by any adequately intelligent person, no matter what his point of view." For the encyclopaedist inquiry is necessarily cosmopolitan. There is nothing we cannot understand. And since understanding does not depend on us in any sort of personally significant way, there is no need to write in anything other than an impersonal sort of style—an objectifying discourse that appears as if no one in particular has written it.[22]

The problem, according to MacIntyre, is that, ironically, "the encyclopaedic mode of enquiry has become one more fideism and a fideism which increasingly

---

17. MacIntyre, *Three Rival Versions of Moral Enquiry*, 12.
18. Rowe, *One True Life*, 176.
19. MacIntyre, *Three Rival Versions of Moral Enquiry*, 14.
20. MacIntyre, *Three Rival Versions of Moral Enquiry*, 16.
21. MacIntyre, *Three Rival Versions of Moral Enquiry*, 24.
22. Rowe, *One True Life*, 178, quoting MacIntyre, *Three Rival Versions of Moral Enquiry*, 60.

flies in the face of contemporary realities."[23] Our contemporary realities function, by way of contrast, as evidence against the assumed social imaginary of the encyclopedist.

First, encyclopedists assumed all intelligent people would affirm a single and significant rationality. Instead, we now live in a world where there is the "presence of, and to some degree a debate between, conflicting, alternative conceptions of rationality."[24] It is difficult to deny today that educated people don't all assume the same rational framework. Different disciplines use different tools and focus on different aspects of the world.[25] Social and vocational location are not deterministic and do not abolish all common ground, but they do make a difference. Once we get past questions of basic logic, we know that intelligent people often still see the world differently, from different angles and using different methods. There is no rationality from nowhere.

Second, encyclopedists believed the result of their rationality "to be the elaboration of a comprehensive, rationally incontestable scientific understanding of the whole, in which the architectonic of the sciences matched that of the cosmos." Instead, the challenge of "a multiplicity of types of enquiry and of interpretative claims" means that "the very concept of an ordered whole, of a cosmos, has been put radically in question."[26]

Third, encyclopedists understood their whole way of life, driven by rationality and science, "as part of a history of inevitable progress." Yet today—due to the works of figures such as Gaston Bachelard, Michael Polanyi, Thomas Kuhn, and Michel Foucault—many can't help but see things through a different lens and recognize "the importance of rupture and discontinuity."[27] Mary Midgley has observed how machine imagery began to prove pervasive in the seventeenth century and still leverages immense influence, so that

> the reductive, atomistic picture of explanation, which suggests that the right way to understand complex wholes is always to break them down into their smallest parts, leads us to think that truth is always revealed at the end of that other seventeenth-century invention, the microscope. Where microscopes dominate our imagination, we feel that the large wholes we deal with in everyday experience are mere appearances. Only the particles revealed at the bottom of the microscope are real. Thus, to an extent unknown in earlier times, our dominant technology shapes our symbolism and thereby our metaphysics, our view about

23. MacIntyre, *Three Rival Versions of Moral Enquiry*, 56.
24. MacIntyre, *Three Rival Versions of Moral Enquiry*, 23.
25. See McGrath, *Territories of Human Reason*, 39, on the shift within the academic field of the philosophy of science, which popularizers have been slow to catch up to.
26. MacIntyre, *Three Rival Versions of Moral Enquiry*, 24.
27. MacIntyre, *Three Rival Versions of Moral Enquiry*, 24.

what is real. The heathen in his blindness bows down to wood and stone—steel and glass, plastic and rubber and silicon—of his own devising and sees them as the final truth.[28]

Thus, we're reminded, first, that people traffic in different myths and metaphors—such as the belief in inevitable progress or the world as machine— that they reason by and, second, that this use of myths and metaphors inevitably impacts conclusions.

For these reasons MacIntyre rightly contends that we cannot presuppose an encyclopedic approach, for such an approach was "devised on the basis of assumptions and within the context of a culture which are not and cannot be our assumptions and our culture."[29] Encyclopedists, even those who follow David Hume's skeptical critique of fellow Enlightenment thinkers, are, as James Peters explains, "unable to recognize that there is no single, neutral standard of rationality by which we can adjudicate substantial philosophical disagreements independently of metaphysical context."[30] Some of the most outspoken modern atheists, and even, ironically, some Christians, who act as if they are just following the data and only using logic, are in some sense descendants of these nineteenth-century encyclopedists. But as we will see next, it was the nineteenth-century genealogists who both critiqued the encyclopedists and helped pave the way for today's spiritual, "Remixed" pagans.

The genealogists did much to help us understand these present realities while they undermined the basic commitments of the encyclopedists. Their type of inquiry takes up a study of history to dig underneath the assumed universal principles of the encyclopedists to "unveil modern scholarly pretentions for what they really are."[31] In contrast to the encyclopedic assumption of progress, the genealogists argued that the notion of progress was rooted in telos, which itself can only be posited contingently and cannot be determined universally by universal methods, and that no cosmopolitan view of progress was achievable. Moreover, there could be no neutral objectivity, because there was no view from nowhere. We cannot view the world impartially, free from our particular context and personal histories.

When the genealogists are charged, as they often are, with appearing to make claims and conduct inquiries into the truth of things that require the same sort of arguments used by the encyclopedists, they reply that they are actually just playing along in order to unmask the universal claims of the encyclopedists

---

28. Midgley, *Myths We Live By*, 7.
29. MacIntyre, *Three Rival Versions of Moral Enquiry*, 24.
30. Peters, *Logic of the Heart*, 22.
31. Rowe, *One True Life*, 180.

and reveal them as parochial expressions. It is easy to see how the genealogical approach helped open the door to subjective feelings taking center stage today. For if there is no way to settle disputes by appealing to a shared rationality and to universal principles, then what, besides our own personal preferences, are we left with? MacIntyre sums up where this leaves us:

> So we have matched against each other two antagonistic views. The encyclo-paedist's conception is of a single framework within which knowledge is discriminated from mere belief, progress towards knowledge is mapped, and truth is understood as the relationship of *our* knowledge to *the* world, through the application of those methods whose rules are the rules of rationality as such. Nietzsche, as a genealogist, takes there to be a multiplicity of perspectives within each of which truth-from-a-point-of-view may be asserted, but no truth as-such, an empty notion, about *the* world, an equally empty notion. There are no rules of rationality as such to be appealed to, there are rather strategies of insight and strategies of subversion.[32]

Given these options, between the genealogical approach—which, when its own sword is thrust against it, fails to escape the blade of deconstruction—and the encyclopedic approach—which clearly affirms universal truth, with humans having a singular, substantive rationality by which to find it—it is understandable that encyclopedic reasoning has held sway for the past two hundred years over much of Christian apologetics. But these aren't the only two paths. All Christians should indeed affirm there is a universal rationality, held by God himself. Yet, by failing to recognize the contingency of human rationality, the finitude of our interpretations of the world, and the impact of sin, apologists have routinely used an encyclopedic approach that, as MacIntyre has shown, can no longer be justified.

So, if the encyclopedic approach cannot be salvaged as a method for settling disputes between rivals, each with their own metarationality, where does this leave apologetics?[33] In other words, how might we overcome the problem of nontransferability so that we can present arguments that will not ineffectively fly past the different rationalities of our interlocutors but will actually register and persuade? MacIntyre suggests a way forward that avoids the self-inflicted problems of a genealogical approach and thereby eschews an arbitrary irratio-nalism or relativism. His third option, which involves comparing traditions—with "traditions" including communal *habits* of thinking and *patterns* of action—asks which tradition has the most explanatory power and the greatest ability to

---

32. MacIntyre, *Three Rival Versions of Moral Enquiry*, 42.
33. MacIntyre, *Whose Justice?*, 399.

provide resources to meet challenges: "The rival claims to truth of contending traditions of enquiry depend for their vindication upon the adequacy and the explanatory power of the histories which the resources of each of those traditions in conflict enable their adherents to write."[34] For our purposes, MacIntyre's third option provides a framework by which to retrieve *Confessions* and *The City of God* for contemporary apologetics, a framework that is also to some extent anticipated by these works. In the remainder of this chapter, we provide examples to display how Augustine's approach enables us to meet the challenges of competing rationalities in our pluralistic world. But first, back to our pagans.

### Our Modern Pagans

The challenge for apologetics of the nontransferability of rational frameworks is even greater given the Remix culture of the twenty-first-century West. The openings left by the critiques of an encyclopedic rationality and the undermining of Christendom have been filled by new authorities that insidiously shape the way we imagine the world—the desires and narratives that we reason from and within. The media and consumeristic forces have been happy to swoop into the space left by the dominance of Christianity and offer grand stories and promises of "salvation," forming our visions of the good and beautiful toward their shows, products, and services. Burton describes the resulting shift:

> Seventy years ago—at the height of institutional, mainline Protestant America, our social options were relatively narrow. We could participate in the culture of our hometown and our family. Or, more rarely, we could participate in one of a few subcultures available to us. If these cultures, these communities, these foundational truths didn't satisfy us, we had little recourse: we'd either adapt or consign ourselves to a life on the margins. But now, we have access [through the internet] to people across the country and the world who think and feel and want the exact same things that we do. And we participate in a culture that incentivizes this individualism, which necessarily extends into our religious and spiritual lives. Why force our beliefs into a narrow category of organized religion, with its doctrines and creeds, when we can cobble together a metaphysical system that demands of us no moral, ethical, spiritual, or aesthetic compromises?[35]

---

34. MacIntyre, *Whose Justice?*, 403. Also see Terry Pinkard's summary of MacIntyre's view of the relationship between reasoning and tradition: "Reasoning is always carried out in terms of shared, socially established standards and in light of what he calls a 'tradition' (a more or less technical term for him, meaning an inquiry directed toward a truth independent of the inquiring mind, whose normative standards are developed over time in light of the problems, anomalies, and clashes with other such traditions that appear in its history)." Pinkard, "MacIntyre's Critique of Modernity," 185.

35. Burton, *Strange Rites*, 88.

As post-Christian sensibilities are formed by a consumeristic individualism that sees personal choice as an ultimate end, Christianity, with Christ's call to die to self and the religion's own checkered past, is deemed the villain of a drama that the West is only beginning to be liberated from. Whether it be the encyclopedist champions of Enlightenment humanism casting aspersions on religious superstitions, the therapeutic spirituality of the progressive Remixed rejecting the structured norms of institutional religion and its suppression of personal identity, or some combination thereof, a normative coming-of-age story with a value-laden telos frames their logic and rejection of Christianity. "Normative" is an apt description because proponents of these worldviews express a moral duty to progress to a superior state. This is evident by the use of terms and phrases like "progress," "human flourishing," and "the right side of history." That their reasoning is guided by unprovable assumptions and toward certain value-laden ends would not take Augustine off guard. For Augustine, as we've seen, "reasoning is an activity of rational agents pursuing some end. The pursuit of any end for Augustine involves the will, for it is the will by which rational agents choose among alternatives and seek to satisfy some desire." Thus, "reason," as Peters aptly summarizes, is not to be "thought of as a mere blind machine, indifferently processing data," but rather as "seeking an end and thus as being passionate and desiring."[36]

The question then becomes how we reason with people in a you-do-you therapeutic culture, which assumes instrumental logic and the freedom to pursue personal preferences as a telos.

If we invite modern-day pagans to simply look more closely at a form of encyclopedic rationality, they won't have much incentive to take us up on the offer, and if they do, this kind of rationality will be unlikely to make much sense to them. As C. S. Lewis warns in *The Abolition of Man*—written in the 1940s!—"fact" has long been severed from "value" in the modern social imaginary.[37] Many of the Remixed would opt out of the proposal of an encyclopedic thought experiment to go on living their life, pursuing what they feel to be fulfilling and imagine to be good, their moral and aesthetic visions being formed not according to syllogisms but rather along the logic of the dominant cultural narratives in which they live and breathe and have their being. And if we turn to the encyclopedist atheists of our day, we still have a problem if we attempt to wield an encyclopedic sword against them. For we'd be entering into this contest on turf that has been shown by the genealogists to be irreparably

---

36. Peters, *Logic of the Heart*, 71.
37. Lewis, *The Abolition of Man*. This is akin to what MacIntyre labels "emotivism" in *After Virtue*.

damaged, that is littered with naturalistic assumptions and utilitarian logic on which Christianity stumbles, and that may be allowing their normative value judgments to remain underground.[38]

Apologists who maintain an encyclopedic rationality in practice and attempt to sideline judgments about the good and beautiful to use "just the facts" will continue to be frustrated by the various forms of modern pagans and their rationalities. This is because, in reality, our moral and aesthetic judgments can't be so neatly separated from our intellectual judgments as they pertain to the big questions of life. Today we need an approach that faces the problem of non-transferability and also avoids wrongly imagining that humans in general—no less our late-modern Remixed neighbors—will, can, or even should bracket out their aesthetic and moral registers when deciding what to give their life to.

## An Augustinian Approach

So we once again turn to Augustine. We acknowledge that the new paganism of our time isn't a mirror image of the ancient paganism Augustine knew so well, but, like classical paganism, modern paganism is devoted to the immanent rather than the transcendent. As Augustine joins us in our pluralistic context, with competing rationalities and rival aesthetic takes in play, he would agree that a narrow encyclopedic approach will not do. It would not have worked for the pagans in Augustine's day either. Augustine had to learn, as Gerald O'Collins explains, to be "rhetorically sensitive to the capacity and interests of various audiences" and convince them of the truth not just by historical data or bits of logic but by "appealing to their imaginations and emotions."[39] Because Augustine had this holistic understanding of persuasion, he used words as surgical tools rather than blunt instruments to reason with the hearts and minds of ancient pagans. As we explore his approach, we will pause along the way to look at some contemporary figures—Catholics and Protestants representing different vocations and academic specialties—who do not fit neatly into the current dominant apologetic schools and who, as we will see, bear an Augustinian family resemblance. In doing so, we will pull on the strands woven throughout the previous chapters and give language to an approach that has an ancient pedigree and is now reemerging, recalibrated to meet the challenges of a new context.

---

38. For examples of this in the work of Steven Pinker, Jonathan Haidt, and Joshua Greene, see J. D. Hunter and Nedelisky, *Science and the Good*, 119–37.

39. Here we are compressing two different sentences (parts of which are quoted directly) in a way that we believe faithfully captures O'Collins's point. See O'Collins, *Saint Augustine on the Resurrection of Christ*, 32–33.

Augustine understood that persuasion was an art more than a science and that different people in different contexts needed to be engaged at different levels with different kinds of arguments.[40] This is especially important for us to take note of considering the piecemeal approach of many of our Remixed neighbors. Such diversity calls for a nimble approach, and Augustine's sprawling corpus testifies to his ability to adjust the way he argues according to the situation and context. And yet, within *Confessions* and *The City of God*, which were written with multiple audiences in mind, a general approach is discernible—one that can be retrieved to provide a framework for apologetic engagement today.

On the surface one could wonder about the links between the two works as well as their apologetic value. For the casual observer, *Confessions* might at first glance appear to be a rather strange spiritual autobiography. Looking back at his life, the famous bishop fixates on seemingly inconsequential events,[41] is prone to apparently meandering asides, and closes with four lengthy books that feel to many like disjointed philosophical musings. *The City of God* is in danger of being read narrowly as a political manual that oddly lacks a concrete, clearly applied political theory and that is laced with digressions. These superficial "hot takes" on Augustine's most celebrated works settle for shallow appraisals and attempt to force modern literary expectations on them both. Moreover, the modern apologist exploring these works in hopes of mining them for golden nuggets of syllogistic arguments that can be cleanly extracted and carted out for use today will not only be disappointed but also be in danger of missing Augustine's rhetorical strategy. Yet, as the bishop joins us at our apologetic table, if we sit patiently with him it will soon be evident that he knows exactly what he is doing and that he does it effectively. As we reach the climax of this work and turn to examine the structure and form as well as the overlapping aims and features of *Confessions* and *The City of God*, we will now see an Augustinian apologetic method emerge.

### Holistic Persuasion: Narrative, History, Feelings, and Logic

Both *Confessions* and *The City of God* have the goal of moving the reader—his mind, beliefs, and affections—toward God, and they employ story as the governing framework for doing so. Summarizing with extreme brevity, Augustine explains in *Revisions* his intentions in writing *Confessions*: "The thirteen books of my confessions praise the just and good God for both the bad and the good that

---

40. This is a central point used in support for the thesis argued in Harrison, *Rethinking Augustine's Early Theology*.

41. To mention just two examples, consider the amount of attention he gives to his prank of stealing pears with a group of other adolescent boys and to his sexual escapades, which are rather mild for a young man in his prime.

I did, and *they draw a person's mind and emotions towards him.*"[42] In this concise description, we are reminded that confession, prayer, and worship are central features of his work. It doesn't occur to Augustine to draw sharp boundaries between a work offering personal confessions and one making apologetic appeals. *Confessions* does both. With the reference to the "bad and the good that I did," he alludes to the central story line of the first nine books. His personal narrative—his birth, the twists and turns of his childhood in a half-pagan, half-Christian home, his departure from his mother's catholic faith, his many little conversions, his reconsideration of Christianity, and his eventual baptism—functions as the scaffolding supporting the work.

Why structure the first nine books of a work dedicated to drawing hearts and minds to God around his own story? Augustine understands people, as Brian Stock explains, as "ceaselessly engaged in mimetic interplay with the persons that they want to be."[43] Augustine knows that humans use their memory to interpret their selves by way of a story and that they look to those around them (à la their social imagination) to provide the hermeneutic. People understand themselves by reading their personal histories through the lens of hero stories they inherit from communities around them.[44] This enables them to link their past experiences along a plotline that then directs their responses in daily life and aims them in certain directions. To put this differently, Augustine is aware that his listeners tacitly see themselves on a quest for something more, whereby they envision their own selves on a historical trajectory toward certain goals. And these goals are based on what they largely assume to be the good, which is judged on the basis of what they absorb from the narratives, symbols, and practices they are surrounded by. "They thereby," as Stock says in explaining Augustine's understanding of humans, "attempt to introduce into their insubstantial narratives something that has both the form and substance that is capable of raising them upwards" to reach these aims.[45] When *Confessions* is seen through these anthropological insights, a reason for the book's form and approach becomes transparent.

Augustine narrates his own story, itself both a profession to the God who is capable of "raising them upwards" and a confession of his own disordered desires

---

42. Augustine, *Revisions* 6.33 (emphasis added).

43. Stock, *Augustine the Reader*, 35.

44. Brian Stock explains Augustine's understanding of the relationship between the individual self and narrative: "If language, from which reading and writing derive, is definable through a community of speakers, then selves, souls, or minds, which depend on language for their human expression, have to have their communities too. Their lives consist of what Charles Taylor calls a 'web of interlocutions.' . . . His story hovers between thought and the world before it enters the world in words that are intended to be interpreted by others. *Confessio* becomes *narratio*, and it is retransformed into a mental confession by its readers." *Augustine the Reader*, 16.

45. Stock, *Augustine the Reader*, 35.

and intellectual errors, which God providentially sorts out in order to heal his soul and open his eyes to divine truth. The narrative functions as a mimetic cautionary tale. It is a subversive coming-of-age story for his time, fashioned after the primordial Adam and after Luke's prodigal son, who travels through the heartaches, misery, and irrationality that come from claiming independence from the Father and feasting with the pigs. Turning contemporaneous coming-of-age stories on their head—such as those illustrating the Manichean mockery of faith carried out in the name of reason—Augustine reveals these moral tales to be more akin to juvenile myths. In their place he offers a better coming-of-age story. For while his mother's piety, which he was once embarrassed by, was quaint, he narrates in the end how she turned out to be more reasonable than his younger self. His sophisticated training and lofty rhetoric, he confesses, functioned as a veneer for his misguided search for love and enlightenment in all the wrong places. Augustine tells his story in a way that would speak to his younger self— who flirts with the rationalism of Manicheism, demands hard proof without faith, and chases the glories that the Roman story of achievement promises—allowing him to show the abyss to which these rival pursuits ultimately lead.

At the same time, *Confessions* offers readers someone they can want to grow up to be. In the story he tells about himself, they can see, as Augustine saw in the pious and erudite Ambrose, that coming of age does not mean casting out faith but rather should involve learning how to reason and feel within the right kind of faith. Humility as opposed to pride is the key to true intellectual maturity and spiritual wisdom. It should then come as no surprise in book 8, after his ecstatic Neoplatonic experience ultimately proves unsustainable and his critical inquiries are unable to move his will, that it is the biographical conversion stories of Ponticianus and Victorinus—whom Augustine tells us he "was fired to imitate"—that convince him.[46] *Confessions* is intended to serve the same persuasive purpose for its readers.[47]

---

46. Jennifer Herdt comments on Augustine's use of these two stories, "Augustine draws on the common inheritance of the Roman rhetorical tradition in his use of exempla, narratives that present actions or attitudes to be imitated or avoided. Exempla were recognized as having particular persuasive and exhortative power, rendering thoughts clearer, more vivid, and more plausible. For Augustine, though, exempla are no longer simply a way to inspire imitation of human virtues but the site of the creation of desire for God." *Putting on Virtue*, 67.

47. Likewise, Hauerwas rightly sees the connection between story, community, and exemplars in persuasion: "In particular practical reason requires acknowledgment of authority, but authority depends on the existence of an ethos that is founded on argument and makes continuing argument possible. Such an ethos consists in narratives that constitute the memory of a community and consequently establish the community's future. We become ethical agents through membership in such communities by initiation of texts and exemplars of the past. Narratives are, therefore, invitations for inclusion. That is why lives matter for the embodiment of narratives as well as for their testing and revision." *With the Grain of the Universe*, 250.

Augustine tells of his own rational, historical, and psychological journey from his departure from the church and back. Within this narrative structure, the intellect matters to Augustine. Through his own pilgrimage, he offers a "Socratic defense of his faith,"[48] inviting readers into his questions and objections to the catholic faith and into his discovery of sufficient responses. History likewise matters within his approach. He offers a historical narrative, recounting events in his life—though they are not always necessarily to be read literally, and certainly these events are interpreted through the eyes of a middle-aged bishop looking back through the lens of his Christian faith. *Confessions* is also psychological. Augustine describes what he thought and felt as he struggled to make sense of his life, was plagued by anxiety, and mourned over the loss of friends and family. Feelings matter for Augustine. They are to be explored, because when they are properly diagnosed, they are a pathway to truth.

His confession of misguided thinking and disordered desires eventually winds its way to the point of showing what it means to encounter God and to live in the present as a believer, and the closing books consider how believers can interpret the world through the opening and foundational scenes of the Christian story. Maria Boulding's explanation of the much-discussed relationship between books 1–9 and books 10–13 aptly summarizes a possible structure of the work: "The prodigal wanders away from God, plunges into misery and frustration, and finds his way back in tears [books 1–9]; but this is the story of all creation writ small [books 10–13]. Augustine's personal story can be read as a particular exemplification of his thesis throughout the last books: that only in turning back to its creator can the creature, sunk in its own darkness, instability, and formless futility, find its destined happiness."[49] In sum, Augustine takes up his personal history and rational reflection to bend people's minds and affections toward God.[50]

As with *Confessions*, Augustine's strategy in *The City of God* is to offer a story, albeit one with a much larger scope. Rather than a personal narrative testimony, it is a far-reaching epic that deconstructs the dominant historical and metaphysical story lines of his sociohistorical context. John O'Meara describes *The City* as "a book which applies Augustine's personal experiences, recounted in the *Confessions*, to the canvas of all mankind."[51]

---

48. Peters, *Logic of the Heart*, 77.

49. Boulding, introduction to Augustine, *Confessions*, 23.

50. "Augustine's story is a narrative demonstration of the failure of autonomous reason and the transformation of the human heart by divine love. And it is a narrative account of the reasonableness of faith, since only through faith can we hope to complete the rational journey toward wisdom." Peters, *Logic of the Heart*, 77.

51. O'Meara, "Virgil and Augustine," 32.

Reminding us that *The City of God* is no dispassionate theoretical exercise, Augustine explains that he started "burning with zeal for the house of God" in response to the pressing apologetic challenge of his day: the need to "answer to their [the pagans who blamed Christianity for the fall of Rome] blasphemies and errors."[52] In his first letter to the unbelieving Firmus, he asks him not only to read all the books of *The City* but to give them to others who "want to be instructed about the Christian people" or "are trapped in some superstition."[53] In a follow-up letter, Augustine makes clear to Firmus that he has written the books of *The City of God* not with the intent of "delighting the reader or making someone know many facts" but for the purpose of "persuading either a person to enter the city of God without hesitation or to remain there with perseverance."[54] For Augustine, apologetics is to be in service of evangelism. His aim in *The City of God* is nothing less than to convert non-Christians and save Christians on the brink of deconversion.

The first five books of *The City of God* respond directly to the pagans who nostalgically argue that Roman citizens should "make the empire great again" by shunning Christianity and returning to the gods who will allow them to flourish as in the imagined golden age of Roman glory. In response, Augustine out-narrates this cultural narrative by using their own sources to recount a more accurate, deflationary account of Rome's founding and history. These opening books also respond to the existential and logical problem of suffering in light of the evils committed against Christians during the sack of Rome. After focusing on the most influential Romans, with Virgil and Varro taking center stage, in the closing books of part 1 Augustine enters into the world of the most revered philosophers of his time, the Platonists.

Then, in a manner reminiscent of *Confessions*'s pivot from critiques of other belief systems to reflections on the Christian faith, the second half of *The City of God* turns from a critique of Christianity's rivals (books 1–10) in order to offer a better account of history, humanity, and the ends to which people were created (books 11–22).[55] Augustine does this by quite explicitly turning to Scripture. This pivot can be seen, for instance, in the contrast between his sources in the first ten books, in which he cites pagan sources far more frequently than he does the Scriptures, and his sources in the second half of the work, in which the vast majority of the references come from the Bible. His approach in part 2 is to follow the trajectory of the biblical story to trace the origin, development,

---

52. Augustine, *Revisions* 43.70.
53. Augustine, *Letter* 1A*.2.
54. Augustine, *Letter* 2*.3.
55. Harrison (*Augustine*, 206) suggests further possible structural similarities between *The City of God* and *Confessions*.

and destiny of the city of God in comparison to those of the earthly city, arguing throughout for the superiority of the former city over the latter.

### A Contemporary Example: Charles Taylor

A contemporary Augustinian use of narrative at a macro and micro level is on display in Charles Taylor's *A Secular Age*. Taylor recognizes that, to be effective, he must engage the larger narratives that often work under the radar and frame the operative logic of his rivals: "We can't avoid [master] narratives. The attempt to escape them only means that we operate by an unacknowledged, hence un-examined and uncriticized, narrative. That's because we (modern Westerners) can't help understanding ourselves in these terms. . . . Our narratives deal with how we have become what we are; how we have put aside and moved away from earlier ways of being."[56] So when people say things like "That approach is medieval" or "That's a progressive thought" or "She is ahead of her time," they are assuming a narrative arc that should be progressing toward certain aims.[57] Taylor, therefore, explains his strategy: because "various tellings of the story of how we have become carry this sense of secularity as an inevitable consequence,"[58] we must counter these with "another story."[59]

Recalling the way in which Augustine's pagan contemporaries leveraged nos-talgic accounts of Roman glory to attack Christianity, modern-day encyclope-dists spin a tale of the Enlightenment's glory, with reason and science pushing religion further to the margins while ushering in the material and medical goods of our modern world.[60] And as the Roman pagans cast blame on the Christians for the fall of Rome, so too these historical narratives blame Christians as part of the counter-Enlightenments whenever the Enlightenment fails to deliver on its promises. Taylor exposes these versions of our shared history as "subtrac-tion stories," since they wrongly cast secular humanism and the best of the late-modern world as what remains once religion—with its socially constructed, superstitious, and oppressive myths—is subtracted. Taylor counters that actu-ally it is secularity that is socially constructed, and he retells the historical nar-rative in a way that better captures the complexities of that history, including the impact of religious reform and Enlightenment movements, answering the question of how we've arrived in a secular age.[61]

---

56. Taylor, afterword to *Varieties of Secularism in a Secular Age*, 300.
57. Taylor, afterword to *Varieties of Secularism in a Secular Age*, 301.
58. Taylor, *A Secular Age*, 29.
59. Taylor, afterword to *Varieties of Secularism in a Secular Age*, 301.
60. See, e.g., Pinker, *Enlightenment Now*.
61. Ashford and Ng, "Charles Taylor," 677. In this case, by "secular" Taylor means not a less religious age but rather an age when traditional religious faith is now only one possibility among many options.

Hence, we could apply Taylor's Augustinian approach to turn the tables on the subtraction story underlying the encyclopedist reasoning Steven Pinker uses in his *New York Times* bestseller *Enlightenment Now* to champion secular science, reason, progress, and humanism (and to pit them against religious belief).[62] To mention just one example of Pinker's subtraction story, he takes it as obvious that "life is sacred" and gauges his notions of progress and humanism on the basis of this principle.[63] But he never explains why he *believes* that this (theological?) statement is true. Given his commitment to naturalism, where does this value judgment come from? Moral sentiment? A leftover inheritance from a Western culture that once grounded such ideas in a divinely given sacred order?

It is not that science, progress, reason, and humanism magically appeared on the scene from nowhere during the Enlightenment. Where these values grew (and they didn't always) among the different figures and various Enlightenment movements, they relied upon the nutrients of a particular kind of Christian soil. Indeed, many Christians are still committed to each of these values precisely because of their faith.[64] And one would understandably wonder what will happen in the future if these values continue to be replanted further away from their native soil—without their original metaphysical and theological grounding. Moreover, Taylor's narrative reveals it is misguided to view reason and science as the primary engines driving the flight from Christianity. Instead, it was the moral aims and sensibilities, ironically, inherited from Christianity itself that ultimately led to the possibility of secular humanism. It was the sense, as Bruce Ashford and Matthew Ng put it, that "ordinary life, benevolence, active reordering, and instrumental reasoning," ideals developed within Latin Christendom, could be best achieved by secular rather than Christian means that led to the plausibility of secularism.[65] Hence, Taylor retells the historical story of how we've arrived in an age where belief in God is only one possibility among others, with the plotlines following the moral and instrumental reasons

---

62. Pinker's *Enlightenment Now* is a recently influential version of this story that is not directly taken up in *A Secular Age*, for it was written over a decade after the publication of Taylor's work. For a brief critique of *Enlightenment Now*, see Peter Harrison, "The Enlightenment of Steven Pinker," ABC Religion and Ethics, February 20, 2018, http://www.abc.net.au/religion/the-enlightenment -of-steven-pinker/10094966.

63. Pinker, *Enlightenment Now*, 213.

64. Pinker, of course, wouldn't have had to look far to find such Christians. For example, see Packer and Howard, *Christianity*, or Alan Jacobs's account of Jacques Maritain, T. S. Eliot, C. S. Lewis, W. H. Auden, and Simone Weil (Jacobs, *Year of Our Lord 1943*). In fact, it would be difficult to find a contemporary Christian intellectual who would not affirm reason, science, humanism, and progress, though they would doubtlessly see each operating differently than Pinker does.

65. Ashford and Ng, "Charles Taylor," 690. Ashford and Ng make a similar comparison between *A Secular Age* and *The City of God*.

secular humanism became a widespread option. And by offering this story in this way, he also shifts the apologetic conversation to a comparison of accounts and resources. Between exclusive humanism and Christianity, which makes the best sense of human experience and can "respond most profoundly and convincingly to what are ultimately commonly felt dilemmas"?[66]

In addition to offering a sweeping sociohistorical narrative that resembles *The City of God*, Taylor mirrors *Confessions* in recognizing the importance of personal and mimetic narratives in persuasion. He closes *A Secular Age* with a chapter entitled "Conversions," in which he tells the stories of "some of those who broke out of the immanent frame; people who went through some kind of 'conversion.'"[67] Like Augustine telling his own life story and the conversion accounts of others for apologetic purposes in *Confessions*, Taylor understands these conversion stories as a way for people to "take on a new view about religion from others: saints, prophets, charismatic leaders, who have radiated some sense of more direct contact."[68] Like Augustine, Taylor offers exemplars so people might see what it looks like and even imagine what it feels like to believe. And as James K. A. Smith observes regarding Taylor's final chapter, "The portraits *are* the apologetic."[69]

So far, we've sketched the basic literary contours of *Confessions* and *The City of God* to see how they share certain features and incorporate logic, history, and psychology to persuade along, and argue for, the Christian story. Yet, for us to hear Augustine clearly and to apply him effectively for today, we need to look at how he weaves these aspects together so we can discern his approach.

### Step 1: Exploratory Surgery—an Immanent Critique

The first step in Augustine's meta-approach is on display in *Confessions*: he interprets his past in order to invite others to journey with him as he tries on a life that follows the narratives of achievement and glory, Manicheism, skepticism, and Neoplatonism. He turns to their authorities—namely, the Roman poet Virgil, Faustus and the other books of the Manichees, Cicero, and the Neoplatonist books—to critically engage them as one who experienced them from the inside. Though *Confessions* is written with a Christian audience in view, by utilizing his training as a rhetor, Augustine layers his narrative so that it is relevant for multiple audiences, including those outside the church. A fifth-century

66. Taylor, *A Secular Age*, 675.
67. Taylor, *A Secular Age*, 728.
68. Taylor, *A Secular Age*, 729.
69. J. Smith, *How (Not) to Be Secular*, 133.

contemporary reading *Confessions* would have seen each of the aforementioned views as plausible options in competition with Christianity, just as modern readers of C. S. Lewis's *Surprised by Joy* might imagine themselves adopting the author's early atheism.[70] In books 1–8 Augustine testifies to how each of the world-and-life-views he adopted before returning to catholic Christianity ultimately failed to deliver on its promises, and he also recognizes how God providentially used each in his conversion, Neoplatonism in particular playing a key role. Augustine autobiographically reflects on the various faults of these other views and how he discovered these errors.

A few select examples illustrate this point. Augustine appreciated Faustus for his humility, yet the latter even admitted to not having the answers his followers believed he was capable of providing. The Manichees gave Augustine a way to process evil, but they critiqued caricatures of Christian doctrine, and their books failed to make good on their scientific and epistemological claims. Cicero's *Hortensius* inspired Augustine to seek truth, yet it lacked the name of Christ. When Augustine later tried on the Academics—at least as he understood them at the time—it led him only to "doubting everything and wavering."[71] And, as we've seen previously, for as much as he praises the Platonists for helping him address some of his intellectual problems concerning the nature of God and evil, their pride led them to attempt to ascend to God through a kind of disembodied contemplation rather than to humbly trust the incarnate God who had descended to mediate for them. Reaching for God on their own terms, Platonists refused the grace needed to cure the human condition, failed to account for the goodness of creation, and proved experientially unstable. In each case, Augustine comments on any common ground available, explains why he found the view attractive, or narrates how it marked an important moment on his journey. And yet each is revealed to lack coherence, explanatory power, or the ability to make good on its claims and aspirations.

This first step of internal critique is apparent also in the opening ten books of *The City of God* as Augustine takes up the Romans' key cultural and philosophical sources and invites readers to come along as he surgically explores their claims. He spends much of his time in these opening books responding to the pagan critique of Christianity, the one that initially prompted him to begin this work. The pagans' story follows a fairly straightforward plot: Rome's glorious rise and reign was due to the favor of the gods and the homage that was

---

70. For more on the parallels between Augustine's *Confessions* and Lewis's *Surprised by Joy*, see McGrath, *Intellectual World of C. S. Lewis*, 10–12.

71. Augustine, *Confessions* 5.25.

paid to them by Rome's citizens; by allowing worship of the gods to wane and a Christian age to emerge, the empire lost favor with the gods, and its citizens accepted a way of life that led to her downfall.

In response, Augustine offers an anti-nostalgic retelling of Rome's history, challenging the coherence and logic of the pagans' claims using their own sources of authority. For example, citing Virgil's *Aeneid*, Augustine asks why they would entrust Rome's fate to the gods who were defeated in Troy. If these gods could not protect Troy—though Augustine does not believe in the gods himself and merely follows the pagans' reasoning for argument's sake—why would they blame the Christian God for not protecting Rome? The pagans' own poets even acknowledge that their fallen gods failed to protect Rome. Augustine provides a long list of historical calamities that came upon Rome long before Christianity arose, again drawing on pagan authorities, to undermine the narrative that cast Christianity as the culprit for the recent disaster.

The theologian Charles Mathewes captures a significant strand of Augustine's argument: "There was no golden age of Rome. Roman rule and the empire it had gained were facts about the world, as much theological as political."[72] Christian beliefs were assumed to be wrong because the people's social imaginary had primed these elite pagans to believe that the Roman way and empire was the good. After all, they had embraced Roman exceptionalism, essentially saying, "We are the world's superpower and hope. The *pax romana* and our march to benevolently civilize the world testifies to the superiority of the Roman way." They reasoned within this normative narrative, which they had inherited through the glorious stories passed down to them along with the pagan practices and symbols that accompanied them. Augustine therefore understands he cannot just offer narrowly construed arguments for Christianity; he must first puncture their inflated story of Rome—the myth that their logic operates within. As we've seen, he does so through appealing to their own sources. But he goes further. Augustine levels the playing field, bringing to the fore the *faith* they have in their political and theological authorities, and then he digs deeper to deconstruct the underpinnings of their assumptions, a strategy that anticipates the nineteenth-century genealogists we saw near the beginning of this chapter.

As part 1 progresses, this political and theological critique increasingly takes center stage. Curtis Chang aptly summarizes Augustine's thesis: "Underneath Rome's rhetoric of justice was simply 'the love of domination, the greed for praise and glory.' Rome's underlying love of domination and greed for praise and glory recur over and over in Augustine's work."[73] Mathewes also elaborates on

---

72. Mathewes, *Books That Matter: The City of God*, 29.
73. Chang, *Engaging Unbelief*, 73, quoting Augustine, *The City of God* 5.12.

Augustine's approach: "All empires are eventually held accountable under God's sovereignty, for every empire eventually falls into the idolatry of self-worship. This theological interpretation of empire gives Augustine tremendous critical leverage—now the argument is not between belief and unbelief, but between rival forms of believing."[74] Four apologetic questions emerge: What are you ultimately seeking? Who do you trust to deliver it? How's that going for you? How will it end? Or, to stay in line with an Augustinian medicinal metaphor, What will make you whole? What physician are you trusting? What are the current results? What is the long-term prognosis?[75]

The Roman myth is not only historically inaccurate, even according to their own authorities, but it lacks explanatory power, is existentially unsatisfying, and fails to deliver on its promises. Those who have embraced it have put their faith in themselves and their own fallen *polis* to deliver peace, justice, and happiness, but these are promises it can never fulfill. The claims to such divine gifts serve only as a mask for their own *libido dominandi*. Self-worship leads to a lust for domination that is self-dominating. In Augustine's words, "In fact it is the very lust for domination itself, to mention no others, that ravages the hearts of mortals by exercising the most savage kind of domination over them."[76] It is widely recognized, as Chang points out, that Augustine "presents a political analysis that was stunningly original for its time and for centuries to come. He takes apart an entire civilization's ideologies to reveal them as masks for raw power."[77]

In the second half of part 1, Augustine turns to the question of the benefit of worshiping Roman gods for life after death. In doing so he takes up the account of the famous Roman intellectual Marcus Varro, whom Augustine himself lauds as "the most acute and undoubtedly learned man of all." Augustine, however, steps inside Varro's "three kinds of explanatory accounts of the gods"[78]—the mythical, the natural, and the civic—to deconstruct them.

Much to Augustine's approval, Varro denounces the poets' mythical stories as "lying fables." Augustine reads Varro as attempting to save his intellectual integrity and make room for the civic gods who prop up Roman society. But Augustine shows that Varro actually treats the popular civic gods in virtually the same way as the mythical gods he denounces, for the mythical and the civic are inseparable. In this regard, Augustine calls Varro to his aid: Varro knows the civic gods are also false myths, though he lacks the courage to say it outright

74. Mathewes, *Books That Matter: The City of God*, 29.

75. After writing these questions, we came across support for this reading in Peters, *Logic of the Heart*, 74–75.

76. Augustine, *The City of God* 19.15.

77. Chang, *Engaging Unbelief*, 74.

78. Augustine, *The City of God* 6.5.

and face the mob of public opinion. Augustine addresses him directly: "You desire to worship the natural gods; you are compelled to worship the civic. You have discovered other gods—the mythical gods—on whom you feel free to vomit out what you think, but in so doing you also splatter the civic gods, whether you want to or not."[79]

Augustine then goes on to take apart Varro's naturalistic theology from the inside. Augustine lists examples of incoherence in Varro's naturalistic account and demonstrates how Varro is unable to overcome the moral evils on display in his attempt to salvage the pagan myths through naturalistic interpretations. The bishop ends book 7 by offering a narrative that better explains Rome's civic gods: they were at one time just humans who were given the status of gods, a development that is best understood as nothing less than demonic. "Pagan religion is on the one hand a false social projection, but on the other a very real den of spiritual forces under Rome's foundation."[80] In responding to a critique of Christianity as the reason for society's downturn, Augustine recognizes the need to dig deep enough into the soil of Rome—hence his engagement with Virgil and Varro, both instrumental architects of the Roman social imaginary—to pull up the very underpinnings of Roman culture.

His strategy of offering an immanent critique is also on display as he steps inside the revered work of the Neoplatonists in the final books of part 1. We've seen already in chapter 4 and earlier in this section, in our discussion of *Confessions*, how Augustine avoids an all-or-nothing approach as he interacts with his rivals. In *The City of God*, Augustine likewise goes out of his way to praise the Platonists. He has left his dialogue with them until the final books of his exploration of other major contemporary options because Platonism serves as the closest stop on the way to Christianity; and, as we saw in *Confessions*, this was certainly the case in his own journey. He uses the Platonists to correct other Roman views and affirms their insights into the nature of God as well as their insights about the need to love God and to see by his light. The Platonists, Augustine writes, "have to some extent, as if through some faint and shadowy image, caught sight of what we should strive to attain."[81] In other words, they have intuitions that Augustine steps inside of and works not just against but also with. They can "see—if only from a great distance and with clouded vision—the country in which we should abide." And yet, he explains, they "do not keep to the path that leads to it," with the "path" referring to the "grace of God through Jesus Christ our Lord."[82] Understanding "grace" as attainable only by the intellectual

79. Augustine, *The City of God* 6.6.
80. Chang, *Engaging Unbelief*, 78.
81. Augustine, *The City of God* 10.29.
82. Augustine, *The City of God* 10.29.

elite, they are bereft of the knowledge of ultimate grace, which comes through the God who humbly became flesh, and thus their lives are characterized by destructive pride and a "false happiness."[83]

### A Contemporary Example: Christian Smith

In sociologist Christian Smith's *Atheist Overreach*, we find an Augustinian-style immanent critique. Smith explores the question "Do people who believe that we live in a naturalistic universe *have good reason* to believe in universal benevolence and human rights—that is, are they *rationally warranted* in asserting and championing such moral claims and imperatives?"[84] Smith is careful to note that his question is *not* whether naturalists can believe in such ideals and live accordingly. The answer to that question is clearly yes. Instead, the question is whether a person can hold to such values as "a rational, compelling, universally binding fact and obligation" rather than as "an arbitrary, subjective, personal preference."[85] Smith has chosen the late modern's highest ideals and deepest aspirations and then asks the questions, (1) Do these values "fit well with and flow reasonably from the facts of a naturalistic universe"?[86] and, (2) Will they be able to be sustained within a culture that has embraced this perspective? After surveying the leading secular theories, he answers the first question with a resounding no, and he's deeply worried that, given this negative answer, these values will steadily erode.

Smith observes that, while secular systems have practical merit in encouraging ethical behavior rooted in a morality of self-interest, they fail to provide a basis for universal obligations to strive for the good of all. To pose a specific and practical question in our own words, Why should, say, an American truck driver exert effort, sacrifice personal comfort, and expend emotional energy seeking the welfare of a South African child or a Mexican immigrant whose happiness is irrelevant to the truck driver's own well-being? Smith gets to the heart of the problem that secular theories face when they rely on self-interest as the rationale and motivator for high moral ideals: "If morality only exists to benefit us, then I will be moral with people I wish to benefit and who might benefit me."[87] Inside their own rationale, this is a logical conclusion. As for the second question, Smith explains that, in order to sustain such high moral ideals over time, a society that practices an ethic based on universal benevolence and human rights will need "at least

---

83. Augustine, *The City of God* 10.28.
84. C. Smith, *Atheist Overreach*, 48.
85. C. Smith, *Atheist Overreach*, 49.
86. C. Smith, *Atheist Overreach*, 48.
87. C. Smith, *Atheist Overreach*, 22.

implicit rationales in order for people to embrace and act on them over the long run."[88] In other words, imagine a scenario—we doubt you will have to work too hard—where a culture has been relying on sentiment or "common sense" to ground these high moral ideals but they are increasingly facing resistance. A growing number begin to question democratic values, seek to place authoritarian leaders in power, find cosmopolitanism revolting, and, in the spirit of "survival of the fittest," see concern for the weak as a weakness. Without an actual rational basis, such as belief in the *imago Dei*, a society desiring to maintain the aforementioned high moral ideals finds itself on shaky ground. An actual rational basis is necessary, and Smith shows that the leading atheists have so far, though not without great effort, failed to provide one. Smith is careful not to suggest that his argument proves Christianity is true and naturalism is false. Rather, his approach is to critique naturalists on their own terms, affirming their deepest aspirations but showing how their own account can't fulfill their most noble longings. In this way and in Augustinian fashion, he overcomes the problem of nontransferability and opens up the late-modern skeptic so that they might at least begin to want Christianity to be true.

In summary, the first step in Augustine's approach is to enter into his opponent's narrative to deconstruct it, revealing its internal conflicts and tracing out its existential implications. By modeling for us an approach that begins by entering into rival narratives and interacting with them on their own terms rather than assuming a singular rational framework or asking them to enter our rationality, he illustrates a way to overcome the problem of nontransferability so we can reason with modern-day pagans. Augustine offers a master class in using his opponents' sources of authorities and logic to bring them to what MacIntyre refers to as an "epistemic crisis"—motivating the person to consider what is lacking in their belief system, what is in contradiction, what is unlivable, and how the system fails to account for certain common observations and experiences.[89] Augustine does this at an individual level in *Confessions* through his own story and at the level of sociohistorical critique in *The City of God*, showing that the individual and the community that makes themselves or itself the absolute is doomed to eventually face problems with ultimate reality at multiple levels.

---

88. C. Smith, *Atheist Overreach*, 53.

89. See MacIntyre, "Epistemological Crisis," 453–72. He notes that "an epistemological crisis is always a crisis in human relationships" and that such a crisis is resolved "by the construction of a new narrative which enables the agent to understand *both* how he or she could intelligibly have held his or her original beliefs *and* how he or she could have been so drastically misled by them." *Confessions* and *The City of God* both offer this kind of narrative explanation.

### Prepping for Healing: More Than a Critique

If Augustine ended here with step 1 and we focused primarily on his critiques of other views or even of the foundations of an entire civilization, we might retrieve something along the lines of how one could use Carl Trueman's historical account, which, as we saw in chapter 2, traces the narrative leading to the late-modern social imaginary to show its contingency and incoherence. But Augustine isn't finished. After all, he's performing exploratory surgery, inviting the pagans to stay awake during the procedure so that they might see their internal problems and become willing to take the medicine the Great Physician offers.

Or, to build upon Chang's metaphor, Augustine enters in and deconstructs these competing narratives, not to annihilate them but to "capture" them within a Christian metanarrative.[90] As Chang explains, in *The City of God* Augustine offers "a metanarrative that contains stories within its story" and so "essentially weaves [the strands of the fallen earthly city with the glorious city of God] into a narrative net that will encompass the challengers."[91] This is a critical point. Augustine is not just showing that the competing narratives are simply wrong. He is also pulling on the strands of their narratives that are true, or at least closer to the truth, and the facts they get right and then reinterpreting them in a way that fits into the gospel story, a more capacious story with greater explanatory power.[92]

For example, Augustine reveals how, in the words of Rowan Williams, "classical society and classical political thought provide ideals for the corporate life of humanity which they cannot provide the means to realize." This critique of society having the "possibility of vision without transformation" has already been on display as he narrates his personal experience with the Platonists in

---

90. Chang, *Engaging Unbelief*, 66. Mathewes comments that, other than Scripture, the two most significant books for *The City of God* are Virgil's *Aeneid* and Augustine's own *Confessions*. Mathewes, *Books That Matter: The City of God*, 86–87.

91. Chang, *Engaging Unbelief*, 66–67.

92. This is the normal pattern for how theories gain prominence. Theories win the day by having the most explanatory power, which includes accounting for the truth in previous paradigms and offering better solutions to the problems and tensions with their predecessor's narrative. In this way, as Chang points out, conquering means not annihilating the other theories but incorporating their insights into a more capacious story (see *Engaging Unbelief*, 84–85). Alister McGrath notes that this is part of what J. R. R. Tolkien and C. S. Lewis meant when they referred to Christianity as the "true myth": it is "telling a story that places and accounts for other stories, and subsequently generating a set of ideas derived from this story." He also adds that this is consistent across disciplines, for proposed theories are "called upon to account for the existence of rival accounts of rationality and alternative narrations of identity and meaning—in other words, to account for something that exists outside that community, in terms of that community's own framework of meaning." *Territories of Human Reason*, 108.

*Confessions*.[93] A fifth-century Neoplatonist reading *Confessions* would be affirmed by Augustine's praise while also being challenged by the humility, incarnation, and resurrection of Christ. For, while Augustine uses their philosophy, he uses it to help prepare them to see that the best of their philosophy promises what only Christ can ultimately deliver. Even for an elite mind such as Augustine's, the ecstatic Platonic experiences are ultimately unsustainable and inadequate. Augustine's own story testifies that Platonism can function as a bridge but that travelers need more than an intellectual bridge to find their way home. They need a person.

While *Confessions* concentrates on the individual, in *The City of God*, as Williams explains, Augustine turns his attention to the social order itself.[94] Augustine's aim is not to destroy the partial or misdirected aspirations for societal harmony and justice wherever he finds them but to show how they can be fully realized only in God. *The City of God*, thus, could aptly be described as a wisdom war with the pagans that includes, as Agostino Trapè puts it, "opposing Christian wisdom to the pagan wisdom on which adherents of the old religions relied; bringing out what was valid and praiseworthy in pagan wisdom; and showing that all this is found more perfectly in Christianity."[95] So, while Augustine is performing exploratory surgery, he is doing so in a way that prepares the patient to be willing to try out the medicine of Christ as the cure for their ailments. But in order to bring healing, he cannot simply remain within their account, deconstructing and retelling their stories, for "the tragic flaw of pride dominates too much of his challengers' terrain, seizes too much of their heart. Their eyes must be lifted to a new land, their heart captivated by a new tale."[96]

### A Contemporary Example: Sarah Coakley

Priest and theologian Sarah Coakley, in her conversation with Robert Lawrence Kuhn, serves as an example of an Augustinian approach to engaging with a modern-day encyclopedist, who rejects the personal and existential in favor of allegedly neutral and independent approaches to the question of God.[97]

Though like any conversation this one has many different twists and turns, at least two strategies are discernible. First, Coakley steps into Kuhn's view and helps him see that his approach to the question is itself "contaminated" and is,

93. Williams, *On Augustine*, 116.

94. Williams, *On Augustine*, 116–17.

95. Trapè, *Saint Augustine*, 232.

96. Chang, *Engaging Unbelief*, 82.

97. Sarah Coakley, interview by Robert Lawrence Kuhn, *Closer to Truth*, episode 1103, "Why Believe in God?," aired July 14, 2015, https://www.closertotruth.com/episodes/why-believe-god. Again, thanks to Bailey (*Reimagining Apologetics*, 242–46) for making us aware of this video.

in fact, wrongly closing him off to the possibility of belief in God. Second, she persistently presses him on the very existential issues—such as desire, joy, and death—that he initially demurs as off-limits.

Kuhn opens by attempting to set the terms of the conversation: "Sarah, I will admit to you two things. One, I would like to believe in God, and two, I really don't. Why should I believe in God?" He's seemingly inviting her to line up her arguments while at the same time undermining any attempt at offering existential reasons to believe.

Coakley, however, wants to first know more: "My answer to that would be very different depending on what's motivating you." Like an effective counselor, she inquires about several possible motivations for even asking the question. Kuhn is reticent at first, but after some back-and-forth, he explains that while he'd like to believe in God for existential reasons, he fears he would be believing because of personal "desire" and would thus "fool" himself. Coakley, keenly aware of how one's overarching approach as well as one's desires and fears impact the way arguments will be received, asks him, "What are the conditions under which you could conceive of being drawn to believe in a way that you weren't duping yourself?"

He admits he doesn't know. Notice how Coakley has avoided rushing in to give proofs. Though she isn't against a wide range of arguments for God, this patience turns out to be wise. Such arguments would not rise to the standard of proof Kuhn requires. Later in the conversation he explains that in his view science gives us "objective reality that pretty much everyone agrees on" and seems to want the same thing out of arguments for God. Coakley thus knows she must work to have him reconsider his framework rather than simply argue within his own social imaginary. Through questions, she points out that his assumptions exclude the very way God could be working. Kuhn essentially has set the rules and then asks why God can't play by them.

Throughout the conversation, she comes back to the question "What do you seek?" and eventually explains why: "The reason I'm asking you this is not to trick you. . . . I don't in any way sneer at [arguments for God's existence] by the way. . . . But arguments as such, they would not engage you unless your will was somehow turned towards the reality that might lie somehow behind them."

Kuhn seems to understand: "So, what you're saying is that if there's some predisposition, some will to believe, that the arguments for God would be received in a different way. That's what scares me. That's exactly what scares me. That's what I don't want." What hasn't seemed to occur to Kuhn, at this point at least, is that a predisposition to believe only on his own terms works in a similar way but with the opposite effect. Coakley therefore replies by asking him to imagine a scenario: "Let's say God is reaching out to you in some way to work on this niggle, this niggle that you have, that you would like to believe in God, and let's say that there are some arenas of your life which have a sort of element of vulnerability in them of love, of desire, of pain, where God could get in. Under what condition do you think those might lead to something?"

She then gets to the heart of her critique to his approach. "You seem to be operating with an extraordinarily individualistic notion of the intellectual life in which you and you alone are responsible for everything you do and think." Kuhn admits, "So, that's one problem I may have," to which Coakley replies, "Yes, and this strikes me as not really true to any of our intellectual endeavors." In other words, as Augustine has taught us, in none of our intellectual endeavors are we *just* calculating the facts, especially not the big questions, such as, Is there a God? By allowing our conversation partners to imagine that they are approaching the big questions of life like a scientist looking under a microscope, we not only allow them to continue to believe something that is evidentially not true, but we close them off from a deeper kind of knowledge that goes beyond the shallow truths of basic data collection and rudimentary logic to questions of meaning, beauty, value, purpose, and, yes, God.

Coakley therefore continues, "It seems to me that the reason you haven't got very far in what you say is a desire to believe in God is that you have this rather strange, abstract, arid vision of a sort of space in which you would be completely uncontaminated by any previous authoritative—[Kuhn interrupts]." Coakley apparently is able to make a breakthrough, at least in that Kuhn admits that he can't be neutral on the matter of God and acknowledges he has, in a sense, been "contaminated" against religion.

She closes the conversation by emphasizing the value of traditional arguments for God, but only once his epistemological pride has been deflated and such arguments are framed by the existential concerns she is bringing to the fore. This final portion of the interview is worth quoting in full:

> So, I would want to say over against a huge number of moves in recent philosophy of religion and theology against arguments for God's existence that I would be very happy to lay out a range of arguments why it seems to me to be very rational to believe in God, including profoundly experiential reasons, which I suspect that you share a little bit more than you're owning up to at the moment. I just have that little feeling as a priest. And then I would say, "Let's look at these arguments," and then I would ask you the big existential question, which is, Where are true joys to be found?
>
> Which is to circle back to that question, What are you seeking? Because if these arguments simply add up to a range of quite arid abstract propositional possibilities, then they're not grabbing you existentially in the way that they would if you were actually prepared to put your life on the line in terms of

practices. Because I as a priest, I as a believer find that it is in silent waiting on God that ultimate transcendent reality impinges on me. And every time I do that, I think of it as a kind of rehearsal for the moment when I finally have to give over control, which will be the moment when I die, and as a priest I think rehearsing for death is actually one of the most important things we do as humans, because once we're no longer afraid of death, then we're no longer afraid of life. And you strike me as a person who is very interested in controlling what you believe in for fear that you might fall victim to some kind of Kantian heteronomy, where you would no longer be in charge, the captain of your own soul. But when you come to think of it, there's going to come a day when you're lying in bed, about to die, and that possibility will no longer be a fantasy that you can maintain. So perhaps what is a little bit different about the way I approach arguments for the existence of God is to think about the context of desire, transformative practices, and ultimate longing, which ultimately I think can't be fully taken account of in terms of totting up the relative value of arguments.[98]

Coakley thus, in the legacy of Augustine, models a way in which desiring, thinking, and trusting can be brought back together in the practice of apologetics to invite others to reconsider the explanatory and existential power of Christianity. As Augustine would, she encourages Kuhn to consider what he truly seeks: control, life after death, freedom from fear? By doing so, Coakley contests Kuhn's illusory ideal of a neutral observer and plants apologetic seeds that can be harvested if he is willing to try on the Christian story.

### Step 2: Holistic Therapy—Subversive Fulfillment through a Better Story[99]

Augustine's apologetic goal was never to simply win; it was to save. He was the doctor of grace in service to the Great Physician; his aim was to administer the medicine of Christ to heal not simply the intellect but the whole self. For as we have seen in chapter 3, and as James Peters concisely summarizes, "For Augustine, as well as Pascal, the rationality of faith is inextricably bound up with a concept of human nature as unhealthy and incomplete apart from divine grace."[100] Thus, his apologetic magnum opus is not properly said to have been written "against the pagans" as the subtitle to *The City of God* suggests. As Gerard O'Daly has compellingly argued, the phrase *contra paganos* ("against the pagans") was a later addition to Augustine's title. This addition threatens

---

98. Coakley, "Why Believe in God?"
99. The language of "subversive fulfillment" comes from Strange, *Plugged In.*
100. Peters, *Logic of the Heart*, 21.

to misrepresent Augustine's intentions.[101] *The City of God* was written for the sake of healing the pagans.[102]

By entering their narratives and critiquing them from the inside while also establishing that we all believe and thus all depend on external authorities, he reminds us that the genealogists weren't the first to make such arguments.[103] By leveling the playing field, an Augustinian approach deconstructs the modern-day encyclopedists' illusions of being able to make progress in understanding the big questions of life without faith of some kind. Yet, cutting through these rationalistic illusions is not an end in itself. Rather, the first step prepares interlocutors to consider the logic of the Christian faith, which Augustine will present by (a) inviting them into the gospel story by narrating how it explains the world and takes up their deepest aspirations and experiences in a redemptive narrative that leads to Christ while (b) offering ad hoc justifications and responses to objections along the way.

Another way to say this is that Augustine (step 1a) speaks *within* his culture's dominant narratives so he can be understood, (step 1b) speaks *against* these same stories to show they are deficient even on their own terms and are ultimately insufficient for those who rely on them, and (step 2a) *redirects* them toward Christ and the biblical story while (step 2b) offering positive support and responding to critics along the way. This second step is seen in how he incorporates pagan sources in both *Confessions* and *The City of God* not simply to critique them but rather to show that their true insights and deepest aspirations can be fulfilled only by Christ.

### Supporting Arguments and Responding to Objections

To understand how step 2b fits with the curative metaphor, imagine a doctor giving a patient the medicine that will heal them or a surgeon inserting a stint, only for the body to reject what is given to save the person's life, at which point the doctor needs to pivot and address the new problems that arise. For Augustine, offering supporting arguments and responding to critics from within the Christian narrative operates analogously. As Augustine seeks to persuade his listeners to take the medicine of the gospel story, he stops along the way to offer positive historical and creational arguments in support of the medicine and to treat objections where he senses the narrative is vulnerable to attack.

---

101. See O'Daly, *Augustine's City of God*, 273–74.

102. We are in debt to Charles Mathewes for emphasizing this point in his lectures, *Books That Matter: The City of God*.

103. He makes this point about belief and authority in both *Confessions* (e.g., 6.6–8) and *The City of God* (e.g., 11.3).

In a work that fills a lacuna in recent scholarship, Gerald O'Collins has brought attention to how, in Augustine's arguments for the resurrection, he appeals to "evidence from creation, from Christian history (including miracles and martyrdom), and the inner 'factors' that include the human hunger for happiness."[104] In *The City of God*, Augustine argues from "'the miracle' of the world and all the marvels we observe in it" for the plausibility of the resurrection.[105] Given such marvels of our world, which he lists, "why, then, would God not have the power . . . to make the bodies of the dead rise again?"[106] Augustine isn't offering a context-free argument. Instead, he is showing that for those who share the "background belief" that the marvels of creation originated with a creator of some sort, the resurrection should be viewed as no less plausible.[107] His arguments here do not *prove* Christianity, but they appeal to observations anyone can make about the natural world and invite listeners to see how these observations cohere with belief in the resurrection.

Augustine also uses history as evidence for the resurrection. He reasons abductively in search of the best explanation for how "a few obscure men, of no standing and of no education, were so effective in persuading the world, including the learned, of something so incredible."[108] O'Collins summarizes the logic of his historical argument: "Augustine argues from the visible *effect* which his readers could see for themselves . . . to the *only adequate cause* for this historical phenomenon, Christ's victory over death. Since the original witnesses to that resurrection were ill equipped, the success of their message of Christ's resurrection cannot be explained on merely human grounds."[109] Moreover, Augustine goes on to cite the testimony of eyewitnesses, the evidence of other miracles within the Christian community, and the witness of martyrs as historical reasons to believe in the resurrection.[110]

In both *Confessions* and *The City of God*, Augustine also regularly responds to potential critiques. Christians or non-Christians struggling with restlessness and doubt stemming from disordered desires, the problem of evil, what they view as the implausibility of the Old Testament, or the seemingly naive faith of a parent—all barriers to the faith Augustine wrestles with in *Confessions*—find in Augustine a figure who understands where they are coming from and responds to their objections autobiographically. And in *The City*, while he is

---

104. O'Collins, *Saint Augustine on the Resurrection of Christ*, 58.

105. O'Collins, *Saint Augustine on the Resurrection of Christ*, 38. See Augustine, *The City of God* 21.7–9.

106. Augustine, *The City of God* 21.7.

107. O'Collins, *Saint Augustine on the Resurrection of Christ*, 37.

108. Augustine, *The City of God* 22.5.

109. O'Collins, *Saint Augustine on the Resurrection of Christ*, 41.

110. Augustine, *The City of God* 22.7–10.

certainly responding to critics from the very beginning, in the second half of
the work he regularly halts his progress in the story to respond to objections
that threaten to undermine the logical or historical plausibility of his account
and offers support for "the truth of the history as it is presented to us in a most
faithful narrative."[111]

These observational and historical arguments can and should be updated and
expanded given the contextual developments in the fields of science and history.
Yet, our point is that Augustine uses forms of them and would almost certainly
advise us to use them in some form today within his larger apologetic framework. An Augustinian apologetic can make use of such historical arguments
as Richard Bauckham's case for the Gospels being composed of eyewitness
testimony, N. T. Wright's narrative and abductive argument for the resurrection,
Craig Keener's two-volume historical case for miracles, and Alvin Plantinga's
answering of defeaters and work on the compatibility of theism and science.[112]
At least the seeds of these kinds of arguments are found in Augustine's work,
and they should be applied as part of a wider Augustinian rhetorical strategy.[113]

### A Contemporary Example: N. T. Wright

A contemporary picture of an Augustinian combination of historical explanation, an epistemology of love, and the existential features of personhood is seen
in biblical scholar N. T. Wright's *History and Eschatology*, which one reviewer
has ranked as the "crowning achievement" of his illustrious academic career.[114]
However, this is no sterile academic volume; throughout, Wright the pastor-
theologian-apologist shines through. Like Augustine, he argues that the resurrection of Jesus is the best explanation of the historical data: "History, in other
words, matters; and thus Jesus and the New Testament ought by rights to be
included as possible sources for the task of 'natural theology.'"[115] But Wright is

111. Augustine, *The City of God* 13.22.
112. Bauckham, *Jesus and the Eyewitnesses*; Wright, *Resurrection of the Son of God*; Keener,
*Miracles*; Plantinga, *Warranted Christian Belief*; Plantinga, *Where the Conflict Really Lies*.
113. This also corresponds with Pascal's use of "proofs" as part of his Augustinian apologetic
strategy. See G. Hunter, *Pascal the Philosopher*, 188.
114. Wright, *History and Eschatology*. John Cottingham says this in an endorsement in the front
matter. The book is an edited version of Wright's 2018 Gifford Lectures.
115. Wright, *History and Eschatology*, xiii. Wright recognizes that "natural theology" can have
many different meanings, but he clarifies which conception he favors: "Is it the attempt to provide
a 'neutral' argument, acceptable to all, irrespective of presuppositions, leading to the existence of
God and perhaps to more specific Christian claims, in such a way as at least in principle to convince
the sceptic? Is it the attempt to sketch, from a Christian point of view, what such an apparently
'neutral' argument might look like? Or might it be a Christian account, 'reading backwards', like
Jesus retelling Israel's story on the road, to show how the 'natural' world had in fact been pointing, however brokenly, to the truth? It might try to be all of these. But something like the last of

quick to clarify, "I am certainly not attempting to revive the kind of rationalist apologetic that would seek to 'prove' the Christian faith by a supposed 'appeal to history.' History is far more complex than that. . . . Neither in method nor in results will I be following normal apologetic pathways."[116] By "normal" he means typical contemporary apologetic approaches; Wright doesn't fit neatly into any of the dominant schools we saw in chapter 2.

In addition to the historical arguments for the resurrection, another affinity with Augustine is evident when Wright submits "'love' as the missing link in those various modernist epistemologies which have either grasped at 'objectivity' as a form of power or retreated into a 'subjectivity' which is in fact a self-serving projection."[117] Though using different labels, Wright, too, is attempting to find a third way, following neither the encyclopedists nor the genealogists. And his epistemological critique and remedy sound rather Augustinian: "Modernism has screened out the dimension of 'love.' . . . But one cannot, I suggest, understand ordinary knowledge of the ordinary world without 'love' in this sense; which means that we must challenge *both* the reductionist visions which have done without 'God' altogether *and* the would-be 'apologetic' strategies which have tried to answer them."[118] Love is thus essential for the deepest forms of knowledge, and by allowing it to be placed out of bounds prima facie, apologists have ceded the game at the start.

For Wright, the historical claim of the resurrection not only unlocks another dimension of an "epistemology of love" but also opens "a new public world in which the questions raised by humans within the present creation can be seen as provisional signposts to God."[119] "The world opened by Jesus' resurrection is the *real* world in its new mode: the new creation which recontextualizes and reinterprets the old."[120] Thus Wright explores the "broken signposts" of our world, the "perceptions and aspirations of human beings across different times and cultures,"[121] with the resurrection serving as a way to make sense of what it means to be human. By interpreting justice, beauty, freedom, truth, power, spirituality, and relationships as aspects of the universal human vocation lived out in a variety of concrete cultural expressions, Wright argues that "the world in general, and human life in particular . . . seem to be pointing to some kind of deeper meaning; yet all of them together will not lead the unaided mind to God

these has, to my mind, most coherence, and that is what I shall be trying to sketch in the present chapter." *History and Eschatology*, 218.

116. Wright, *History and Eschatology*, xiii.
117. Wright, *History and Eschatology*, xviii.
118. Wright, *History and Eschatology*, xviii.
119. Wright, *History and Eschatology*, xvii.
120. Wright, *History and Eschatology*, 190.
121. Wright, *History and Eschatology*, 223.

who is the Father of the crucified and risen Jesus."[122] Therefore, the apologist is given an "explanatory task"[123] to uncover the paradoxes of life:

> The resurrection compels the fresh evaluation of the stories and signposts [available within history and culture], leading to the shocking conclusion that the place above all where the true and living God is revealed is actually in the event which appeared to destroy hope and falsify the story. . . . Precisely in their brokenness, the stories and signposts were gesturing toward the truth all along. This, I suggest, is why the crucifixion of Jesus—both the event and the story of the event—carries such power.[124]

In this approach to "natural theology," we meet an additional side of Wright that his historian and New Testament colleagues might be surprised by: Wright the Augustinian incarnational phenomenologist, appealing to universal human experiences and then reasoning through Christ. In doing so, he asks today's skeptics and pagans not to follow him down the customary apologetic roads built over the past three hundred years[125] but to join with Christians to see whether they might just be able to hear the "echoes of a voice, perhaps, calling us from just out of sight, telling us meanings at which we grasp but which always just elude us."[126]

### With, Against, and Beyond a Virgilian Social Imaginary

Now that we have outlined Augustine's apologetic strategy, we are ready to return to the concept of social imagination to see how he applies his therapeutic approach. In chapter 2 we saw how profoundly Virgil's *Aeneid* shaped and reflected the social imaginary of Augustine's context. Augustine's interaction with Virgil in both *Confessions* and *The City of God* serves as an example of how he uses this rhetorical strategy to persuade his pagan contemporaries as he ultimately moves beyond the narrative of the *Aeneid*. Sabine MacCormack stresses the role Virgil's masterpiece plays in both of Augustine's most influential works:

> In the *Confessions*, Augustine gave shape to his life as he remembered it . . . ; here the long journey of Vergil's Aeneas and incidents on that journey provided both a model and precedents to be rejected. In the *City of God*, Vergil was the spokesman of Rome, of Roman virtue and glory, and of Roman expectations,

122. Wright, *History and Eschatology*, 224.
123. Wright, *History and Eschatology*, 220.
124. Wright, *History and Eschatology*, 224.
125. Wright, *History and Eschatology*, 219–20.
126. Wright, *History and Eschatology*, 225.

as Augustine construed them, of life after death. . . . Throughout, Augustine's engagement with Vergil was propelled by the endeavor to see *beyond* what the great poet had said.[127]

As Augustine recounts his trip from Carthage to Italy and his journey to the Christian faith, he clearly echoes Aeneas's voyage: "But the goal of Aeneas, which was to find a home for his people and to found Rome, was no proper antecedent for Augustine's goal, which was to find God."[128] Augustine leaves no doubt in *Confessions*; it is his journey to find rest for his soul in God, rather than the quest for Roman glory, that is universally proper. And as with *Confessions*, MacCormack explains, "in the *City of God*, Vergil's Rome could be no more than a shadow, if that, of the heavenly city. The life of the saints in the heavenly city would be a social life, just as the life of the Romans in their city had been a social life, which Vergil and others had described, criticized, and extolled. Here also what Augustine sought was only indicated in some terrestrial and thus imperfect fashion, by what Vergil had said."[129]

The narrative of the *Aeneid* unfolds so that readers don't forget the rationality behind Rome's universal charge:

> But you, Roman, remember, rule with all your power
> the peoples of the earth—these will be your arts:
> to put your stamp on the works and ways of peace,
> to spare the defeated, break the proud in war.[130]

In the opening to *The City of God*, Augustine quotes the final phrase of this famous line, setting his narration of the Christian story in dialogue with Virgil. The introduction challenges not the Roman desires for peace and happiness and justice in their entirety, for he will go on to affirm versions of each within the Christian narrative, but *how* these desires are pursued and the existential repercussions of the Roman way of pursuing them. For while Christianity teaches that "by humility we reach a height . . . which transcends all these earthly pinnacles that totter with the shifts of time," the earthly city "seeks dominion, even though whole peoples are its slaves, [and] is itself under the dominion of its very lust for dominion."[131] Augustine will go on, alluding to the *Aeneid*, to show how humility, the way of Christ and the city of God, is the only path to true peace. For while everyone desires peace, "pride is a perverse imitation of

---

127. MacCormack, *Shadows of Poetry*, 227 (emphasis added).
128. MacCormack, *Shadows of Poetry*, 227.
129. MacCormack, *Shadows of Poetry*, 227.
130. Virgil, *Aeneid* 6.981–84 (trans. Fagles, 210).
131. Augustine, *The City of God* 1, preface.

God"[132] that puts oneself or one's tribe in the place of God and "hates a society of equals."[133] The result of the ensuing disordered affections is the feeling of pain as well as hatred and wars between humans, which all serve as indicators that something is not right.

Notice Augustine doesn't sideline their feelings but rather explores them and offers an interpretation: "For anyone who feels pain at the lost peace of his nature feels this due to some remnant of that peace by virtue of which his nature still shows its care for itself."[134] When human nature, even in its fallen form, rebels against God and the fabric of his created order, it eventually feels the consequences. But those who allow God to be God, humbly submitting to him while on pilgrimage to their true home with him, are able to live in peace, accepting the good things of this life as gifts without futilely clinging to them:

> God is, therefore, the supremely wise creator and supremely just orderer of all natures. He established the mortal human race as earth's highest ornament, and he bestowed on human beings certain goods suited to this life, namely, a temporal peace appropriate to the brief measure of a mortal life, consisting in bodily health and soundness, and the society of one's own kind, as well as whatever is necessary to maintain or recover this peace (such as those things which are readily and conveniently on hand for our senses—light, speech, air to breathe, water to drink—and whatever is suited to feeding, clothing, healing, and adorning the body). He did this, however, on the wholly just condition that any mortal who makes right use of such goods, which are meant to serve the peace of mortals, will receive fuller and better goods, namely, the peace of immortality and the glory and honor appropriate to it, in an eternal life meant for the enjoyment of God and of one's neighbor in God, but that anyone who uses them wrongly will not receive these eternal goods and in fact will lose those temporal goods.[135]

In summary, an Augustinian approach is *realistic*: in the present evil age, the good life is limited by a fallen world. Jesus's prescription to die to self can seem like a radical treatment, and experiencing grace will not always mean immediately "feeling better." Such an approach is also *hopeful*: as the gospel and nature proclaim, death leads to new life. The standard for the good life is Jesus, who is both the picture of human flourishing and the "man of sorrows." In a postlapsarian world, Jesus's life demonstrates that true flourishing is possible for us only when we are opened to the wounds of love, which will mean the agony of feeling a good creation gone wrong. But even the tears of sorrow

132. Augustine, *The City of God* 19.12.
133. Augustine, *The City of God* 19.13.
134. Augustine, *The City of God* 19.13.
135. Augustine, *The City of God* 19.13.

will be accompanied by hope: for to have the capacity to experience the deepest of joys, we must refuse to numb ourselves with the prescriptions written by late-modern consumerism and refuse to dupe ourselves with the hopes of human "enlightened" progress. The medicine of the cross serves as evidence that our suffering has a purpose. The remedy of the resurrection stands as a sign that our fleeting and fragile joys were always meant to direct our hearts to an eternal love calling us to himself. The Augustinian apologist reasons with our world about who we should trust to heal what is broken and fulfill our deepest aspirations. The claim of the Great Physician is that the wisdom of Christ is the way to restoration.

## Therapeutic Apologetics in *Confessions* and *The City of God*

In naming this chapter "A Therapeutic Approach," we mean two things.[136] First, Augustine diagnosed distorted aspirations within the narratives of his culture and sought to show how they could be fully restored only within the story of Christ. Second, in our age, when the goal of feeling better has become a central aspiration, our approach follows Augustine in diagnosing sin as a disease, exploring its ravaging effects on human life, and offering Christ as the path by which to begin healing in the present—though only fully realized in the eschaton.

This approach, which we saw in the previous section in relation to Virgil, is on display as a metadialectical approach throughout *Confessions* as Augustine signals to his readers that in his own passage through other competing views he discovered truths that he could still affirm, though they needed to be situated within a more intellectually capacious and existentially satisfying story.[137] The cure for his restlessness, as he declares in his introduction, will be found only in God. Beginning with his conversion in book 8 and continuing in books 9 and 10, Augustine reflects on Christianity from within his own experience as a believer, illustrating, with his own life story and his thoughts on memory, the answer to the question, What might it look like to live a life of faith in Christ?

---

136. Without by any means denying the legitimacy and proximate goods of contemporary therapy, an Augustinian approach would at times come into conflict with certain standards and assumptions of modern therapy. Or to put this differently, a spiritually healthy person should not simply be equated with a particular fallen culture's conception of a mentally healthy person. Augustine, as we've seen, would have us take a more dialogical approach, which includes both affirmation and challenge.

137. For even more support for the "therapeutic" in Augustine, see Kolbet, *Augustine and the Cure of Souls*; Brown, *Augustine of Hippo*, 151–75, 324–29, 375–77.

Through his depictions of his life as a believer, readers are invited to consider the difference that the grace in Christ makes to one's life:

> How you loved us, O good Father, who spared not even your only Son, but gave him up for us evildoers! How you loved us, for whose sake he who deemed it no robbery to be your equal was made subservient, even to the point of dying on the cross! Alone of all he was free among the dead, for he had power to lay down his life and power to retrieve it. For our sake he stood to you as both victor and victim, and victor because victim; for us he stood to you as priest and sacrifice, and priest because sacrifice, making us sons and daughters to you instead of servants by being born of you to serve us. With good reason is there solid hope for me in him, because you will heal all my infirmities through him who sits at your right hand and intercedes for us. Were it not so, I would despair. Many and grave are those infirmities, many and grave; but wider-reaching is your healing power. We might have despaired, thinking your Word remote from any conjunction with humankind, had he not become flesh and made his dwelling among us.[138]

By way of Augustine's introspective and personal narrative, readers are invited to imagine what it would feel like to live a life that hasn't arrived home yet but is on a pilgrimage compelled by the love of God. Then *Confessions* goes meta. In the first eight books, Augustine's story is woven together with the Scriptures, which suggests that his story is a microcosm of God's much bigger story. But with books 11–13, he zooms out to begin exploring the foundations of the larger biblical story and the philosophical questions of time and memory it raises.

As we've seen already in books 1–10 of *The City of God*, Augustine offers an internal critique of the Christian challengers, using their own sources, authorities, and terms. He "imaginatively entered into their worldviews, apprehending both their insights and what made them worry about his own views."[139] A clear shift occurs beginning in book 11 and extending through book 22 as Augustine invites his readers to try on the Christian story; the terms and authority in the second stage of his apologetic approach are explicitly drawn from the Scriptures.

Along the way, with keen linguistic sensitivity Augustine *converts* the popular pagan language of his day—including concepts such as "peace," "happiness," and "justice"—so that it fits within the Christian narrative and testifies to how these ideals are ultimately fulfilled only in Christ and his eschatological community.[140]

---

138. Augustine, *Confessions* 10.69.

139. Mathewes, *Books That Matter: The City of God*, 26.

140. Carol Harrison concludes concerning Augustine's relationship to the classical literature and culture of the Roman Empire in which he was educated, "He did not leave his past behind and attempt to root out any traces of it in his new Christian identity: he was too well aware of the futility of such a task and of the pervasiveness, importance, and usefulness of secular culture to make such an attempt. Rather, he attempted to come to terms with secular culture, to appreciate

For instance, he doesn't ask his reader to cease striving for happiness. The pursuit of happiness is a universal feature of the human race. Rather, he asks them to reconsider what happiness in our world means and how it should be pursued. So in book 19 Augustine sobers his readers with a long discussion of the miseries of this life. Even "innate goods" common in this life are fleeting, and our experience of them is undercut by the surety of our eventual loss: "The life, therefore, which is weighed down by the burden of such great and severe evils, or is subject to the chance that such great and severe evils might afflict it, should by no means be called happy."[141] Hence, this instinct to search for happiness in the midst of the inescapable suffering of this life leads Augustine to ask his readers to try on—intellectually and experientially—another kind of happiness:

> If anyone uses this life in such a way that he directs it to that other life as the end which he loves with ardent intensity and for which he hopes with unwavering faithfulness, it is not absurd to call him happy even now, although *happy in hope* rather than in this reality. Without that hope, in fact, this reality is only a false happiness and a great misery. For it does not make use of the true goods of the soul, because no wisdom is true wisdom if it does not direct its intention—in everything that it discerns with prudence, bears with fortitude, constrains with temperance, and distributes with justice—to the end where God will be all in all in assured eternity and perfect peace.[142]

Like Ted Lasso in this chapter's introduction, Augustine believes in hope too. In fact, it is the only way to true happiness and peace. What Ted and his fans are looking for exists. The moments of grace and forgiveness throughout the episodes are intimations of a divine source whom the human heart was made for. Yet, to be made whole they must learn to hope in the right way, looking through the gifts to cling to the giver.

Curtis Chang insightfully points to Augustine's apologetic telos:

> In *City of God* Augustine seeks to move pagans by showing them that their story properly belongs at a wider table. Like the master in Jesus' parable of the great banquet, he 'compel[s] people to come in' to his metanarrative. He compels by demonstrating that the pagans' deepest hungers, properly understood, can be satisfied only in this wider story. Thus for all his deconstruction of the challenger's story, Augustine does not obliterate it totally. He seeks to redeem it.[143]

---

but also to criticize; to assimilate but also to reject—in other words, to 'convert' it to Christianity."
Harrison, *Augustine*, 78.

141. Augustine, *The City of God* 19.4.
142. Augustine, *The City of God* 19.20 (emphasis added).
143. Chang, *Engaging Unbelief*, 86.

Within an Augustinian view of the creational goodness (though now also the fallen state) of all things, we can apply his approach today by searching for the shared features and experiences of humans that point as "broken signposts" to God.[144] By looking for overlapping interests and connecting points with his interlocutors, Augustine models how we can find common ground with our modern pagans. By stepping inside their account and finding ideas and aspirations that overlap with Christianity, we are able to relevantly appeal to their concerns and our shared humanity. Augustine thus, with this second step, provides a way by which we can show not just common concerns but how the deepest hopes and noblest ideas of our contemporaries will reach their fulfillment only within the true story of reality.

### A Few Contemporary Examples: J. I. Packer, Thomas Howard, and Charles Taylor

In 1985, the respected Anglican theologian J. I. Packer, together with his close friend English professor Thomas Howard, wrote *Christianity: The True Humanism*, a largely forgotten apologetic work. This was the same year that Howard announced his conversion from Anglicanism to Catholicism. Robert Webber, in a review from the same year, spotlights the cultural context that gave shape to the title and approach of the book. Five years earlier the Religious Right had begun to set its target on humanism as "public enemy number one."[145] Tim LaHaye and Jerry Falwell, to note just two prominent examples, had come out fighting head-on against humanism. Packer and Howard, however, took a different approach. Christianity, they explain, is not the enemy of humanism but the only path to the truest form of the human life. Their approach is not to bludgeon secularist humanists but, instead, to convert them.

To do so, Packer and Howard offer "a vision of Christian life as the only true, full, and authentic humanness" while pointing out where their rivals fall short. They argue that Christianity is *wisdom*—the path to the good life—in contrast to "folly."[146] Webber compares their approach to the second-century apologist Justin Martyr:

> *Christianity: The True Humanism* is similar in methodology, then, to the second-century *First Apology* written by Justin Martyr. His appeal to the emperor Titus to become a Christian was based on the very thing the emperor sought. Titus,

144. Wright, *History and Eschatology*, 217–49.
145. Robert Webber, review of *Christianity* by Packer and Howard, *Christianity Today*, March 1, 1985, https://www.christianitytoday.com/ct/1985/march-1/special-book-section.html.
146. Packer and Howard, *Christianity*, 231.

a man of enormous intellect, placed reason above all things. Justin called upon him to receive Jesus the Logos (reason) incarnate, the one in whom his life would find complete fulfillment. Packer and Howard, like Justin, are appealing to the humanist on the basis of what the humanist respects and desires most of all: a true experience of the human for himself and others. Come to Jesus Christ, the authors urge, for in him and him alone is found the true and ultimate source of humanity.[147]

The central apologetic question that guides Packer and Howard's book is, "What analysis, what story will account for our remorseless quest for identity, purity, peace, truth, beauty, joy, adoration, love and meaning?"[148] Webber is right to compare Packer and Howard with Justin on the basis of how they situate their arguments to appeal to what their particular audience "respects and desires most of all." However, with respect to the actual inspiration and source of their approach, Packer and Howard don't leave it in question: the book is, in their own words, "a footnote on Augustine's dictum: 'You made us for yourself, and our hearts are restless till they find rest in you.'"[149]

Since 1985, culturally the envelope has only been pushed further in embracing a therapeutically humanistic mode of life. In the midst of the consumerism and fragmentation that has come to dominate our society, people desire a way to cope with the disappointments of life, to live "authentically," and to find a deeper meaning to it all. Rather than refusing to engage opponents on the level of "authenticity" or rejecting the language of "therapeutic" wholesale, an Augustinian approach sees an apologetic opportunity. For example, Charles Taylor's *Ethics of Authenticity* models a way of entering into the therapeutic "you do you" ethos of progressive paganism, affirming certain aspirations while exposing their inability to fulfill their own ideals. Taylor doesn't simply chide modern-day pursuits of "authenticity" as nothing but selfish and narcissistic quests. Instead, while he critiques what he calls "expressive individualism"—the sense that the most profound way to be human is to do what *you feel* is right—he nonetheless recognizes in this feature of the late-modern social imaginary a desire that should be explored rather than simply criticized. This late-modern approach to purpose and identity is a corrective to the traditional hierarchal ordering of society, which narrowly limited social standing on the basis of birth and sex. Taylor's approach is to "enter sympathetically into [the culture of authenticity's] animating ideal and try to show what it really requires."[150] This would be music to Augustine's ears. And he surely would sing along with Packer, Howard, and

---

147. Webber, review of *Christianity* by Howard and Packer.
148. Packer and Howard, *Christianity*, 51–52.
149. Packer and Howard, *Christianity*, 231.
150. Taylor, *Ethics of Authenticity*, 79.

Taylor, reminding us that the quest for an authentic human life and the desire to be healed, which are prevalent within today's religiously Remixed landscape, are aspirations we can subversively work with rather than simply rail against.

### Many Tools in Service of a Single Aim

Aimed ultimately at redemption rather than destruction, Augustine's apologetic approach allows for flexibility. His is not what we would call today an evidential or classical apologetic, though, as we saw earlier in this chapter, he does give logical and historical arguments in defense and support of the faith. Neither is his approach simply narrative-based or aesthetic, though, as we've seen, he leverages narrative apologetically and appeals to "a knowing that is loving."[151] So James K. A. Smith is certainly correct when he stresses that "Augustine is writing [in *Confessions*] to the imagination, appealing to the affections, to *move* people into a different story" and when he understands Augustine to be giving "us the drama of narrative instead of the arguments of a treatise . . . because his apologetic is aesthetic . . . [and] Augustine knows the heart traffics in stories."[152] Yet, this doesn't capture the *whole* of Augustine's apologetic approach. As Augustine narrates the biblical story and shows how his opponents' longings make rational and existential sense within this true narrative of the world, he offers ad hoc arguments—drawing on metaphors, analogies, history, logic, and empirical evidence from nature—in support of his claims and in response to the critics. As we've seen, his approach is multidimensional, as is his theological anthropology and his diagnosis of the human problem. An Augustinian approach thus not only allows us to respond to the challenge of nontransferability but also provides us with the resources to engage relevantly with today's Remixed culture.

This leads to a central point of this chapter. While a clear framework has emerged, it is Augustine's apologetic *aim* that grounds the elasticity of this approach. His aim is not to bury the dead but to heal the sick. Rather than a battlefield with assassins or a morgue with undertakers, Augustine envisions the church as a hospital and himself as being in service to the Great Physician. Augustinian apologists go into surgery knowing they must cut, and they therefore bring along, as any skilled surgeon would, many different instruments—but the incisions are carefully made so the wounds are accessible to the healing balm of Christ.

---

151. This last phrase is Gerald O'Collins's description of how Augustine understands the Spirit to work with the "human hunger for happiness" as part of the bishop's "broad, triple-shaped apology for the resurrection." *Saint Augustine on the Resurrection of Christ*, 58.

152. J. Smith, *On the Road with Saint Augustine*, 173.

# Conclusion

## The Return of the Bishop

In the introduction we noted the surprising lack of direct engagement with Augustine, arguably the greatest postbiblical apologist in the history of the church, by those who have taken up the helm of contemporary apologetic leadership. This book has sought to fill this void by imaginatively teleporting Augustine into the present to see whether he might have something to teach us.

What have we learned from his return?

In Augustine we have met a sage pastor-theologian-apologist who grew up in and then ministered in a time that in some ways feels far away from us but that also features significant bridges to our present situation. In our imaginative scenario, upon his arrival in the twenty-first-century West, Augustine would discover innumerable differences between the world as it is now and his world of late antiquity. Modernization and the Enlightenment have happened, and the world cannot pretend as if they hadn't. In turning to Augustine for our apologetic retrieval, we have endeavored to call a great doctor of the church to our side to see how he might help us re-narrate our world *after* disenchantment—a situation Augustine never had to face.[1] And even if Augustine were to help the West return to organizing society around the Christian story, we would still at least know that we had run through the winds of secularism. If we benefit from the Augustine we have met in this project, he will have helped us *through* the storm of secularism rather than returned us nostalgically to the premodern period.

---

1. In fact, we live in a situation that no society has had to face—until now. As Philip Rieff explains, the "notion of a culture that persists independent of all sacred orders is unprecedented in human history." *My Life among the Deathworks*, 13.

Nevertheless, we've stressed that any discussion of Augustine's context that assumes that catholic Christianity was the default option fails to take into account young Augustine struggling through several different world-and-life-views in *Confessions*, the attention Augustine recognizes he must give to a range of pagan beliefs in *The City of God*, or his many writings *against* various groups threatening the church. The Italian scholar Agostino Trapè's remarks concerning Augustine's debates with the Manichees could easily be applied to his tireless engagement with various opponents: "His pastoral duty of responding to these accusations and errors . . . impelled him to . . . elucidate a wide-ranging metaphysical doctrine, explain the morality of the Gospel, defend the unity of Christian revelation, and provide solid apologetic arguments for it."[2]

Though we have focused much of our attention in this book on *Confessions* and *The City of God*, both were birthed out of Augustine's pastoral ministry— from which we can draw even more evidence for the apologetic pressures present within his context. In his sermons we hear a pastor facing "the constant presence of the unpersuaded, the indifferent and the downright disobedient."[3] In reading his homilies we find a preacher who is at times "struggling with all the rhetorical and didactic resources at his disposal to keep the Christian congregation from being absorbed back into a world in which Christianity had *by no means yet captured the cultural high ground*."[4] His ministry included challenges from people who would not easily digest the Christian story.[5] He had to constantly practice apologetics or risk seeing his flock wander away.

Still, we have not attempted to repackage Augustine's arguments hamfistedly, expecting something wondrous to happen. We can only imagine that if Augustine were by our side, he would rebuke us himself if we attempted a wholesale repackaging. For in the midst of epochal changes in the fifth century, Augustine remained faithful to the church's teaching while also demonstrating a willingness to hold certain exegetical non-load-bearing walls provisionally, to introduce nuance, and to calibrate arguments depending on the context.[6] His perceptive attention to his opponents and listeners enabled him to nimbly reach for their hearts, seeking not simply to convince but to convert. While

---

2. Trapè, *Saint Augustine*, 161.

3. Brown, *Augustine of Hippo*, 446.

4. Brown, *Augustine of Hippo*, 45 (emphasis added).

5. Brown, *Augustine of Hippo*, 445–47.

6. The terminology of "non-load-bearing walls" is inspired by Trevin Wax's reflections on Matthew Lee Anderson, "Will the Controversies 'Fade Away'?," Respectful Conversation, January 3, 2016, https://respectfulconversation.net/2016-1-3-will-the-controversies-fade-away-html. See Trevin Wax, "Is Marriage an 'Architectural Doctrine' of the Christian Faith?," The Gospel Coalition, February 29, 2016, https://www.thegospelcoalition.org/blogs/trevin-wax/is-marriage-an-architectural-doctrine-of-the-christian-faith.

he never departed from the rule of faith, staying the same wasn't an option for Augustine.[7] So rather than a spot to land on, Augustine has offered us a trajectory we have sought to follow, resources to build on, and a rhetorical strategy flexible enough to be employed in different contexts. The exemplars surveyed in chapter 5, for instance, imbibe the *spirit* of Augustine rather than abide by the *letter* of his arguments.

## Going Back for the Future

In order to hear what Augustine might say to us today, we first traveled back in time to appreciate Augustine's ancient world. Before entering fourth-century North Africa, we started in a surprising and, for me (Josh), a nostalgic time and place: the 1990s in Georgia. By opening here, we narrated what it was like to grow up in a modern context, experiencing (1) different available world-and-life-views that increasingly feel like livable options, (2) a growing moral imperative, accompanying the prospect of social advancement—especially with geographical moves to cities and cultural centers—to intellectually "come of age" beyond childhood religious experiences, and (3) the expectation that one will forge an identity rooted in merit and personal achievement. These are all common experiences for late moderns, and—as we saw—Augustine's early life was characterized by similar intellectual and existential pressures. Therefore, his journey to Christianity, by which he *worked through* these challenges with serious rigor and introspection, can help us today. The fact that Augustine relied upon the lessons of his conversion to respond in compelling fashion to a resurgent paganism later in life should not be lost on us.

Years after his conversion, Augustine the bishop, busy helping seekers and skeptics navigate the aforementioned challenges, had before him the formidable task of responding to the fall of Rome. The sack of Rome was an epoch-shaping event that wrought feelings that in some ways corporately mirrored the fragility and disintegration Augustine had once felt personally as he searched for peace. In the final quarter of his life, Augustine set out to bring peace to the restless soul of an empire as people felt the reverberating shocks of having their nationalistic hopes dashed, the grief that follows such terrible destruction and death, and the anxiety of a future that now felt miserably uncertain. For Augustine, the uncertainties were just as palpable. Who would wrest control of the highest places in society after Rome's fall? And what story would they tell? As Curtis Chang writes, Augustine "was well aware that this educated

---

7. Michael Fiedrowicz describes Augustine's thought as having a "continuity-amid-development." Introduction to *True Religion*, in Augustine, *On Christian Belief*, 16.

class of pagan challengers could define the dominant perspective of Roman culture."[8] Augustine knew the pagan elites could still assert power over the social imaginary, making Christianity seem rationally implausible and turning it into a scapegoat for the evils that were upon the empire. Before his conversion, Augustine had climbed the ladder all the way to the emperor's inner circle in Milan, the imperial seat of the empire, and along the way had learned that the "intelligentsia could easily seize events like the sack of Rome and produce a widely accepted interpretation that would 'harden a prestigious tradition against the spread of Christianity.'"[9] Uniquely qualified, having traveled in and been educated by such circles, the seasoned bishop was compelled to help those whose confidence was shaken and, like the younger version of himself, were in search of a coherent, unifying narrative. In *The City of God*, Augustine set out to do what Ambrose's sermons had done for him: help him see that the faith "was in fact intellectually respectable."[10]

While going back to Augustine's context gave us perspective, bringing him into the present gave us fresh eyes to reconsider contemporary methodological debates. Though contemporary apologists have offered the church many important insights, the dominant apologetic schools of our day have framed the methodological discussions in a way that has too often led to certain blind spots in how the discipline is taught and practiced. The main problems do not lie in the particulars of apologetic arguments but rather go deeper. We saw that the dominant contemporary approaches have not adequately taken into account the late-modern social imaginary—that intuitive cultural soil in which people's objections are rooted. This soil can produce a misguided default perception of "rationality" and is infected with assumptions that yield objections to the aesthetic and moral features of Christianity. To the extent that apologists choose to plant in late-modern dirt while neglecting to sample and till the soil—that is, to understand and interact with the opportunities and challenges our era presents—the crop is in danger.

Moreover, in both methodological discussion and methodological practice, contemporary apologetics has not sufficiently recognized the importance of humans being doxological creatures. The result has too often been a reductionist anthropology that leads to a failure to strike the right chords with our contemporary audience. These two problems, the anthropological and the sociohistorical, go hand in hand. For by not fully integrating sociocultural analysis into our training, and thus minimizing the fact that the effectiveness of particular

---

8. Chang, *Engaging Unbelief*, 14.
9. Chang, *Engaging Unbelief*, 14; cf. Markus, *Saeculum*, 28–39.
10. Augustine, *Confessions* 5.13.23, 5.14.24.

arguments is contingent upon specific contexts, our apologetic pedagogy has lacked a clear model that can guide us in engaging the social imagination and human affections. In other words, the most popular pedagogical approaches have not offered their students enough "mass" to effectively persuade within post-Christendom. Hence, part 2 turned to Augustine to see how he might be able to help.

## An Augustinian Vision for Today

Part 2 opened by returning to the contemporary struggle for faith in a cross-pressured world in which truth seekers are often led by the carrot of epistemological delusions. As Rhett McLaughlin explains in his autobiographical account, when he began to "come of age," exploring the intellectual and existential pressure points he was sensing, he turned to apologists, who did much to reassure him that Christianity could answer his questions. Except it didn't. At least not with the kind of certitude he was looking for. After a long and painful process of "maturing," struggling under the weight of competing world-and-life-views, he walked away from the faith. Augustine, however, showed us another way to grow up.

In *Confessions* we found a boy who was raised in church with his mother, only to walk away from the faith as he came of age and searched for certainty—as well as respectability and recognition from the intelligentsia, the "inner ring" of his day. *Confessions* is an account of his truly growing up. But more than this, as Peter Brown puts it, Augustine wrote *Confessions* to "come to terms with himself."[11] It "was an act of therapy" long before the modern "triumph of the therapeutic," and it used a radically different approach to healing.[12] In contrast to self-actualization through freedom from authority and overconfident trust in oneself, for Augustine the grace discovered through humility before an authority that could be rightly trusted and loved was the path to restoration and thereby to understanding. We might call this his re-coming-of-age story, which began in earnest once he put aside a quest for certainty through reason alone and could confess his own arrogance—his prideful nature and the inheritance of a social imaginary informed by his early miseducation at the hands of teachers breathing the air of Roman glory. Looking back, he realized that all along he had been driven by his desire both to be loved and to know. And in the end, he came to see that these two desires couldn't be neatly separated. Nor should they be. Indeed, faith has to precede understanding. But so too one must learn to love

11. Brown, *Augustine of Hippo*, 158.
12. Brown, *Augustine of Hippo*, 158; Rieff, *Triumph of the Therapeutic*.

rightly in order to know rightly. Logic chopping alone would never lead to the ultimate truth behind the universe. The big questions of life can't be answered by reducing life to its smallest component parts.

*Confessions* models a way to live the Christian faith amid doubt and the cross-pressures of a pluralistic society. For Augustine, experiencing God's grace is not the end of the pilgrimage but rather the beginning of a new set of questions. Believing will lead to understanding, but *understanding* does not mean all questions are fully or definitively answered. Rather than promising us that we will have all of our questions answered, Augustine shows us how to learn to ask the right questions and live as contingent beings; he shows us how to live in accordance with our humanity. In *Confessions* he tells his own story overlaid with the story of Scripture in order to invite us to grow up so we can begin again in God's story. Augustine thus not only invites us to call others to consider a new posture for contemplating the question of God but also supplies the resources for contemporary apologists to reconsider their own posture.

Augustine offers a big picture with explanatory power, a metanarrative marked by internal consistency and rational appeal, but he does not stop there. For Augustine, human frailty and sinfulness undermine true rationality, right belief, and ordered desires. And since these problems are intertwined—for our choices not only mingle "reason and longing" but also include "a reasoning that is always interest-bound and a desire that is always haunted by a self-obsession"[13]—a holistic apologetic treatment is required.

Despite the popular impression of Augustine as a sour critic of the physical world, including our bodies, Augustine challenges his contemporaries with a radically positive doctrine of creation, comparing his creational metaphysics to that of his opponents and offering a better story about the human desire for peace. A metaphysics of creation makes for a compelling part of apologetics and stands in stark contrast to contemporary narratives of metaphysical chaos and violence. And yet, while Augustine views all of creation as being structurally good, east of Eden the world is disordered. Human loves are aimed in the wrong direction. Our lives are marked by pride, *libido dominandi,* and splendid vices, each rooted in the false worship of the creation rather than the Creator. Idolatry has had catastrophic implications on everything from human thinking, relationships, and agency to a corrupted physical creation.

Augustine's unflinchingly positive affirmation of creation, coupled with the universal impact of the fall, furnishes an account that makes sense of seemingly contradictory yet powerful human intuitions: our present world is a wonderful gift, and at the same time it is dreadfully cruel. Our world, says Augustine, is a

13. Williams, *On Augustine,* 101.

paradox: beauty exists alongside a disorder in creation; humans are wondrous and wretched. When the apologist is no longer restrained by an epistemological straitjacket that limits one to attempting to "prove" God from the ground up, these paradoxes can be fruitfully explored and developed in multiple apologetic directions.

For Augustine, the incarnation illuminates how human history and our individual histories are to be interpreted. All of history was leading up to the Christ event, pointing ahead to him "through veiled allusion and hints."[14] Subsequent history should be viewed in light of the God who climactically entered into history as a person. Hence, our personal stories (*Confessions*) and metastories (*The City of God*)—with our individual histories functioning as a microcosm of larger cultural stories—play a significant role in how God makes himself known. Christ is the lens for making sense of each of our lives as well as human history, and because he himself existed in human history, he is also open to historical inquiry. Augustine thus out-narrates his opponents in interpreting human history and experience *and* makes evidential arguments. Out-narrating his opponents is his metastrategy, but it is supplemented throughout by his answers to defeaters and by a variety of supporting arguments.

As we saw with his departure from Manicheism, empirical evidence really does matter for Augustine. In his apologetic for a historical resurrection, he argues from creation, history, and human desire,[15] though he does determine that history's ultimate *significance* depends on holding the interpretive key. Christ is the key that unlocks the mystery of history and the profound human experiences of a created but fallen world. The person and work of Christ opens the door to God, shepherding unbelievers from angst to wonder, conflict to peace, bondage to freedom, tyranny to justice, judgment to grace, misery to joy, and despair to hope.

Christ also reveals humility to be the fundamental disposition required for knowing God. Though Augustine often praises certain pagan philosophers, especially the Platonists, and is willing to plunder their ideas, his most strident critique is that they are unwilling, because of their pride, to open themselves up to the revelation of God. The humility of Christ opens our eyes to see God's revealed truth and gives us the clarity of vision to perceive the world rightly. The cure for our own self-delusions and self-absorptions that hold us captive and blind us to the truth are found at the right hand of the Father, who is ultimate truth and joy. And for Augustine, a community of grace guided by the Scriptures—the church as a hospital for sinners—is the means by which our

14. Chang, *Engaging Unbelief*, 69.
15. O'Collins, *Saint Augustine on the Resurrection of Christ*, 32–59.

ability to see the truth and experience true joy is healed. The church is to be an embodied, living apologetic.

Augustine's apologetic, as with his broader theology, orbits around love. Years of personal reflection and confession—not typically a feature emphasized in apologetics programs today—contributed to the kind of apologist Augustine became: an apologist who attended to the deep desires of his opponents. *Confessions* is a testament to the years of critical reflection to which Augustine had committed his own life in light of God's story. He learned to comb through the layers of his own experiences to identify the deepest sources of his own malaise: the sources of error, the roots of his restlessness, and his many misdirected loves. *Confessions* is the product of a disciplined habit of theological and psychological self-reflection directed toward repentance before God. His Christ-centered therapeutic practices—appropriated from the classical tradition, which was in turn transformed by his theology[16]—sharpened his ability to perceive deeper motivations as well as the underlying causes of his own anguish. Through confession, Augustine grew in understanding his own humanity and developed a thorough perception of the malformities Roman culture had wrought in his own life, preparing him to speak persuasively to common human experiences. Anticipated by this relentless examination of his own story, *The City of God* critiques the layers of his opponents' arguments as well as the assumed social structures of his day. The deep contemplation about his early life enables him to see how earnest human and cultural aspirations are meant to point to God.

Augustine's training as a rhetor taught him to attend to the way words work and to leverage them for effective persuasion. The Scriptures taught him how to attend to the world—to read the world correctly. However, it was through the work of *Confessions* that attention to his own soul taught him how to attend to the souls of his opponents—to know how it felt to be lost and how apologetics could be applied to the wounds of the unbeliever. Augustine is able to use apologetics to attend to the souls of others in *The City of God* because he has attended to the vagaries in his own story and to the existential angst of being a person with a disintegrated and wondering self who is yearning to come of age.

In *Confessions* we hear how God transformed Augustine's life by changing what he loved. Through this reorientation of his loves, Augustine also realigned his polemical aims. While previously he had used rhetoric in service of his own ambition, with the goal of winning acclaim and gaining power, *Confessions* testifies to a divinely wrought transformation. Years later, as an aging bishop, he would say of *Confessions* that his rhetoric was meant to "draw a person's mind

---

16. Kolbet, *Augustine and the Cure of Souls.*

and emotions towards [God]."[17] As a mature apologist Augustine was no longer writing in the hopes of "delighting the reader or making someone know many facts," as he would explain in a letter concerning his goals in writing *The City of God*, but was trying to persuade people to enter the city of God.[18] In Augustine we find an apologist whose aim is directed by a pastoral desire for people to be "set free by the grace of God."[19]

Yet, for Augustine, such an apologetic endeavor of love could not be separated from a community of divine love. For the church was both the communal apologetic witness displaying the logic of God's love and the community in which faithful witnesses were formed. Through the catechesis of the church, one learned to read the world by way of reading the Scriptures. Though Augustine's stated purpose and occasion for writing *The City of God* was clearly apologetic, often scholars view him as sliding into pedagogy for the church. Such observations aren't wrong, but they do draw solid lines where, for Augustine, the boundaries are more porous. Spiritual formation and apologetics are two sides of the same coin for him. While contemporary apologetics has too often failed to integrate the two within the life of the church, living out the drama of the Scriptures in word and deed is the means by which wisdom, sanctification, and love are attained—all essential characteristics of an Augustinian apologist.

Augustine's eschatological vision of the future restoration of the world enables him to offer a radical societal critique aimed at the structural pillars of Roman society—the first of its kind in history. While he does not deny the relative virtue and temporal goods of the earthly, post-fall city, the biblical vision of a future new Jerusalem gives Augustine the vantage point to deconstruct the foundational myths and ultimate aims of the Roman Empire (*The City of God* books 1–10) and then to replace them with the true story of the world and the transcendent aim for which people were made (books 11–22). Augustine's thinking here is marked by a realism that leads to hope rather than despair: God will gather the strands of history together for a final judgment, even though we must live with the mystery of not knowing exactly how this will be accomplished. *The City of God* maps a rationally coherent narrative within which the common features of human experience fit, and it does so without making overrealized, utopian promises. True happiness is available in the present, though it is an anticipatory happiness rooted in the fulfillment of promises that are not yet fully consummated. By contrasting this happiness with the transitory and shallow pursuits of

17. Augustine, *Revisions* 6(33), par. 1
18. Augustine, *Letter* 2*.3.
19. Augustine, *Letter* 2*.2.

happiness found in immanent approaches, Augustine charts a path that makes better emotional and logical sense than his contemporaneous opponents do.

With *Confessions* and *The City of God* applied in tandem—for, as we have seen, the two are connected structurally, theologically, and literarily—an apologetic strategy emerged in our final chapter. Today's challenges include not simply a dizzying array of different spiritual, religious, and secular world-and-life-views that are available because of technology, globalization, and the intermixing of cultures; these changes also bring with them competing traditions of rationality as well as conflicting moral and aesthetic assumptions. What is considered rational, good, and beautiful is, in part, dependent on one's assumed cultural metanarrative and the social imaginary it fosters. Hence, apologetic methods that assume a universally recognized frame for apologetics fail to meet the challenge of persuasion within modern pluralism. Having ministered before the advent of a full-fledged Christendom and within a context that had multiple plausible worldviews, Augustine offers us a meta-apologetic strategy that can be applied in multiple contexts and can meet the challenge of the nontransferability of arguments between different framing narratives.

Augustine's apologetic goal was never simply to convince; it was to convert. He was a pastor who cared for souls; his aim was to move not only people's intellect but also their desires. Toward this aim, his meta-approach allowed for flexibility. In his return to speak to us today, Augustine offers not a one-dimensional evidential apologetic, though it does give logical and historical support for the faith. Nor is his approach simply a narrative or aesthetic apologetic, though he offers a narrative framework and is sensitive to pathos in persuasion. Augustine is nimble in his tactics, and to understand his approach and faithfully apply it in any context, it must be stressed that Augustine's apologetic telos was therapeutic—and thus equips us to engage our present culture's longings by affirming its concern with the therapeutic but challenging the ways it is pursuing this aim.

### Augustine's Invitation

As we close, we can imagine a response to our proposal that is worth addressing: Is it practical for the everyday minister, missionary, and Christian?[20]

20. A second question someone might pose is related to biblical support. On the one hand, we need to be careful in our answers not to give the impression that the Bible offers a singular and straightforward apologetic methodology. The Bible makes various types of apologetic appeals and uses different kinds of persuasive strategies. On the other hand, this biblical diversity actually supports Augustine's multipronged and contextual approach. Paul, to mention just one example, takes a different approach with the Jews in Acts 17:1–15 than he does with the philosophers in

After all, you might reason, it is one thing for a fifth-century theological genius such as Augustine, or for today's intellectuals like Charles Taylor or N. T. Wright or Sarah Coakley, to leverage the strategy in their writings, but where does that leave the rest of us, the "typical" Christians who find ourselves needing a practical approach to guide everyday conversations? I (Josh) have addressed that question by writing what can be viewed as a practical Augustinian guide for apologetics in a previous book, *Telling a Better Story*. In some ways, this current project is an academic prequel to this more practical and popular-level book.

We can also both bear witness to how, in our own lives, we've seen the difference that this perspective and posture makes in our apologetic interactions with others. For example, I (Mark) work at a university and serve as a pastor in a church in the same town, so most of the apologetics I do on a daily basis happens with college students. I try to speak wise and healing words to them that will get inside their felt memory in a way that echoes back years from now.

When I assume that they are doxological creatures who, at the core of their being, deeply desire to love and be loved, it seems as if most are aware I am speaking to something real within the core of who they are and who they desire to be. It does something to them that apologetic appeals stripped down to a bare-bones rationalism cannot. I still bring in various "traditional" arguments in different ways, but these arguments are framed by appeals to their deepest desires as humans.

When I share with them an Augustinian vision for what it means to be a human, they feel the existential weight of their disordered loves, the restlessness that comes from clinging to creation, and the despair of death. After I call upon Augustine to help me diagnose these disorders, the power of a crucified Mediator begins to attract them to the logic of Christ's humble wisdom and healing. It often rings true to them and awakens hope within them, but not the kind of hope that believes that everything will get easier and work out for the best. They begin to discover a hope that sees that suffering can be meaningfully

---

Athens (vv. 22–34). The mixture of different biblical genres and rhetorical tools used to persuade in the Scriptures supports the case for an approach that is flexible enough to incorporate these different tools. We've also seen how Augustine offers theological resources that can shape our approach. While moving from the Bible to theology to apologetics always entails creativity, Augustine remains firmly moored to a fully orthodox theological interpretation of the Scriptures and an orthopraxy centered on the two greatest commandments. And Augustine's apologetic aim to heal is in line with one of Jesus's metaphors for his ministry: "Those who are well have no need of a physician, but those who are sick. I came not to call the righteous, but sinners" (Mark 2:17 ESV). Finally, Augustine's use of narrative to frame an immanent critique of his opponents and to present Christianity as the fulfillment of our deepest desires finds support throughout the Bible. This is not surprising given Augustine's commitment to and retention of the Scriptures. I (Josh) have previously summarized, starting with Jesus himself, how a similar narrative approach takes center stage throughout the Bible. Chatraw, *Telling a Better Story*, 45–47.

healing and redemptive, that life's enigmas can teach them more wisdom than easy answers, and that persuading others to open themselves up to God is not the same thing as backing them into an intellectual corner. Hence, even before I have believers memorize arguments and learn to detail historical evidence, through their participation in Christ's body they begin to become the right kind of apologists.

Augustine offers us a useful posture and pattern from his own context, using a creativity born out of a humble scriptural and doxological community—the kind of ecclesial community that is essential for a holistic and timely apologetic. A similar reinvigoration of apologetic communities, along with an application of theological resources and persuasive arguments, remains the challenge for each new Christian generation.

It's as if Augustine, by way of the well-worn pages of his most popular works, has long been speaking through time, inviting whoever will listen to develop his approach for their own day. Yet, while listening carefully for Augustine's theological reflections, for too long the church has been distracted from hearing his apologetic voice. Our hope is that this book has faithfully retrieved the Augustine way for our day so that people will hear the nature of his invitation more clearly and join together in carrying on the task of persuading others to enter the blessed city of God.

# Bibliography

Allen, Mark D. "The City of God and the City of Man." *Faith and the Academy* 6, no. 1 (Fall 2021): 8–11.

Ashford, Bruce, and Matthew Ng. "Charles Taylor: Apologetics in a Secular Age." In Forrest, Chatraw, and McGrath, *History of Apologetics*, 674–95.

Augustine. *The Advantage of Believing.* In *On Christian Belief*, edited by Boniface Ramsey, translated by Ray Kearney, 104–48. The Works of Saint Augustine I/8. Hyde Park, NY: New City, 2005.

———. *On Christian Belief.* Edited by Boniface Ramsey. Introduction by Michael Fiedrowicz. The Works of Saint Augustine I/8. Hyde Park, NY: New City, 2005.

———. *The City of God.* Translated by Henry Bettenson. Introduction by John O'Meara. London: Penguin, 1987.

———. *The City of God (1–10).* Edited by Boniface Ramsey. Translated by William Babcock. The Works of Saint Augustine I/6. Hyde Park, NY: New City, 2012.

———. *The City of God (11–22).* Edited by Boniface Ramsey. Translated by William Babcock. The Works of Saint Augustine I/7. Hyde Park, NY: New City, 2013.

———. *Confessions.* Edited by John E. Rotelle. Translated by Maria Boulding. The Works of Saint Augustine I/1. Hyde Park, NY: New City, 1997.

———. *Confessions: A New Translation.* Translated by Sarah Ruden. New York: Modern Library, 2017.

———. *Letters 100–155.* Edited by Boniface Ramsey. Translated by Roland Teske. The Works of Saint Augustine II/2. Hyde Park, NY: New City, 2002.

———. *Letters 156–210.* Edited by Boniface Ramsey. Translated by Roland Teske. The Works of Saint Augustine II/3. Hyde Park, NY: New City, 2004.

———. *Letters 211–270, 1\*–29\*.* Edited by Boniface Ramsey. Translated by Roland Teske. The Works of Saint Augustine II/4. Hyde Park, NY: New City, 2005.

——. *The Literal Meaning of Genesis*. In *On Genesis*, edited by John E. Rotelle, translated by Edmund Hill, 153–506. The Works of Saint Augustine I/13. Hyde Park, NY: New City, 2002.

——. *Revisions*. Edited by Roland Teske and Boniface Ramsey. Translated by Boniface Ramsey. The Works of Saint Augustine I/2. Hyde Park, NY: New City, 2010.

——. *Sermons 51–94*. Edited by John E. Rotelle. Translated by Edmund Hill. The Works of Saint Augustine III/4. Hyde Park, NY: New City, 1991.

——. *Sermons 184–229Z*. Edited by John E. Rotelle. Translated by Edmund Hill. The Works of Saint Augustine III/7. Hyde Park, NY: New City, 1993.

——. *Sermons 341–400*. Edited by John E. Rotelle. Translated by Edmund Hill. The Works of Saint Augustine III/2. Hyde Park, NY: New City, 1992.

——. *Teaching Christianity*. Edited by John E. Rotelle. Translated by Edmund Hill. The Works of Saint Augustine I/11. Hyde Park, NY: New City, 1996.

——. *The Trinity*. 2nd ed. Edited by John E. Rotelle. Translated by Edmund Hill. The Works of Saint Augustine I/5. Hyde Park, NY: New City, 2015.

——. *The Two Souls*. In *The Manichean Debate*, edited by Boniface Ramsey, translated by Roland Teske, 105–34. The Works of Saint Augustine I/19. Hyde Park, NY: New City, 2006.

Ayres, Lewis. "Christianity as Contemplative Practice: Understanding the Union of Natures in Augustine's *Letter 137*." In *In the Shadow of the Incarnation: Essays on Jesus Christ in the Early Church in Honor of Brian E. Dailey, S.J.*, edited by Peter W. Martens, 190–211. Notre Dame, IN: University of Notre Dame Press, 2008.

Bailey, Justin Ariel. *Reimagining Apologetics: The Beauty of Faith in a Secular Age*. Downers Grove, IL: IVP Academic, 2020.

Bauckham, Richard. *Jesus and the Eyewitnesses: The Gospels as Eyewitness Testimony*. 2nd ed. Grand Rapids: Eerdmans, 2017.

Bavinck, Herman. *The Wonderful Works of God: Instruction in the Christian Religion according to the Reformed Confession*. Glenside, PA: Westminster Seminary Press, 2019.

Becker, Enrest. *The Denial of Death*. New York: Free Press, 1997.

Bray, Gerald. *Augustine on the Christian Life: Transformed by the Power of God*. Wheaton: Crossway, 2015.

Brown, Peter. *Augustine of Hippo: A Biography*. 2nd ed. Berkeley: University of California Press, 2000.

Burge, Ryan P. *The Nones: Where They Came From, How They Are, and Where They Are Going*. Minneapolis: Fortress, 2021.

Burton, Tara Isabella. *Strange Rites: New Religions for a Godless World*. New York: Hachette, 2020.

Carnell, Edward J. *Christian Commitment: An Apologetic*. 1957. Reprint, Eugene, OR: Wipf & Stock, 2007.

Cavadini, John C. "Ideology and Solidarity in Augustine's *City of God.*" In *Augustine's City of God: A Critical Guide*, edited by James Wetzel, 93–110. Cambridge: Cambridge University Press, 2012.

———. *Visioning Augustine: Challenges in Contemporary Theology.* Oxford: Wiley-Blackwell, 2019.

Chadwick, Henry. *Augustine of Hippo: A Life.* New York: Oxford University Press, 2009.

———. "On Rereading the *Confessions.*" In *Saint Augustine the Bishop*, edited by Fannie LeMoine and Christopher Kleinhenz, 139–63. New York: Garland, 1994.

Chang, Curtis. *Engaging Unbelief: A Captivating Strategy from Augustine and Aquinas.* Downers Grove, IL: InterVarsity, 2000.

Chatraw, Joshua D. *Telling a Better Story: How to Talk about God in a Skeptical Age.* Grand Rapids: Zondervan, 2020.

Chatraw, Joshua D., and Mark D. Allen. *Apologetics at the Cross: An Introduction for Christian Witness.* Grand Rapids: Zondervan, 2018.

Chatraw, Joshua D., and Jack Carson. *Surprised by Doubt: How Disillusionment Can Invite Us into a Deeper Faith.* Grand Rapids: Brazos, 2023.

Clark, Gillian. "Paradise for Pagans? Augustine on Virgil, Cicero, and Plato." In *Paradise in Antiquity: Jewish and Christian Views*, edited by Marcus Bockmuehl and Gary G. Stroumsa, 166–78. Cambridge: Cambridge University Press, 2010.

Craig, William Lane. *On Guard: Defending Your Faith with Reason and Precision.* Colorado Springs: David C. Cook, 2010.

———. *Reasonable Faith: Christian Truth and Apologetics.* 3rd ed. Wheaton: Crossway, 2008.

Douthat, Ross. *The Decadent Society: America before and after the Pandemic.* New York: Avid Reader, 2020.

Drobner, Hubertus. "An Overview of Recent Research." In *Augustine and His Critics: Essays in Honor of Gerald Bonner*, edited by Robert Dodaro and George Lawless, 18–34. London: Routledge, 2000.

Dulles, Avery. *A History of Apologetics.* 2nd ed. San Francisco: Ignatius, 2005.

Ehrman, Bart. *Jesus, Interrupted: Revealing the Hidden Contradictions in the Bible.* New York: HarperOne, 2010.

Eliade, Mircea. *The Sacred and the Profane: The Nature of Religion.* New York: Harcourt, Brace, 1959.

Ellingsen, Mark. *The Richness of Augustine: His Contextual & Pastoral Theology.* Louisville: Westminster John Knox, 2005.

Evans, Stephen. *The History of Western Philosophy: From Pre-Socratics to Post-Modernism.* Downers Grove, IL: InterVarsity, 2018.

Fitzgerald, Allan. "Jesus Christ, the Knowledge and Wisdom of God." In *The Cambridge Companion to Augustine*, edited by David Vincent Meconi and Eleonore Stump, 108–24. 2nd ed. Cambridge: Cambridge University Press, 2014.

Forrest, Benjamin, Joshua D. Chatraw, and Alister McGrath. *The History of Apologetics: A Biographical and Methodological Introduction*. Grand Rapids: Zondervan, 2020.

Geisler, Norman L. *Christian Apologetics*. 2nd ed. Grand Rapids: Baker Academic, 2013.

Gilson, Etienne. *Introduction à l'étude de Saint Augustin*. Paris: J. Vrin, 1929.

Gonzalez, Justo L. *The Mestizo Augustine: A Theologian between Two Cultures*. Downers Grove, IL: InterVarsity, 2016.

Gould, Paul M. *Cultural Apologetics: Renewing the Christian Voice, Conscience, and Imagination in a Disenchanted World*. Grand Rapids: Zondervan, 2019.

Haidt, Jonathan. *The Happiness Hypothesis: Finding Modern Truth in Ancient Wisdom*. New York: Basic Books, 2006.

Harrison, Carol. *Augustine: Christian Truth and Fractured Humanity*. Oxford: Oxford University Press, 2000.

———. *Rethinking Augustine's Early Theology: An Argument for Continuity*. Oxford: Oxford University Press, 2006.

Hart, David Bentley. *Atheist Delusions: The Christian Revolution and Its Fashionable Enemies*. New Haven: Yale University Press, 2009.

Hauerwas, Stanley. *With the Grain of the Universe: The Church's Witness and Natural Theology*. Grand Rapids: Baker Academic, 2013.

Herdt, Jennifer. *Putting On Virtue: The Legacy of Splendid Virtues*. Chicago: University of Chicago Press, 2008.

Holland, Tom. *Dominion: How the Christian Revolution Remade the World*. New York: Basic Books, 2019.

Horton, Michael. "The Enduring Power of the Christian Story: Reformation Theology for a Secular Age." In *Our Secular Age: Ten Years of Reading and Applying Charles Taylor*, edited by Collin Hansen, 23–38. Deerfield, IL: Gospel Coalition, 2017.

Hunter, Graeme. *Pascal the Philosopher: An Introduction*. Toronto: University of Toronto Press, 2013.

Hunter, James Davison, and Paul Nedelisky. *Science and the Good: The Tragic Quest for the Foundations of Morality*. New Haven: Yale University Press, 2018.

Huxley, Aldous. *Aldous Huxley: Complete Essays*. Edited by Robert S. Baker and James Sexton. 6 vols. Lanham, MD: Ivan R. Dee, 2001.

Jacobs, Alan. *How to Think: A Survival Guide for a World at Odds*. New York: Currency, 2017.

———. *The Year of Our Lord 1943: Christian Humanism in an Age of Crisis*. Oxford: Oxford University Press, 2018.

Keener, Craig S. *Miracles: The Credibility of the New Testament Accounts*. 2 vols. Grand Rapids: Baker Academic, 2011.

Kelly, J. N. D. *Jerome: His Life, Writings, and Controversies*. New York: Harper & Row, 1975.

Kolbet, Paul R. *Augustine and the Cure of Souls: Revising a Classical Ideal*. Notre Dame, IN: University of Notre Dame Press, 2009.

Koukl, Gregory. *Tactics: A Game Plan for Discussing Your Christian Convictions*. 10th anniversary ed. Grand Rapids: Zondervan, 2019.

Kreeft, Peter. *Christianity for Modern Pagans: Pascal's Pensées*. San Francisco: Ignatius, 1993.

Lewis, C. S. *The Abolition of Man*. New York: Collier, 1955.

———. *Mere Christianity*. New York: Macmillan, 1960.

———. *Miracles*. 1960. Reprint, San Francisco: HarperOne, 2015.

———. *The Weight of Glory*. 1941. Reprint, San Francisco: HarperSanFrancisco, 2001.

MacCormack, Sabine. *The Shadows of Poetry: Vergil in the Mind of Augustine*. Berkeley: University of California Press, 1998.

MacDonald, George. *God's Words to His Children: Sermons Spoken and Unspoken*. New York: Funk & Wagnalls, 1887.

MacIntyre, Alasdair. *After Virtue*. 3rd ed. Notre Dame, IN: University of Notre Dame Press, 2007.

———. "Epistemological Crisis, Dramatic Narrative, and the Philosophy of Science." *Monist* 60, no. 4 (October 1977): 453–72.

———. *Three Rival Versions of Moral Enquiry: Encyclopedia, Genealogy, and Tradition*. Notre Dame, IN: University of Notre Dame Press, 1990.

———. *Whose Justice? Which Rationality?* Notre Dame, IN: University of Notre Dame Press, 1988.

Markus, Robert A. *Christianity and the Secular*. Notre Dame, IN: University of Notre Dame Press, 2006.

———. *Saeculum*. Cambridge: Cambridge University Press, 1970.

Marrou, Henri-Irénée. *Histoire de l'éducation dans l'antiquité*. 2nd ed. Paris: Éditions du Seuil, 1950.

Mathewes, Charles. "Another City: Augustine before the Modern." *Hedgehog Review* 23, no. 3 (Fall 2021): 98–114.

———. *Books That Matter: The City of God; Course Guidebook*. Chantilly, VA: Great Courses, 2016.

———. "The Liberation of Questioning in Augustine's 'Confessions.'" *Journal of the American Academy of Religion* 70, no. 3 (September 2002): 539–60.

McClay, Wilfred M. "The Strange Persistence of Guilt." *Hedgehog Review* 19, no. 1 (Spring 2007): 40–52.

McGilchrist, Iain. *The Master and His Emissary: The Divided Brain and the Making of the Western World*. Rev. ed. New Haven: Yale University Press, 2018.

McGinn, Colin. *Mindset: Image, Dream, Meaning*. Cambridge, MA: Harvard University Press, 2004.

McGrath, Alister. *The Genesis of Doctrine: A Study in the Foundation of Doctrinal Criticism*. Cambridge: Blackwell, 1990.

———. *The Intellectual World of C. S. Lewis*. Oxford: Wiley-Blackwell, 2014.

———. *The Territories of Human Reason: Science and Theology in the Age of Multiple Rationalities*. Oxford: Oxford University Press, 2019.

Meister, Chad. "Augustine of Hippo: Apologist of Faith and Reason Seeking Understanding." In Forrest, Chatraw, and McGrath, *History of Apologetics*, 137–63.

Midgley, Mary. *The Myths We Live By*. New York: Routledge, 2003.

Milbank, John. *Theology and Social Theory: Beyond Secular Reason*. 2nd ed. Malden, MA: Blackwell, 2006.

O'Collins, Gerald. *Saint Augustine on the Resurrection of Christ: Teaching, Rhetoric, and Reception*. New York: Oxford University Press, 2018.

O'Daly, Gerard. *Augustine's City of God: A Reader's Guide*. New York: Oxford University Press, 1999.

O'Donnell, James J. *Commentary Books 1–7*. Vol. 2 of *Augustine's Confessions*. Oxford: Oxford University Press, 1992.

Oliphint, Scott. *Know Why You Believe*. Grand Rapids: Zondervan, 2017.

O'Meara, John. "Virgil and Augustine: The *Aeneid* in the *Confessions*." *Maynooth Review* 13 (1988): 30–43.

Ortlund, Gavin. *Retrieving Augustine's Doctrine of Creation: Ancient Wisdom for Current Controversy*. Downers Grove, IL: InterVarsity, 2020.

Packer, J. I., and Thomas Howard. *Christianity: The True Humanism*. Waco: Word, 1985.

Pascal, Blaise. *Pensées*. Translated by A. J. Krailsheimer. New York: Penguin, 1995.

Pennington, Jonathan. *Jesus the Great Philosopher: Rediscovering the Wisdom Needed for the Good Life*. Grand Rapids: Brazos, 2020.

———. *The Sermon on the Mount and Human Flourishing: A Theological Commentary*. Grand Rapids: Baker Books, 2017.

Peters, James R. *The Logic of the Heart: Augustine, Pascal, and the Rationality of Faith*. Grand Rapids: Baker Academic, 2009.

Pinkard, Terry. "MacIntyre's Critique of Modernity." In *Alasdair MacIntyre*, edited by Mark C. Murphy, 176–201. Washington, DC: Georgetown University Press, 2003.

Pinker, Steven. *Enlightenment Now: The Case for Reason, Science, Humanism, and Progress*. New York: Penguin, 2019.

Plantinga, Alvin. *Knowledge and Christian Belief*. Grand Rapids: Eerdmans, 2015.

———. *Warranted Christian Belief*. Oxford: Oxford University Press, 2000.

———. *Where the Conflict Really Lies: Science, Religion, and Naturalism*. Oxford: Oxford University Press, 2011.

Rieff, Philip. *My Life among the Deathworks: Illustrations of the Aesthetics of Authority*. Charlottesville: University of Virginia Press, 2006.

———. *The Triumph of the Therapeutic: Uses of Faith after Freud*. Chicago: University of Chicago Press, 1987.

Rowe, C. Kavin. *One True Life: The Stoics and Early Christians as Rival Traditions*. New Haven: Yale University Press, 2016.

Smith, Christian. *Atheist Overreach*. Oxford: Oxford University Press, 2018.

———. "Does Naturalism Warrant a Moral Belief in Universal Benevolence and Human Rights?" In *The Believing Primate: Scientific, Philosophical, and Theological Reflections on the Origins of Religion*, edited by Jeffrey Schloss and Michael Murray, 292–317. Oxford: Oxford University Press, 2011.

Smith, Christian, and Melina Lundquist Denton. *Soul Searching: The Religious and Spiritual Lives of American Teenagers*. Oxford: Oxford University Press, 2005.

Smith, James K. A. *Awaiting the King: Reforming Public Theology*. Vol. 3 of *Cultural Liturgies*. Grand Rapids: Baker Academic, 2017.

———. *Desiring the Kingdom: Worship, Worldview, and Cultural Formation*. Vol. 1 of *Cultural Liturgies*. Grand Rapids: Baker Academic, 2009.

———. *How (Not) to Be Secular: Reading Charles Taylor*. Grand Rapids: Eerdmans, 2014.

———. *Imagining the Kingdom: How Worship Works*. Grand Rapids: Baker Academic, 2013.

———. *On the Road with Saint Augustine: A Real-World Spirituality for Restless Hearts*. Grand Rapids: Brazos, 2019.

———. *You Are What You Love: The Spiritual Power of Habit*. Grand Rapids: Brazos, 2016.

Smith, Steven D. *Pagans and Christians in the City: Culture Wars from the Tiber to the Potomac*. Grand Rapids: Eerdmans, 2018.

Stock, Brian. *Augustine the Reader: Meditation, Self-Knowledge, and the Ethics of Interpretation*. Cambridge, MA: Harvard University Press, 1996.

Storey, Benjamin, and Jenna Silber Storey. *Why We Are Restless: On the Modern Quest for Contentment*. Princeton: Princeton University Press, 2021.

Strange, Daniel. *Plugged In: Connecting Your Faith with What You Watch, Read, and Play*. London: Good Book Company, 2019.

Taylor, Charles. Afterword to *Varieties of Secularism in a Secular Age*, edited by Michael Warner, Jonathan VanAntwerpen, and Craig Calhoun, 300–324. Cambridge, MA: Harvard University Press, 2010.

———. *The Ethics of Authenticity*. Cambridge, MA: Harvard University Press, 1991.

———. *Modern Social Imaginaries*. Durham, NC: Duke University Press, 2003.

———. "Reason, Faith, and Meaning." In *Faith, Rationality, and the Passions*, edited by Sarah Coakley, 13–27. Malden, MA: Wiley-Blackwell, 2012.

———. "Reply and Re-articulation." In *Philosophy in an Age of Pluralism: The Philosophy of Charles Taylor in Question*, edited by James Tully, 213–57. New York: Cambridge University Press, 1994.

———. *A Secular Age*. Cambridge, MA: Harvard University Press, 2007.

Trapè, Agostino. *Saint Augustine: Man, Pastor, Mystic*. Translated by Matthew J. O'Connell. New York: Catholic Book Publishing, 1986.

Trueman, Carl. *The Rise and Triumph of the Modern Self: Cultural Amnesia, Expressive Individualism, and the Road to Sexual Revolution*. Wheaton: Crossway, 2020.

———. *Strange New World: How Thinkers and Activists Redefined Identity and Sparked the Sexual Revolution*. Wheaton: Crossway, 2022.

Van Til, Cornelius. "My Credo." In *Jerusalem and Athens: Critical Discussions on Philosophy and Apologetics of Cornelius Van Til*, edited by E. R. Geehan, 1–22. Phillipsburg, NJ: P&R, 1993.

Virgil. *The Aeneid*. Translated by Robert Fagles. New York: Penguin, 2006.

Wallace, Daniel B. "The Gospel according to Bart: A Review Article of *Misquoting Jesus* by Bart Ehrman." *Journal of the Evangelical Theological Society* 49, no. 2 (June 2006): 327–49.

Ward, Graham. *Unimaginable: What We Imagine and What We Can't*. London: I. B. Tauris, 2018.

Ward, Michael. *After Humanity: A Guide to C. S. Lewis's "The Abolition of Man."* Park Ridge, IL: Word on Fire Academic, 2021.

Warfield, Benjamin B. *Selected Shorter Writings of Benjamin B. Warfield*. Edited by John E. Meeter. Nutley, NJ: Presbyterian and Reformed, 1970.

Watkin, Christopher. *Biblical Critical Theory: How the Bible's Unfolding Story Makes Sense of Modern Life and Culture*. Grand Rapids: Zondervan Academic, 2022.

Watson, Thomas R. "Enlarging Augustinian Systems: C. S. Lewis's *The Great Divorce* and *Till We Have Faces*." *Renascence* 46, no. 3 (1994): 163–74.

Wetzel, James, ed. *Augustine's City of God: A Critical Guide*. Cambridge: Cambridge University Press, 2012.

Williams, Rowan. "Augustine's Christology: Its Spirituality and Rhetoric." In *In the Shadow of the Incarnation: Essays on Jesus Christ in the Early Church in Honor of Brian E. Dailey, S.J.*, edited by Peter W. Martens, 179–89. Notre Dame, IN: University of Notre Dame Press, 2008.

———. *On Augustine*. New York: Bloomsbury Continuum, 2016.

Wilson, Todd A., and Gerald Hiestand, eds. *Becoming a Pastor Theologian: New Possibilities for Church Leadership*. Downers Grove, IL: IVP Academic, 2016.

Wright, N. T. *History and Eschatology: Jesus and the Promise of Natural Theology*. Waco: Baylor University Press, 2019.

———. *The Resurrection of the Son of God*. Minneapolis: Fortress, 2003.

# Index